J. R. (John Read) Dore

Old Bibles : An Account of the Early Versions of the English Bible

J. R. (John Read) Dore

Old Bibles : An Account of the Early Versions of the English Bible

ISBN/EAN: 9783337099060

Printed in Europe, USA, Canada, Australia, Japan

Cover: Foto ©Lupo / pixelio.de

More available books at **www.hansebooks.com**

OLD BIBLES:

An Account of the Early Versions of the English Bible.

BY

J. R. DORE.

Second Edition,

WITH THE PREFACE TO THE VERSION OF 1611 ADDED
AT THE REQUEST OF THE LATE
RIGHT REV. CHRISTOPHER WORDSWORTH, D.D.,
Lord Bishop of Lincoln.

Printed and Published by
EYRE AND SPOTTISWOODE
Her Majesty's Printers.
1888.

DEDICATED

(BY PERMISSION)

TO

HIS GRACE THE LORD ARCHBISHOP OF CANTERBURY.

b

Preface.

THAT pearl of great price, the English Bible of 1611, *remained so long without alteration, that many of us had forgotten that it was only one of a series of versions.*

English folk being (Laus Deo) slow to make changes, it is probable that another generation will pass away before any other version of Holy Scripture will fully take the place of the translation that has been in use so many years.

About forty years elapsed before King James's revision superseded the Bishops' and Genevan versions.

Copies of early versions of the Bible, in a more or less imperfect condition, are in the possession of many families, but their owners, for want of knowing how to identify the books, frequently place an exaggerated value on comparatively worthless copies, while rare ones are insufficiently estimated; I have, therefore, endeavoured to place within the reach of all, easy directions by which to ascertain, from internal evidence, to what edition any copy belongs; the title page being often missing, and not always trustworthy when it exists, owing to titles being sometimes bound up with books to which they do not belong.

All the statements I have made are based on most careful investigation of original copies of the books to which they refer, and I have spared no efforts to insure the utmost accuracy.

The original spelling has been preserved in all quotations from the texts and notes of early versions: for to modernise the orthography, is to destroy one of the charms of these old Bibles, and seems to me to be in as bad taste as attempting to improve their quaint diction.

Most gratefully I acknowledge the kind assistance I have received during past years from Mr. Francis Fry, Mr. Bradshaw, and Mr. H. Stevens, all of whom have recently been taken from us; also from Mr. Geo. Bullen, of the British Museum, the Rev. N. Pocock, M.A., of Clifton, Colonel Thomas Brooke, the Rev. W. E. Smith, M.A., W. T. Lynn, M.A., and other men of eminent learning, who have ever been ready to afford help in bibliographical difficulties.

I also thank the Right Rev. the Lord Bishop of Salisbury for his kind permission to avail myself of the consent of the late Right Rev. Lord Bishop of Lincoln to have his name placed on the title page.

This year being the tercentenary of the publication of the first Bible in the Welsh language, perhaps it is not inappropriate to add as an Appendix a few notes on Welsh Bibles, which have been read and approved by the Right Rev. the Lord Bishop of S. David's.

The first edition of this book was received with greater favour than I now think it deserved, as ten more years devoted to the study of early printed Bibles have shown me how many faults it contained, of which I was then unconscious. I hope this edition is made more worthy the acceptance of those who value the English Bible.

J. R. DORE.

Huddersfield, 1888.

Contents.

Index.

OLD BIBLES,

By J. R. Dore.

Introduction.

IT is very difficult to say at what time the Bible was first translated into the English language.

It is certain that there is no English Bible known to be in existence of earlier date than the fourteenth century.

On one hand, we have the evidence of Sir Thomas More, "as for olde translacions, before Wycliffes time, they remain lawful and be in some folkes handes.

Sir Thomas More says he could show English Bibles earlier than Wycliffe's.

"Myself have seen, and can show you, Bybles fair and olde, in Englyshe, which haue been known and seen by the Byshoppe of the Diocese, and left in laymanes handes and womenes."

Again, in his "Dyalogues," p. 138, ed. 1530, Sir Thomas says, "The hole byble was long before Wycliffe's days by vertuous and well learned men, translated into the English tong;

and by good and godly people with devotion, and soberness, wel and reverendly red."

This evidence is corroborated by Archbishop Cranmer, who, in his prologue to the second edition of the Great Bible, says,

Cranmer's evidence.

"If the matter shoulde be tried by custome, wee might also alledge custome for the reading of the scripture in the vulgar tongue, and prescribe the more auncient custome. For it is not much aboue one hundred yeare ago, since scripture hath not bene accustomed to be read in the vulgar tongue within this realme, and many hundred yeares before that, it was translated and read in the Saxons tongue, whiche at that tyme was our mother tongue, where of there remayne yet diuerse copies found lately in olde Abbeyes, of such antique maner of wryting and speaking, that fewe men nowe be able to read and vnderstande them. And when this language waxed olde and out of common vsage, bycause folke should not lacke the fruit of reading, it was again translated into the newer language, where of yet also many copies remayne, and be dayly founde."

The Bible translated in the second century.

Another reason in favour of there having been an early English Bible is, that it was the custom of the Church in primitive days to translate the Bible into the language best understood by her children.

The Vulgate itself is a proof of this fact. It was translated into Latin for the use of the Latin speaking Church of North Africa.

The writings of S. Ephrem read in the early Church after the usual lessons.

S. Jerome, speaking of the veneration in which the writings of S. Ephrem the Syrian were held, says they were read in the Churches immediately after the usual lesson from Holy Scripture.

The Gospel and Epistle a part of the liturgy.

From a very early period in the history of the Church the reading of the Gospel and Epistle formed a portion of the liturgy. In Colossians, chapter iv., verse 16, we have, "And when this epistle is read among you, cause that it be read also in the Church of the Laodiceans; and that ye likewise read the epistle from Laodicea."

The rubric prefixed to an early English translation of S. Matthew, chapter i., is, "This Gospel is to be read on midwinters mass even."

No trace of an English Bible earlier than the 14th century.

On the other hand it is strange that if the whole Bible had been translated into early English, all traces of it should have been lost.

As the Latin tongue had become the universal ecclesiastical language, and all who could read were familiar with Latin, there was at that time little need of an English Bible.

That the Psalter and other portions of the Old and New Testament were translated from the Latin into English at various times from the 7th century to the 14th there can be no doubt.

Cædmon's paraphrase.

A paraphrase or metrical translation was made by Cædmon, a Whitby monk, in the 7th century. Bede tells us that Cædmon sang of the creation of the world, the origin of man, and made many verses on the departure of the Children of Israel from Egypt, and their entering into the land of promise, and other histories from Holy Writ; the incarnation, passion, resurrection of our Lord, and His ascension into Heaven.

Guthlac's English Psalter.

About the close of the 7th century the Psalter was translated by Guthlac, a Saxon anchoret, at Crowland, near Peterborough.

S. Aldhelm's Psalter.

S. Aldhelm, Abbot of Malmsbury, and afterwards Bishop of Sherborne, made another version of the Psalter in the year 706; the first fifty Psalms of this translation are in prose and the remainder in verse.

The Venerable Bede.

The Venerable Bede, who is one of the brightest gems in the crown of the Church of England, left, as a precious legacy to the Church he loved, a translation of the Gospel of S. John; and a touching memorial of his last labours has been given us by a monk named Cuthbert, in a letter to his fellow reader Cuthwin.

King Alfred.

The historian to whom we owe so much, William of Mamesbury, tells us that King Alfred, at the end of the 9th century, had his memory stored not only with the Psalms and the New Testament, but with the Old Testament also, and had learned that the laws of God are the best basis and models for human legislation; and that at the time of his death he was engaged in making a new version of the Psalter for the use of his people.

Next we have the Lindisfarne MS., an early English interlinear translation of the Latin text written by Aldred, a priest, early in the 10th century, on a copy of the Gospels in Latin formerly belonging to Eadfrith, Bishop of Lindisfarne.

This gloss was copied by Farmen, a priest at Harewood, in Yorkshire, and a monk called Owun, between the lines of a Latin MS. written by Macregol, and is known as the Rushworth gloss.

In the latter part of the 10th century Ælfric collected various early translations of portions of the Bible, and clothed them in the language of his day. His work consisted of the five books of Moses, Joshua, Judges, Esther, Job, part of Kings, Judith, and Maccabees.

In the 13th century some portions of the Bible were translated into Anglo-Norman, indicating that a desire for Bible reading existed amongst the upper class of that day.

The Psalter has always been an especial favourite with English people, its melodies have ever vibrated in their hearts, and it has often been translated both into prose and verse. Three versions dating from soon after 1300 still exist, and bear witness to this fact; one of these was by the Yorkshire hermit, Richard Rolle, of Hampole, a learned man who lived at a hermitage near Doncaster. He thus spoke of his own translation: "In this worke I seke no straunge Ynglys, bot lightest and communest, and swilk that is most like vnto the Latyne, so yt thai that knawes noght ye Latyne be the Ynglys may com to many latyne wordis. In ye Translacione I felogh the letter als-mekille as I may, and thor I fyne no proper Ynglys I felogh ye wit of the wordis, so that thai that shall rede it them thar not drede errynge. In the expownyng I felough holi Doctors. For it may comen into sum envious mannes honde that knowys not what he suld saye that will saye that I wist not what I sayd, and so do harme tille hym and tylle other."

At the end of this ancient Yorkshire translation and gloss of the Psalms were several canticles or hymns to be sung in English during Divine service. His translation of the New Testament included the Epistle to the Laodiceans, mentioned in Colossians iv. 16.

Hampole died in the year 1349.

Probably the first entire Bible in English was the work of Nicholas de Hereford and John Wycliffe, about the year 1380.

Wycliffe's Bible.

Wycliffe was born near Richmond, Yorkshire, early in the 14th century.

He was educated at the University of Oxford, and held office in three colleges; he was ultimately presented to the Rectory of Lutterworth, in Leicestershire.

Wycliffe held views which if carried into practice would have been totally subversive of morality and good order, but he never separated himself from the Church of England.

He died on S. Silvester's day (Dec. 31) 1384, having been struck with paralysis on S. Thomas a Becket's day (Dec. 29) while assisting at Mass at Lutterworth Church.

Wycliffe had many powerful patrons, and was allowed to disseminate his views with little molestation.

Nicholas de Hereford was tried, and found guilty of heresy, but recanted his errors, and died in communion with the English Church.

A revision of Wycliffe's Bible was made by some of the leaders of the Lollards, the chief of whom was John Purvey. Purvey's Bible.

Purvey removed many of the glosses introduced by Hereford and Wycliffe, some of which were restored in Matthew's Bible of 1537.

There must have been a great many copies made both of the earlier and the latter edition of this Bible, for in spite of the large number that must have been destroyed by the various enemies of books during the four centuries that have passed since they were written, even at the present day a large number survive. Wycliffe's Bible extensively circulated.

The following is Psalm 66 from a 15th century MS. Bible, and its translation by Wycliffe, Purvey, and the Douai College in 1610:—

Liber Soliloquiorũ.

¶ In finem in ẏmnis psalmus cātici Dauid. lxvj.

Deus misereatur nostri et bñdicat nobis: illumĩet vultu suum sup nos: et misereaĩ nri. Ut cognoscam⁹ in terra via tua: in omib⁹ gentibus salutare tuũ. Confiteanĩ tibi ppli de⁹: confiteanĩ tibi ppli oēs. Letent et exultēt gētes: qm̄ iudicas pplós in equitate: et gētes Vulgate version of the 66th Psalm.

in terra dirigis. Confiteant tibi ppli deus cōfiteant tibi ppli oēs terra dedit fructum suum. Bn̄dicat nos deus de9 noster bn̄dicat nos deus: et metuāt eū oes fines terre.

WYCLIFFE.

In to the ende; in ympnes, the salm of the song to Dauyd.

Wycliffe's version of the 66th Psalm.

God haue merci of vs, and blisse to vs, liȝte to his chere vpon vs; and haue mercy of vs. That wee knowe in the erthe thi weie; in alle Jentilis thi helthe ȝiuere.

Knouleche to thee puplis, God; knouleche to thee alle puplis.

Gladen and ful out ioȝe Jentilis, for thou demest puplis in equite; and Jentilis in the erthe thou dressist. Knouleche to thee puplis, God, knouleche to thee all puplis; the erthe ȝaf his frut. Blesse vs God, oure God, blesse vs God; and drede hym alle the coostus of erthe.

PURVEY.

The titil of the sixe and sixtithe salm. In Ebreu thus, To the victorie in orguns, the salm of the song. In Jerome thus, To the ouercomer in salmes, the song of writing of a delitable thing with metre.

Purvey's version of the 66th Psalm.

God haue merci on vs, and blesse vs; liȝtne he his cheer on vs, and haue merci on vs. That we knowe thi weie on erthe; thin heelthe in alle folkis. God, puplis knowleche to thee; alle puplis knowleche to thee. Hethen men be glad, and make fulli ioye, for thou demest puplis in equite; and dressist hethene men in erthe. God. puplis knowleche to thee. alle puplis knowleche to thee. the erthe ȝaf his fruyt. God. oure God blesse vs. God blesse vs; and alle the coostis of erthe drede hym.

The Douai version of this Psalm is,

Psalme LXVI.

The prophet prayeth for (and withal foresheweth) the propagation of the Church of Christ.

1. Vnto the end, in hymes, a Psalme (*a*) of Canticle to Dauid.

a The Psalme beginning to be [illegible]ngue by voices, instruments [illegible]

2. God (*b*) haue mercie vpon vs, and (*c*) blesse vs: (*d*) illuminate his countenance vpon vs, and (*e*) haue mercie on vs.

b God first remitte our sinnes: [illegible] then giue vs thy manifold [illegible] grant faith and repentance [illegible] and so f[illegible]

3. That we may know thy way vpon earth: in al nations thy saluation.

4. Let peoples ô God confesse to thee: (*f*) let al peoples confesse to thee.

f Al nations shal be conuerted.

5. Let nations be glad & reioice: because thou iudgest peoples in equitie, and the nations in earth thou doest direct.

6. Let peoples ô God confesse to thee: let al peoples confesse to thee:

7. the earth hath yelded her fruite.

8. (*g*) God, (*h*) our God blesse vs, (*i*) God blesse vs: and let al the endes of the earth feare him.

g God the Father. h God the Sonne. i God the Holie Ghost [illegible] the [illegible] of al nations, by Euangelical preaching [illegible] thee, the most blessed Trinitie.

The Printing Press necessary for the general distribution of the Bible.

It is plain that something more than a written translation of the Bible was necessary, in order to multiply copies with sufficient rapidity, and so to reduce their price, as to bring them into common use. The time alone taken to transscribe a manuscript so lengthy as the Bible, made it costly. The clerk or scribe was so frequently in holy orders, that when a man was described as a clerk, it was taken for granted that he was an ecclesiastic, but not all the clergy were able to write, and very few indeed of the laity.

Block Books precursor of printing, 14th century.

Block books were the glimmering light in the East that gave promise of day-break. About the end of the 14th century we first hear of their being used for pictures of the saints, accompanied by a few lines of letters cut in the block; gradually entire pages were impressed in this manner, and thus began what are called block books, printed in fixed characters, but never exceeding a very few leaves. The great improvement from blocks to moveable type was made by Coster, of Haarlem, and perfected by Guttenberg, of Mentz.

Coster the inventor of moveable type.

The first book printed was, very appropriately, the Bible.

It was issued without date, and the precise time it was printed cannot be fixed.

The Guttenberg Bible.

From an inscription on a copy in two tomes in the National Library of Paris, we know this copy was illuminated and bound in the year 1456, therefore the work must have been completed a year or more before August 1456.

The inscription at the end of the first volume, in red ink, is,

"Et sic est finis prime partis biblie seu veteris testamenti. Illuminata seu rubricata et ligata p henricum Albch alius Cremer Anno dm̄i MCCCClvi festo Bartholomei apli.

Deo gracias . . . . . . Alleluia."

On the second volume the English translation of the inscription is,

"This book, illuminated and bound by Henry Cremer, vicar of the collegiate church of S. Stephen, at Mentz, was completed on the Feast of the Assumption of the Blessed Virgin Mary. A.D. 1456. Thanks be to God, Alleluia." Date of Cremer's illumination.

The Guttenberg Bible is without title page, pagination, or signatures. It consists of 641 leaves, printed in double columns from most beautiful type. A certain number of copies were printed on vellum, and the remainder on paper of excellent quality.

It is a magnificent book; its typography has never been surpassed.

The first printed book with a date and printer's name is the Mentz Psalter, "per Johannem Fust civem maguntinum et Petrum Schœffer de Gernszheim anno domini MCCCCLvij. In vigilia Assumpcionis." The Mentz Psalter, 1457.

The first printed Bible with a date was also produced by Fust and Schœffer.

The date is 1462.

Bibles soon began to be printed in almost all languages except English. Bibles printed in many languages.

No less than six editions were printed in

German before Luther was born, by Metelin, Eggestein, Fyner, Sensenschmidt, and Zainer.

W. Caxton prints James de Voragine's Golden Legend.

In the year 1483 Caxton printed at Westminster a translation of the Golden Legend.

This contained most of the five books of Moses and the Gospels.

The 7th verse of Genesis IIIrd is thus rendered :—

"And thus they knewe then that they were naked. And they toke figge leuis and sewed them togyder for to couere theyr membres in maner of brechis."

This book was published by the order of William, Earl of Arundel, and may be considered the first printed English Bible.

Penitential Psalms by Bishop Fisher.

About the same time Fisher, the good Bishop of Rochester (who afterwards approached the block with the New Testament in his hands, and opening it read aloud the words, "This is life eternal to know Thee, the only true God"), translated the seven penitential Psalms, many editions of which were printed by R. Pynson, Wynken de Worde, and others.

Bishop Gardyner.

Soon after this Bishop Gardyner, of Winchester, was engaged in the work of Bible translation. Early in the 16th century the authorities of the English Church took into consideration the desirability of introducing a vernacular Bible into England, and the great majority of the Council were of opinion that considering the religious troubles on the Continent, and the unsettled state of things at home, at this juncture the translation of the

Bible into the vulgar tongue, and its circulation among the people, would rather tend to confusion and distraction, than to edification.

Translation of the Bible into English postponed.

The postponement of the issue of an English Bible, translated by competent men, under the authority of the Church, was a most unfortunate event, although it was decided on after calm deliberation by the best and wisest men in the land, as it led to versions being published containing bitter glosses, which caused contentious disputations and wranglings in alehouses and other places, and the irreverent use of God's Holy Word.

Mischief done by contentious notes.

While giving Archbishop Wareham and the Council full credit for being influenced by conscientious motives alone, we cannot but deeply lament this error of judgment.

Those who were living at the time, and cognizant of all the circumstances of the case, imputed no blame to them.

Cranmer, for instance, says, "I can wel think them worthie pardon, which at the comming abrode of the Scripture doubted and drew backe."

We must remember that the universal desire for a Bible in England, we read so much of in most works on the subject, existed only in the imagination of the writers.

No general desire in England for a vernacular Bible.

So far from England then being a "Bible-thirsty land," there was no anxiety whatever for an English version at that time, excepting among a small minority of the people.

Evidence of George Constantyne.

George Constantyne, Vicar of Llanhuadaine, Registrar of S. David's, the father-in-law of the Archbishop of York, says, "How mercifully, how plentifully and purely hath God sent His Word to us here in England. Again, how unthankfully, how rebelliously, how carnally, and unwillingly do we receive it!

"Who is there among us that will have a Bible, but he must be compelled thereto."

Much more evidence could be adduced from sermons printed at the time, but the fact that the same edition of the Bible was often re-issued with fresh titles and preliminary matter, is sufficient to prove that there was no general demand for Bibles from the millions of people living in Great Britain.

Even the Clergy were not enthusiastic on the subject.

Hugh Latimer ignored the English Bible.

Hugh Latimer almost entirely ignored the English Bible, and always took his text from the Vulgate. Nearly the only reference made in any of his sermons is in his sixth sermon, preached in the year 1552 (Ed. 1562), from Romans 13th, in which he says, "I maruell that the English (Bible) is so translated 'in eating and drynking;' the Latine Examplar hath '*non commessationibus*,' that is to say, not in too much eating and drinkyng," and the marginal note is, "A fault in the English translation."

In the 12mo edition of Latimer's Sermons "Imprinted at London by Ihon Daye, dwellinge at Aldersgate, and William Seres, dwellinge in

Peter Colledge. A.D. 1549." there is an address, on Sig. A ij, from Thomas Some, "to the right vertuous and gracious Lady Katherin Douchesse of Suffolk," and one "To the Reader," of 15 pages, containing many quotations from Scripture, but not one in the words of any English Bible then existing.

The writer draws a dark picture of the state of religion and morals in England at that time:—

"Such a lousenes of lacyuyouse lyuing as the lyke has neuer bene hard of hereto fore."

"The Heathen were neuer so poisoned with the contagion of the most horryble heresies as some of vs Christians which are not ashamed to brag and boste of the spirite. But it is a phanaticke spirite, and a malingnante spirite."

Statement of Foxe untruthful.

The statement made by Foxe that "It was wonderful to see with what joy this book of God was received, not only among the learneder sort, and those that were noted for lovers of the reformation, but generally *all England over* among all the vulgar common people," is not more true than are many other statements made in the Acts and Monuments.

If the people all England over were so anxious to possess the new translation, what need was there of so many penal enactments to force it into circulation, and of Royal proclamations threatening with the King's displeasure those who neglected to purchase copies.

We have documentary evidence that the inhabitants of Cornwall and Devonshire unanimously objected to the new translation, and during "the pilgrimage of grace" in the North of England the Bible in Durham Cathedral was destroyed.

It is strange that this statement of Foxe should have been so often quoted by writers who must have known it to be exaggerated.

We have cause for deep thankfulness that each new version of Holy Writ is an improvement on its predecessor.

While preserving all the beauties of that Past Master in the art of writing pleasant English, William Tyndale, blemishes have been removed, and our translation of the Bible is worthy of the throne it occupies in the hearts of all true Englishmen.

We now proceed to describe the various versions of the English Bible in chronological order.

The Editions of the New Testament of Wm. Tyndale's Translation, and his Version of the Pentateuch.

TYNDALE'S NEW TESTAMENT.

THE first portion of Holy Scripture printed in the English language was Tyndale's New Testament.

The exact date of Tyndale's birth is not known, but it was between 1484 and 1486.—Edward, William, and John Tyndale were brothers of the first Richard Tyndale, of Melksham Court, Gloucestershire. William Tyndale.

The family assumed the name of Hytchins, and in this name he was in boyhood sent to S. Mary Magdalen's Hall, the grammar school of S. Mary Magdalen's College, Oxford. He supplicated for his B.A. May 13th, 1512; was admitted July 4th, 1512; determined 1513; created M.A. July 2, 1515.

Tyndale afterwards removed to the University of Cambridge, but the precise date at which he left Oxford is unknown. Most biographical notices of Tyndale are taken from John Foxe's Acts and Monuments of Martyrs, but no reliance can be placed on the truth of any uncorroborated statement made by Foxe.

Foxe's statements untrustworthy.

The late Mr. Brewer, than whom no man had a better opportunity of forming a correct estimate of the veracity of historical statements, says in his "Reign of Henry VIII.," edited by Mr. J. Gairdner, of the Public Record Office (I., 52, fn), "Had Foxe, the martyrologist, been an honest man, his carelessness and credulity would have incapacitated him from being a trustworthy historian.

"Unfortunately he was not honest; he tampered with the documents that came into his hands, and freely indulged in those very faults of suppression and equivocation for which he condemned his opponents." Tyndale left Cambridge about the end of the year 1521, and accepted the appointment of Chaplain to Sir John Walsh, Kt., of the Manor House, Little Sodbury, Gloucestershire, and became tutor to Sir John's children.

Tyndale at Little Sodbury.

Tyndale describes himself as being "evil favoured in this world, and without grace in the sight of men, speechless and rude, dull and slow witted." Having made himself disagreeable to the guests who visited the Manor House, and offended the neighbouring Clergy, he was cited to appear before the Chancellor of the Diocese, but when before Parker, the Chancellor, Tyndale gave such an explanation of the opinions that had been complained of, that he convinced the Chancellor the views he held were in harmony with the Catholic Faith.

During his residence at Little Sodbury, Tyndale formed the resolution to translate the Bible into the English language. He says in his preface to the Pentateuch, "I perceived by experience how that it was impossible to establish the lay people in any truth, except the Scripture were plainly laid before their eyes in their mother-tongue," "which things only moved me to translate the New Testament."

For this purpose he proceeded to London and applied for support to Cuthbert Tunstall, who had recently been appointed Bishop of that See, and was well known to be one of the greatest scholars of the day, and who on account of his eminent attainments as a linguist was afterwards selected, in conjunction with Bishop Heath, to revise two editions of the Great Bible. The Bishop of London having his house full of dependents already, was unable to accede to Tyndale's request, but advised him to find employment in London. Tyndale in London.

Tyndale was soon after appointed preacher at S. Dunstan's-in-the-West, where he made the acquaintance of Humphrey Monmouth, a wealthy cloth merchant, who took him into his service as Chaplain from the middle of the year 1523 to May 1524, when Tyndale left England for Hamburg. Tyndale leaves England.

During that time Monmouth declared that Tyndale "conducted himself like a good priest. He studied most part of the day, and of the night, at his book, and he would eat but sodden meat by his good will, nor drink but small single beer."

Monmouth promised to pay him £10 a year on the condition that he prayed for the souls of Monmouth's father and mother. Humphrey Monmouth was afterwards knighted, and served as Sheriff of the City of London in 1535.

Humphrey Monmouth.

He died in the year 1537, and was buried at Alhallow's Church.

Tyndale did not remain long at Hamburg, but joined Luther at Wittemberg, where he finished the translation of the New Testament which he had commenced in England.

Luther's influence on Tyndale.

Tyndale's Testament bears impress of the influence of Luther's translation of 1522.

From Luther's general introduction Tyndale transferred to his prologue sixty lines, or nearly one half, and adopted 190 of Luther's marginal references; these stand against the same chapters and verses, and form the same inner margin.

The notes on the outer margin yield the same evidence.

On Tyndale's outer margin are nearly all Luther's glosses.

It cannot therefore excite wonder that Tyndale's translation was at the time usually called "Luther's Testament in English."

Friar Roye.

Tyndale was assisted at Wittemberg in the work of translation by William Roye, a Friar, of whom he speaks in violent terms, as he did of his other assistants.

As soon as Tyndale's manuscript was ready

for the press he returned to Hamburg to receive the £10 promised to him, which Monmouth forwarded by a Stilyard merchant, named Hans Collenbek; he then hastened to Cologne, and arranged with Peter Quentel to bring out an edition of the New Testament in quarto, with prologue, marginal notes, and references; but by the time the printing had proceeded as far as signature K, further progress was prohibited by the Senate of Cologne, and there is no evidence that the book was ever completed. It is true that we have the official statement that two editions of the New Testament were introduced into England at the same time, one with glosses and the other without, but the one with glosses may not have been a complete book.

Just as the Old Testament which Tyndale intended to complete was issued in six separate parts, viz., the five books of Moses and the book of Job, so rather than waste the copies of the Gospels printed at Quentel's press at Cologne, Tyndale may have sent them to England with his complete octavo Testament.

This will account for the fact that no perfect copy of the Cologne quarto exists. The only fragment known is in Case xiij., No. 8, of the Grenville Library, British Museum, and consists of the prologue, the list of the books, and the Gospel of S. Matthew, so far as the 12th verse of xxij^nd chapter. The Col quarto.

When disturbed at Cologne by the city authorities, urged on by the exiled Dean of the

Church of the B.V. at Frankfort, Tyndale and his assistant fled to Worms, and from the press of Peter Schoeffer, of that city, was issued the first New Testament ever printed in English.

Peter Schoeffer.

Peter Schoeffer was the second son of the celebrated printer of Mayence, at one time the partner of Fust.

The book is very small 8vo. size, and contains 348 leaves. Signatures in 8's.

The text begins on fol. i, A ij, and ends on the recto of T t i., numbered 353 in error for 343.

There are 12 woodcuts.

The first English New Testament, 1525.

It was published without the translator's name and without date, unless the date was on the title page, now lost.

There are only two copies known, one is in the library of a College in Bristol, and is perfect except the title page.

The other in the library of S. Paul's Cathedral is imperfect.

The exact date at which it was issued cannot be positively stated; in all probability it was early in March of the year which, by our present mode of reckoning, would be called 1526, but as at that time the year began on Lady day, it may be said that the printing of the first English Testament was finished at the end of the year 1525.

Foxe states that "Tyndale first translated the New Testament about the year 1527." It is inexcusable that so loose and inaccurate a statement should have been made by one professing to be an ecclesiastical historian, and who at that time, with very little trouble, might have ascertained the true date.

We have the testimony of Cochlaeus that it was in 1525 Tyndale left Cologne for Worms, and as his copy was ready, there is no doubt it was at once placed in the printer's hands, and it bears marks of having been passed rapidly through the press.

Dean Cochlaeus.

It was conveyed to England immediately, in order that it might be distributed before the warning to prevent its importation could be acted on.

The following is Tyndale's address:—

"*To the Reder.*

"Them that are learned Christenly I beseche, for as moche as I am sure, and my conscience beareth me recorde that of a pure entent singilly and faythfully I have interpreted itt as farre forth as god gave me the gyfte of knowledge and vnderstandynge, that the rudnes off the worke now at the fyrst tyme offend them not, but that they consyder howe that I had no man to counterfet, nether was holpe with englysshe of eny that had interpreted the same, or sache lyke thinge in the Scripture before tyme. Moreover, even very necessitie and combraunce (God is recorde) above strengthe, which I will not rehearce lest we shulde seme to bost oureselves, caused that many thynges are lackynge whiche necessaryly are required, count it as a thynge not havynge his full shape, but

Tyndale's Epistle to the Reader.

as it were borne afore hys tyme, euen as a thynge begunne rather then fynnesshed.

"In tyme to come (yf god have apoynted us there unto) we will geve it his full shape, and pull out yf ought be added superfluusly and adde to yff ought be over sene thorowe negligence: and will enfoarce to brynge to compendeousnes that which is nowe translated at the lengthe and to geve lyght where it is requyred and to seke in certayne places more proper englysshe and with a table to expounde the wordes which are nott comenly used and showe howe the scripture useth many wordes which are otherwyse understonde of the commen people and to helpe with a declaracion where one tonge taketh nott another and will endever oure selves as it were to sethe it better, and to make it more apt for the weake stomakes, desyrynge them that are learned and able to remember their duetie and to helpe there unto."

The Testament from which Tyndale made his translation was the second edition of Erasmus, printed in Latin and Greek by J. Froben, Bâsle in 1519, folio size.

Tyndale adopted some of the alterations made by Erasmus in his third edition of 1522; for example, he inserted the passage in the fifth chapter of the first epistle of S. John (the three Heavenly Witnesses).

Tyndale's translation is in some places more accurate than Erasmus' text, owing to the influence of the Vulgate.

[illegible]

At this time Tyndale knew little or nothing of Hebrew, but was a good Greek and Latin scholar. He had a wonderful faculty for acquiring foreign languages, and was thorough master of English. To him we owe the exceeding beauty and tender grace of the language of our present New Testament, for in spite of many revisions, almost every sentence is substantially the same as Tyndale wrote it in 1525. It is true that improvements have been made by the more correct rendering of certain words which Tyndale purposely mistranslated, such as "Church" for "Congregation," &c. Tyndale acknowledged that his first translation was very imperfect, "euen as a thynge begunne, rather than fynnesshed;" and in his prologue to the 1534 edition he says, "I haue weeded out of it many faultes which lacke of helpe at the begynning, and ouersyght did sow therein."

[illegible]

The only wonder is that Tyndale's animosity to the Church of England, and his strong Lutheran bias, did not produce a still greater crop of errors.

The English Bishops carefully examined Tyndale's translation, and instead of making a better one, as they ought to have done, endeavoured to suppress it.

They had the greatest reverence for what Tunstall calls "the most holy word of God," and considered Luther's Testament to be a profanation of it, they therefore felt it their duty to destroy every copy they could obtain.

Burning the works of opponents.

Whilst we condemn the burning of Tyndale's work, we must not forget that it was the custom of the age to burn the works of opponents, as Luther a few years before burnt the books of the canon law, and the bull of Pope Leo, outside the walls of Wittemberg, and in 1552 John Calvin burnt all the copies he could collect of Servetus' Bible, at Geneva, because they contained some notes he did not think to be orthodox.

Tyndale's Testaments burnt.

Tyndale made a great outcry against the iniquity of burning the word of God; but as he sold the books to Augustine Packington, well knowing the purpose for which they were being purchased, he was a participator in the crime, and as much to be blamed as the Bishop of London.

The fact is the books were full of errors and unsaleable, and Tyndale wanted money to pay the expense of a revised version, and to purchase Vostermann's old Dutch blocks to illustrate his Pentateuch, and was glad to make capital in more ways than one by the transaction.

Tyndale sold his books to be burnt.

"I am glad," said he, "for these two benefits shall come thereof: I shall get money to bring myself out of debt, and the whole world will cry out against the burning of God's word, and the overplus of the money that shall remain to me shall make me more studious to correct the said New Testament, and so newly to imprint the same once again, and I trust the second will much better like you than ever did the first."

Sir Thomas More.

It is only just to the memory of Sir Thomas More to record that, although he was fully aware of the errors contained in Tyndale's translation, he used his utmost influence with the Bishop of London to prevent their destruction.

Tyndale fully expected from the first that his translation would be burnt. In his preface to "Wicked Mammon," published May 8th, 1527, he says, "In brenninge the Newe Testamente they did none other thynge then I loked for."

Pirated editions.

Tyndale allowed nine years to elapse before issuing a second edition of the New Testament: it is not therefore to be wondered at that pirated editions were produced: how many such cannot be told.

The record of one has recently come to light in the archives of the Town House at Antwerp.

It appears that in the year 1531 a sentence was pronounced in the Alderman's Court in the case of John Silverlinke *versus* the guardians of the children of Francis Birckmann. The plaintiff had delivered to Francis Birckmann 2,025 copies of the New Testament printed in English, for which he was to be paid £28 17*s.* 3*d.* and had only received 20 Carolus florins, equal to £3 7*s.* 3*d.*

No trace of a single copy of this edition is known.

Editions of which no trace remain.

Another edition of which no trace remains, excepting one title page now in the possession of the Revd. Dr. Angus, of Regent's Park College, was printed in 1532.

It reads: The Newe Testa | ment in Englysh translated | after the Greeke contay | ninge these bookes. | The Gospels |

Matthew.	Luke.
Mark.	Ihon.

The Actes of the Apostles.

The Epistles of S. Paul.

To the Romaynes.	The I. Thessalonians.
The I. Corinthians.	The II. Thessalonians.
The II. Corinthians.	The I. Tymothe.
To the Galathians.	The II. Tymothe.
To the Ephesians.	To Titus.
To the Phillippians.	To Phylemon.
To the Collossians.	To the Hebreues.

The Epistle of S. James.

The i. of S. Peter.	The i. of S. John.
The ii. of S. Peter.	The ii. of S. John.
The Epistle of S. Jude.	The iij. of S. John.

The Reuelation of S. Ihon.

The Epistles taken out of the Olde Testament.

Anno 1532.

All printed in black letter, the words underlined are in larger type.

Dr. Angus informs me that there were two men burnt that year (1532) for dealing in

Tyndale's Testaments, and yet no edition is known between 1525 and 1534.

Of the second New Testament of Tyndale's version only one copy is left: it is in the Grenville Library, British Museum.

It has two title pages. The first has ten lines printed in red and eleven lines in black ink. Tyndale's 2nd edition.

The words within the woodcut border are,

"The New Testament as it was written/ and caused to be written by them which herde yt Whom also oure saueour Christ Jesus com | maunded that they shulde preach it vnto al crea tures.

The Gospell of S. Mathew.
The Gospell of S. Marke.
The Gospell of S. Luke.
The Gospell of S. Ihon.
The Actes of the Apostles.

"Joelis ij. I will poure oute of my spyryte vpon all fleshe and youre sonnes and youre doughters shall prophesy youre yonge men shall se visions ād youre olde men shal dreame dreames."

It is strange that this quotation should be given in the words of our present Bible, although this New Testament was issued a year before the first English printed Bible made its appearance.

The Colophon reads,

¶ Here endeth the new Testament diligently ouersene and correctedt and prynted now agayne at Antwerpe/ by me wydowe of Christoffel of Endhouen. In the yere of oure Lorde mccccc and xxxiiij in August.

The size of the book is 16mo. There are twelve pages of preliminary and thirteen leaves of tables at the end.

George Joye. This Testament was revised by George Joye, one of the translator's assistants, who being tired of waiting for Tyndale to fulfil his promise to issue a revised and improved edition, ventured, at the solicitation of the printer, to see an edition through the press; this he had a right to do, but ought not to have made substantial alterations in Tyndale's renderings without acknowledging he had so done.

Tyndale was very indignant, and rated Joye in the most unmeasured language.

Joye's apology. Joye justified himself by saying that, in consequence of Tyndale's long delay, Dutchmen, totally ignorant of the English language, had issued several editions full of printers' errors, and "England hath enough and too many false Testaments, and is now likely to have many more; yea, and that whether Tyndale correct his or no, yet shall these, now in hand, go forth uncorrected too, except somebody correct them."

George Joye could not have been influenced by any mercenary motive in undertaking this work, for the entire remuneration he received was about a half-penny a leaf, and the alterations made by him were not very important; the principal one was that he substituted for the word "resurrection," "the life after this."

Certainly there was nothing in Joye's version to justify the bitter, reproachful, and unchristian terms in which Tyndale poured out the vials of his wrath upon Joye.

In the Cambridge University Library is a pamphlet, the title of which is,

¶ An Apology made by George Joye to satisfye (if it maye be) W. Tindale: to pourge and defend himself ageinst so many sclaunderouse lyes fayned vpon him in Tindals vncharitable and vnsober Pystle so well worthye to be prefixed for the Reader to induce him into the vnderstanding of hys new Testament diligently corrected and printed in the yeare of oure lorde M.ccccc. and xxxiiij in November. George Joye 14 Feb. 1535.

¶ I knowe and beleue that the bodyes of euery dead man shall ryse agayne at domes daye.

¶ Psalme cxx.

Lorde, delyuer me from lyinge lyppes/ and from a deceatfull tongue. Amen.

1535.

in which George Joy records,

"my grete greif and sorowe for that he (Tyndale) shulde so falsely belye and sclaunder me of syche crymes which I neuer thought spake/ nor wrote/ and of siche which I knowe wel his owne conscience doth testifie the contrarie/ euen that I denied the Resurreccion of the bodie/ but beleue it as constantly as himself.

"He rayleth vpon me/ he belyeth me/ he slaundereth me and that most spightfully with a perpetual infamie: whiche al yf yt be not of enuy/ malice/ and hatered of what els shulde yt spring?

George Joye's statement of Tyndale's dependence on Luther.

"An euen here for all his holy protestacions/ yet herd I neuer sobre and wyse man so prayse his owne workis as I herd him praise his exposicion of the v. vj. and vij. ca. Mat. in so myche that myne eares glowed for shame to here him/ and yet it was Luther that made it/ T[yndale] onely but translating and powldering yt here and there with his own fantasies, which praise methought yt then better to haue ben herde of a nother mannis mouth/ for it declared out of what affeccion yt sprang euen farre vnlyk and contrarye vnto these whiche he now professeth and protesteth so holely, for wordis be messageris of mennis myndis."

Tyndale breaks his word.

G. Joye had an interview with Tyndale, who promised to correct and reform his epistle, but did not keep his word. Joye was therefore obliged in self-defence to republish Tyndale's epistle with comments on each paragraph.

Joye says, "I wounder how he coude compare yt (Tyndale's New Testament) with greke sith himselfe is not so exquysitely sene there yn." "I know wel (Tyndale) was not able to do yt with out siche an helper which he hathe euer had hitherto."

Joye then proves that he could not have been actuated by covetous motives, as the printer paid him only 4½*d.* for the correction of each 16 leaves, "so that in al I had for my labour but xiiij shylyngis flemesshe. and yet saith T[yndale] I did it of couetousnes: If this be couetousnes/ then was Tindal moche more couetouse/ for he (as I her say) toke x. ponde for his correccion."

Joye disapproved of "fryuole gloses." "I wolde the scripture were so puerly and plyanly translated that it neded nether note/ glose nor scholia so that the reder might once swimme without a corke."

Joye's objection to notes.

A copy of the second edition of the New Testament revised by Tyndale is in the Chetham Library, Hunts Court, Manchester.

Chetham Library copy.

It looks like a 12mo., but as the seam wires go down the leaf it must be small octavo.

It has two titles within woodcut borders, the first reads,

☾ The ne we Testament/ dyly | gently corrected and compared with the | Greke by Willyam Tindale: and fynes shed in the yere of ou re Lorde God A.M.D & xxxiiij in the moneth of | Nouember.

The second title is,

☾ The ne we Testa | ment. Imprinted at Anwerp by Marten | Emperowr. Anno | M.D. xxxiiij.

Martin Emperowr was of Dutch extraction: his original name was Martin de Keyser; this he translated into the language of the book he was printing; thus, Dutch books have Martin de Keyser; Latin ones have Martinus Cæsar; French books, Martin Le Empereur; and English ones, Marten Emperowr.

Martin de Keyser.

On the reverse of title page begins,

"☾ W T vnto the Reader" "Here thou hast (moost deare reader) the new Testamet or covenaunt made wyth vs of God in Christes bloude. Which I have looked over agayne (now at the last) with all dylygence/ and compared it vnto the Greke/ and have weded oute of it many fautes/ which lacke of helpe at the begynninge and oversyght/ dyd sowe therin. If ought seme chaunged/ or not all to gether agreynge with the Greke/ let the fynder of yt faute consider the Hebrue Phrase or maner of speche lefte in the Greke wordes."

It finishes with an excuse for employing the word "repentance" in place of "penance," and "Seniors" or "Elders" for "Priests."

Elders.

"¶ Elders. In the olde testamēt ye tēporall heedes & rulers of ye Jues which had ye gouernaunce ouer ye laye or cōmen people are called elders/ as ye maye se in ye foure euangelystes. Oute of which custome paule in his epistle & also peter/ call ye prelates & spirituall goueners which are bysshopes & prestes/ elders.

"Now whether ye call them elders or prestes/ it is to me all one/ so that ye vnderstande that they be offycers & seruaūtes of the worde of God/ vnto the which all men both hie & lowe that will not rebell agaynst Christ/ must obeye as longe as they preahe & rule trulye & no longer." This occupies 18 pages; then,

Collation.

"¶ A prologue to the iiij Euangelystes shewynge what they were & their auctoryte," 3½ pages;

"¶ A warninge to ye reader if ought be scaped thorow necligence of the prynter/ as this text is yt foloweth/ which if thou fynde anye more soche: cōpare ye englyshe to ye other bookes that are all readye prynted/ & so shalt thou perceaue the truthe of the ynglish," ½ page;

"Willyam Tindale/ yet once more to the christen reader," 8½ pages and 1½ blank, making 16 preliminary leaves.

The second title is Sig. A 1. At the bottom is the printer's trade mark with the letters M. K.; on the other side, "❡ The bokes conteyned in the newe Testament."

The text ends with four lines on folio 484, in mistake for 384; then the Epistles, &c. after the use of Salisbury, 18 pages. At the end, "These things have I added to fill up a leaf with all."

There are prologues to the epistles; that to Romans occupying 34 pages.

The woodcuts number 39; but some of them are repetitions.

Tyndale's notes.

There are 232 marginal notes. Many of them exhibit the great change that had taken place in Tyndale's religious opinions, and show that he had ceased to be an Episcopalian.

Anne Boleyn.

One of the British Museum copies of this book is imperfect, and is remarkable for having on its edges the words Anna Regina Angliae. It is supposed to have been the property of Anne Boleyn, one of the wives of Henry VIII.; but there is no evidence that the assertion, that it was presented to her by Tyndale, is correct.

This copy was bequeathed to the British

Museum in the year 1799, by the Rev. C. M. Cracherode.

The last New Testament revised by the translator was printed in the year 1534–5; that is, the text was printed in 1534, and the general title added in 1535.

Tyndale's final revision.

As it is Tyndale's final revision, it is the most important of all editions.

It was adopted by Tyndale's personal friend, John Rogers, as the basis of the Testament of Matthew's Bible of 1537.

On the second or text title is the monogram or trade mark of the publisher,

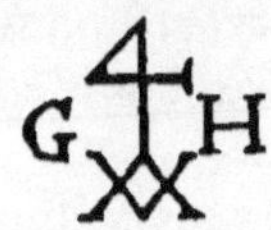

and therefore to distinguish Tyndale's finally revised edition from all others, it is usually called the "GH" edition. This mark has been a fruitful source of speculation.

For some time it was thought to be the initials of the translator's name in its Latin form, Guillaume Hytchins; for in his first publication Tyndale signed himself "Willyam Tindale" otherwise called "Hytchins," and that the other part represented the printer, (I. V. M.) Jacob van Meteren: but owing to some books having turned up with precisely the same trade mark and letters, published at Antwerp by Godfridus Dumæus, it is now known that this monogram was his trade mark.

He, like de Keyser, was of Dutch extraction. His original name was Godfried van der Haghen; but in publishing works in Latin he employed the equivalent of Godfridus Dumaeus: both words signifying in English, "a thicket of bushes."

Godfried van der Haghen.

He was closely associated, if not in partnership, with the well-known Antwerp printer, Marten Emperowr, and their joint names appear on the imprint of many books; for example, on the imprint of a work by Erasmus of Rotterdam, entitled "Enchiridion militis Christiani," may be seen "Apud Martinum Caesarem impensis Godfridi Dumaei," and on another book, "Impress. per Martinum Caesaris impensis honesti viri Godfridi Dumaei."

Marten Emperowr.

As "G H" was the publisher of the 1535-4 edition, there can be little doubt that it was printed by de Keyser. Why he should have declined to allow his name to appear it is impossible to do more than conjecture; perhaps it was a similar reason to that which induced him about the same time to change his motto from "Sola fides sufficit" to the far better one, "Spes mea Jesus."

The size of the book is small octavo. The title page reads,

Tyndale's 8vo. of 1535

"The ne | we Testament yet once agay | ne corrected by Willyam Tindale: | Where vnto is added a Kalendar | and a necessarye Table wherin ea | sely and lightelye maye be foun | de any storye contayned in the | foure Euangelistes and | in the Actes of the | Apostles.

"❡ Prynted in the yere of oure | Lorde God. MD | & xxxv."

Collation.

On reverse of title is, "❡ An Almanack for xxj. yeares" (1535 to 1555). The Kalendar, &c., probably 8 leaves. Address to reader, 15 pages. "A prologe into the iiij Euangelistes" &c., 3 pages. A table as stated on title page, 20½ pages, reverse of the last blank, making in all 28 preliminary leaves.

The prologues are in the same kind of type as the text, but rather smaller size.

There are 36 woodcuts; some of them very small, others nearly filling a page.

The order of the Gospels and Epistles is as follows—

Order of books in the G H edition.

❡ The bokes conteyned in the | newe Testament.

i. The Gospell of S. Mathew.
ij. The Gospell of S. Marke.
iij. The Gospell of S. Luke.
iiij. The Gospell of S. John.
v. The Actes of the Apostles, writtē by S. Luke.

vj. The Pistle of S. Paul to the Romayns.
vij. The. j. Pistle of S. Paul to the Corinthyās.
viij. The. ij. pistle of S. Paul to the Corinthyās.
ix. The pistle of S. Paul to the Galathyans.
x. The Pistle of S. Paul to the Ephesians.
xj. The Pistle of S. Paul to the Philippians.
xij. The Pistle of S. Paul to the Colossians.

xiij. The. j. Pistle of S. Paul to the Tessa-
loniãs.
xiiij. The. ij. Pistle of S. Paul to the Tessa-
loniãs.
xv. The fyrst Pistle of S. Paul to Timothe.
xvi. The second Pistle of S. Paul to Timothe.
xvii. The Pistle of S. Paul to Titus.
xviij. The Pistle of S. Paul to Philemon.

xix. The fyrst Pistle of S. Peter.
xx. The second Pistle of S. Peter.
xxj. The fyrst Pistle of S. John.
xxij. The second Pistle of S. John.
xxiij. The thyrd Pistle of S. John.
The pistle vnto the Hebrues.
The Pistle of S. James.
The Pistle of S. Jude.
The reuelacion of S. John.

This is the last Testament for which Tyndale is personally responsible. The many changes made in subsequent editions were the work of others; for on the 23rd of May 1535 Tyndale was arrested and imprisoned in the Castle of Vilvorde, 24 miles from Antwerp.

Tyndale arrested.

The agents employed to capture Tyndale were Gabriel Donne and Henry Phillips.

Donne was rewarded by being made Abbot of Buckfastleigh Abbey, in Devonshire, in 1539, and afterwards made Prebendary of S. Paul's, London.

Strange to say, John Rogers, the friend of Tyndale, and Gabriel Donne, his betrayer, occupied stalls at S. Paul's at the same time.

Only one document is known to exist in the handwriting of Tyndale; this was discovered by M. Galesloot in the Archives of the Council of Brabant. This touching letter was written, as its contents will show, during his imprisonment at Vilvorde, and was addressed to the Marquis of Bergen-op-Zoom, the governor of the castle. The letter was written in Latin, contracted as usual at that period. The handwriting is thoroughly characteristic of the man. The following is a literal translation :—

Tyndale's letter to the Marquis of Bergen-op-Zoom.

"I believe, right worshipful, that you are not ignorant of what has been determined concerning me (by the Council of Brabant) therefore I entreat your Lordship and that by the Lord Jesus, that if I am to remain here (in Vilvorde) during the winter, you will request the Procureur to be kind enough to send me from my goods which he has in his possession, a warmer cap, for I suffer extremely from cold in the head, being afflicted with a perpetual catarrh, which is considerably increased in the cell, a warmer coat also, for that which I have is very thin, also a piece of cloth to patch my leggings; my overcoat has been worn out, my shirts are also worn out. He has a woollen shirt of mine, if he will be kind enough to send it. I have also with him leggings of thicker cloth for putting on above, he also has warmer caps for wearing at night.

"I also wish his permission to have a candle in the evening, for it is wearisome to sit alone in the dark. But above all I entreat and beseech your clemency to be urgent with the Procureur, that he may kindly permit me to have my Hebrew Bible, Hebrew Grammar, and Hebrew Dictionary, that I may spend my time with that study. And in return, may you obtain your dearest wish, provided always it be consistent with the salvation of your soul. But if any other resolution has been come to concerning me, before the conclusion of the winter, I shall be patient, abiding the will of God to the glory of the grace of my Lord Jesus Christ, Whose spirit, I pray, may ever direct your heart. Amen.

W. Tyndale."

Tyndale's martyrdom.

Tyndale's imprisonment lasted one year and 135 days, and on Friday, October 6th, 1536, the sentence pronounced by the Court was executed; Tyndale was strangled, and his body burnt.

The Court was composed of four members of the Council of Brabant - Godefroid de Meyère, Charles T'Serraets, Jacques Boonen, and Theobald Cotereau, and four theologians of the University of Louvain.

The commission was nominated by the Regent, Mary of Hungary, as representative of the Emperor.

The next edition in chronological order is one that amply justifies George Joye's action in correcting the press at Antwerp, by showing the singular orthography introduced by Flemish printers ignorant of the English tongue.

The place at which it was printed and the name of the publisher are unknown. It has on the text title, "Fynesshed 1535."

Tyndale's Testament of 1535.

Like the first edition of 1525, no copy of this book is known to exist with the first title page.

It is octavo size.

The prologue of 16 leaves to the Romans, and the Table of the Gospels, were evidently corrected by some competent person, as they exhibit the ordinary spelling of the period; but the rest shows the attempt of a Flemish compositor to give the equivalent of the English vowel sounds.

The following is a list of some of the words showing the variation in spelling between this edition and that of 1534:—

Peculiar spelling.

1535.	1534.
abstaeyne	abstayne
abyede	abyde
boedy	body
boeke	boke
boeldely	boldely
clocke	cloke
cloethe	clothe
coelde	colde
coele	cole
coete	cote
daey	day
faele	faule
faeont	faynt
gaeye	gaye
haest	hast

1535.	1534.
haet	hate
haeven	haven
maed	mad
neadeth	nedeth
noane	none
obtaeyned	obtayned
paert	part
paeynted	paynted
praeyer	prayer
reage	rage
rewaerde	rewarde
roope	rope
sae	say
saefe	safe
saeynctes	sayntes
taecklynge	tackylnge
tappe	tope
te	the
toekens	tokens
unfeayned	unfayned
vaele	vayle
veoyce	voyce
waelke	walke
whoo	who
woere	where
wroete	wrote
wreath	wroth
yought	youth

Uniformity of spelling is not to be expected in books printed in the early part of the 16th century. In one of my copies of Tyndale's New

Testament the word Saint is spelt four different ways in as many lines.

In the 1535 edition a few words are almost always spelled the same, such as "Faether" and "Moether," but the spelling of other words varies greatly.

Flemish printers.

No doubt the compositor set up the type to represent, as nearly as he could, the pronunciation of the English words by the Flemish reader.

At any rate, Tyndale had nothing to do with the spelling, and most likely never saw a single copy of the book.

First folio edition.

The first New Testament ever printed in folio size was the edition of 1536.

It is supposed to have been printed in England at the very time its translator was being put to death.

The title is,

¶ The Newe te | stament yet ones agayne corrected by | W. Tyndale:

And in many places a | mēded, where it scaped before by negly | gence of the printer.

Also a Kalender | and a necessary table, wherin easely & | lyghtly may be founde any story cō | teyned in the foure Euangelystes, | and in the Actes of the apostels. | Also before euery pystel of S. | Paul is a prologue very | frutefull to the reder. | And after the newe testament | foloweth the Epystels of | the olde testament. &c. |

¶ Newly printed/ in the yere of | our lorde M.D. XXXVI.

Outside is a woodcut border representing boys, without clothing, climbing up the sides, and going in procession with musical instruments.

The Almanac on reverse of title is from 1535 to 1557. There are 14 leaves of preliminary. After the tables, &c. at the end is, "These thinges are added to fyll vp ye leffe with all"

"Infernus & Gehenna dyffere moche in sygnificacion though we haue none other interpretacion for either of them than this engltssh worde Hell."

The book ends with, "God saue the kynge/ and all his well wyllers."

There are no woodcuts, nor is the order of the Epistles changed.

As in several other editions of Tyndale's Testaments, and also in the Primer of Queen Mary, printed by Robert Valentine in 1555, the word "not" is spelled "nat" wherever it occurs in this edition.

This Testament was set up from that of 1534.

Printer's errors.

It has a curious printer's error in the 10th chapter of S. John's Gospel, 12th verse: "The Wolf eateth them" for "the wolf catcheth them," and in I. S. Peter iij. and 6th v., "be nat afraid of every man" for "be not afraid of every shadow."

Three quartos of 1536.

Three quarto editions were issued the same year (1536) so much alike, that it is difficult to distinguish one from another, and as they all read together. Sometimes a copy contains leaves from all three editions.

They have no publisher's nor printer's name, but whoever had them printed was aware that the edition of 1535-4, known as the G. H., contained the translator's final emendations, and selected that edition for reproduction.

The title pages of all three appear to have been printed at the same press and at the same time; *i.e.* all three have the same title.

They follow the G. H. excepting that reference to a Kalender is omitted, and a quotation from the 16th of S. Mark is added: "Go ye into all the worlde/ and preache | the glad tydynges to all creatures | he that beleueth and is bapti | sed shal be saued.

There are many woodcuts, and that of S. Paul affords the readiest means of differentiating the editions.

In the first, the stone on which the Apostle's foot is placed is blank.

In the second it has a mole, and the third has the engraver's mark,—

Blank stone edition.

One of my copies of the blank stone has a printer's error which the other has not; so this edition must have been corrected while passing through the press.

The same woodcuts in different books.

There must have been some way in which woodcut blocks were passed from one printer's hands to another in early times, for we often find impressions from the same block in Bibles and Testaments printed hundreds of miles away from each other.

For instance, the woodcut of S. John in each of these three editions is the same as that in the Endhoven edition, and some of the cuts in these three editions are in Matthew's Bible of 1537.

My copy of Coverdale's New Testament, printed by Matthew Crom in 1538, has the same cuts in Revelation as these three quartos.

The puzzle is, that sometimes the same cuts appear in two books published at the same or nearly the same time, at considerable distances from each other.

No. 10. " 11. " 12. " 13 Four 8vo editions of 1535.

Beside the folio, and three quarto, there were also four octavo editions of Tyndale's Testament published in the year 1536. Three of them are dated, and they all so much resemble each other that there can be little doubt that all four were issued from the same press, and were most likely printed at Antwerp.

All of them have woodcuts, and are printed in black letter without imprints; and, as some of the copies of each edition are perfect, it is certain they were published anonymously. They have all the same number of lines to a page, and the leaves of all four editions are not numbered.

All four follow the last Testament revised by the translator in omitting the words: "this cup is the new testament in my blood," I. Corinthians xi. and 25th verse. They have all on the second title merely the words, "The newe | testament | newlye | corrected."

No. 14. Redman's duglott.

The first New Testament printed in Latin and English came from the press of Robert Redman in 1538. Quarto size. The title, in red and black, within a woodcut border, is "The newe | Testament in Englyshe | and Latyn accordyng to the | translacyon of doctour Eras | mus of Roterodam &c. Anno MCCCCC. xxxviiii.

"Iermie xxij: Is nat my worde lyke a fyre sayeth the Lorde, and lyke an hammer that breaketh the harde stone?

"Prynted in Flete streete by Robert Redman. Set forth vnder the kinges moste gracious lycence;" and below the border "cvm privilegio ad imprimdvm solvm."

The English is on the left side in large black letter, and the Latin occupies about one-third of the space, being printed in smaller type. No doubt the issue in the two languages was intended to enable the English clergy easily to compare the two, and satisfy themselves of the accuracy of the English rendering, and so overcome their prejudice to a vernacular translation.

It seems a pity that the Vulgate was not selected instead of the Latin of Erasmus; for although Erasmus never separated himself from the Church, he, like Nicolas de Lyra, was not above suspicion.

Nicolas de Lyra.

Certainly his rendering is not equal to that of S. Jerome; for example, "In principio erat sermo, et sermo erat apud Deum. Et Deus erat ille sermo," is no improvement on "In principio erat verbum et verbum erat apud," &c.

On the reverse of first title is an Almanac for 22 years; then follows six pages of Kalendar in red and black ink.

The second title reads,

"The newe Testament in Englyshe & in Latin. Novvm Testamentvm Anglice et Latine. Anno Dni 1538." On the back is the list of books. The imprint is,

Redman's diglot of 1538.

"Thus endyth the newe Testament bothe in Englyshe and in Laten of mayster Erasmus translacio, with the Pystles take out of ye Old Testamet. Set forthe with the kynges moste gra ious lycence, and Imprinted by Robert Redman dwellyng in Flete strete at ye signe of the George nexte vnto saynte Donstons Churche. The yere of our Lorde. M.CCCCC. XXXViij. and the thyrty yere of the Kynges most gracious reygne. God saue the kynge."

There are references in the margin, but no contents or notes, nor are there contents at the head of the chapters. A full page has forty lines.

Text follows the G. H.

The text generally follows Godfried van der Haghen's edition; this accounts for it having been mistaken for a reprint of the Testament attached to Matthew's Bible of 1537, both being taken from the same source.

A printer's error occurs in II. Corinthians, 10th chapter, 11th verse, which should be, "think on this wise," but is here made to read, "think on his wife."

No. 15.

The other quarto edition of this year, although it does not bear on it the name of printer, or place at which it was printed, was the work of Jacob van Meteren at Antwerp, who, the year before, had issued "Matthew's" Bible.

The title is,

"The newe testa | ment of oure sauioure Jesu | Christ, newly and diligently | translated into Englysshe | by Thomas Mathew | with annotations in | ye mergent to helpe | the reader to the | vnderstādyng of ye Texte | ✠

"Set forth with the kynges | moost gratious lycence. Anno M.D. xxxviii."

Thomas Mathew was a pseudonym used to enable Tyndale's translation to obtain the King's licence to circulate.

Two editions printed at the same time.

There were two editions of this book printed the same year and at the same press; one with woodcuts and one without.

This is not at all an uncommon circumstance. I have met with several Bibles which were undoubtedly printed, up to a certain part, from the same setting up of the type, as they not only read together, but contain the same printer's errors and faults in the arrangement of the type, but in a part of the edition woodcuts have been introduced which obliged the rest of the volume to be set up again.

No. 16, Powell's duglott.

The second duglot of Tyndale's version was printed by Robert Redman's successor in business, William Powell.

It may be described as a reprint of the first duglot, the same type and woodcuts having been used for both editions, and it is most difficult to distinguish an imperfect copy of one book from one of the other; indeed, imperfect copies of the 1538 are often completed with leaves from the 1548–7.

The title of this book is,

"The Newe Testa ment in Englishe and in Latin. Novvm Testamen | tvm Anglice et Latine. Anno Dni 1548."

All in black ink. The woodcut border is the same as was used for the 1538 edition.

The same year (1548) Thomas Petyt, of London, printed a quarto edition. No. 17. Petyt's quarto.

On the title the book is said to be "Imprinted in the yeare of oure Lord God mccccc | xl. viij. And in the seconde | yeare of the Reygne of our | moste dread souerayne Lorde Kynge Ed warde the vj.

"¶ Cum priuilegio."

The initials of the printer (T. P.) occur twice on the title page,—on slates at the feet of the figures which form the sides of the border, and again below the title.

The text is printed in very plain and distinct black letter.

In the preliminary matter appears, for the first time,

"¶ A compendyous and brief rehersal of

al ye contētes of the bokes of the new testamente

Matthew. The stock of christe after ye fleshe Mathew doth tel

And his kired, by order in the Gos.

Mark. Jhon ye baptist preching penaunce in wyldernes.

Sayet Mark, very cōpendeously doth expresse.

Luke. Luke describeth in an ordre necessary.

How Jesus christ was borne of the vyrgyn Mary.

Jhon. Ihō sheweth hys diuine byrth inestigable.

Speakig of the lyght & word impenetrable.

Actes. The noble actes of the triumphe apostolicall.

Luke receyueth in goodly style hystoricall."

There are no woodcuts, but there are contents, notes, and references in the margins. The leaves are not numbered.

No. 18, Tylle's quarto.

The next edition was printed by William Tylle, 1549-8, in quarto. The title reads,—

"The newe Te | stament of the last trans | lacion by William Tyndall with | the Prologes and annotacions in the mergēt, declaryng many harde | places conteyned in the texte | also in the later ende folo | weth the Epistles | of the old Te | stament.

"¶ Imprinted in the yere of oure Lorde | God M.D. xlix. and in the thyrd | yere of the reigne of our moost | dreade soueraync Lorde | Kynge Edwarde | the sixte |

"Cum priuilegio ad imprimendum solum."

The woodcut border is very much like that used by John Cawoode for the 4to. editions printed by him of the Great Bible.

The imprint is, "Imprinted at London wythin

Aldrichgate in the parisshe of Saynete Anne and Agnes by Wyllyam Tylle in the yeare of oure Lorde God 1548."

The date on the title being 1549, and on the colophon 1548, shows the book was put to press the latter end of the year 1548, and completed in 1549.

The first New Testament bearing the names of the celebrated Bible printers, John Daye and Wm. Seres, came out in the year 1548, in small octavo size.

No. 19. Daye and Seres' octavo edition of 1548.

In this edition the practice is begun of substituting other notes for those of the translator. Probably they are from the pen of John Daye, who is known to have held very extreme views, although they profess to be taken from "the Testament which goeth under the name of Thomas Matthew," with certain additions.

Some good judges are of opinion that the notes were written by the fanatical Bishop of Ossory, because in them John Bale's Commentaries are praised.

Bale supposed to be the author of some of the notes.

Daye and Seres must have been in communication with Bale, as about that time they printed his "Image of both Churches."

The woodcuts in this Testament were used in several other editions, as well as in the 1549 Bible, issued by the same printers. Those in Revelation, with the doggerel couplets at the sides, are unmistakable.

Richard Jugge, who afterwards printed so many editions of the Bishops' Bible, brought

No. 20. Jugge's 16mo., 1548.

out, in the year 1548, a very small Testament (16mo.). The title is,

"The newe | Testament of oure | Sauyour Jesu | Christ."

Below this is a medallion of our Lord, certainly more appropriate for the New Testament than the likeness of Edward VI., which was afterwards substituted.

Below the woodcut is a quotation from Romans xv., A. "Whatsoeuer thinges are wrytten afore tyme, are wrytten for oure learnynge," and on reverse of title is, "Translated by Wyllyam | Tyndale, after the | laste copye correc | ted by his lyfe."

The colophon is, "Imprynted at London by Rychard | Jugge, dwellynge in Paules | Churchyarde at the sygne | of the Bible.

"An. M.D. xlviij."

No. 21, Wm. Powell's duglot of 1549, 4to.

Were it not for one or two variations, the Latin and English Testament printed by William Powell in 1549 might be stated to be the same book as he issued in 1548-7, with a new title page added.

New title and preliminary often added to old editions.

This plan was frequently adopted by Bible printers. When they had a large remainder they added a new title and fresh preliminary matter, and tried to sell the book as a newly revised and corrected edition, as Bibles and Testaments did not meet with so ready a sale in the 16th century as writers on the subject have represented.

No. 22, Copland's 8vo., 1549.

William Copland, "dwellynge in Fletstrete, at the sygne of the Rose Garland," printed an octavo edition of Tyndale's Testament on the 23rd of May 1549. A copy of it is in the Chetham Library, Manchester, which I have examined very carefully, but do not find it differ mu h from the edition printed by Daye and Seres in 1548, from which it was evidently taken.

On the title it is said to have "ye annatacion of Thomas Matthew." but this statement is not accurate. Unfortunately the title pages of Bibles and Testaments can seldom be relied on to furnish truthful information.

8vo. edition of 1549 without printer's name.

Another 8vo edition, without record of printer's name or place, is dated 1549. The title is,

"¶ The Newe Te stament of oure Sa | uiour Jesus Christ translated by | M. Wil. Tyndall yet once agay ne corrected with newe Annota cyons very necessary to better on derstondynge. Where vnto is ad ded an exhortacion to the same of Erasmus Rotero. with an En gelshe Calender, and a Ta | ble necessary to finde ea | sly and syghtly any sto | ry contayned in the fowre Euangeli | stes and in the Actes of the Apo stles | MCCCCC. xlix."

About the same time a 16mo. edition was issued, of which no title page is known.

Froschover's 16mo. New Testament of 1550.

An interesting edition was printed the following year by Christopher Froschover, of Zurich. It is without woodcuts. The type is similar to that used in the 4to. edition of the Bible of 1535, the introductory matter of which was revised by Coverdale himself.

The first title reads,

"The newe | Testament faythfully trans | lated by Miles Couerdal | Anno 1550." Below is the same medallion of our Lord as appears on Jugge's 16mo. of 1548.

The second title page is,

"The | Newe Testa | mēt of our sauiour | Iesu Christ, Newly | & faythfully ouer | sene & corrected. | S. Paul. Colloss. iij. | Let ye worde of Christ | dwel in you plēteously | in al wysedome."
in the Gothic type with which all possessors of the second edition of Coverdale's Bible are so familiar.

The statement on the title that this Testament is Coverdale's translation is incorrect: it is an edition of Tyndale's translation.

Title pages not to be relied on.

In fact, no dependence can be put on the titles of many Bibles and Testaments: often printers made inaccurate statements from ignorance; but in other cases the title page was composed in order to sell the book, without any regard to truth.

After the title come six leaves of Kalendar, then,

"¶ A Table to fynde the Epistles and Gospels newly set forth by the kynges commaundement, after the copy, called the Seruyce boke or communion," 9 pages.

On the reverse of the fifth leaf are six texts out of the New Testament. The next three leaves contain "The Gospel of S. Mathew, what S. Mathew conteyneth;" then follows the second title.

The Public Library at Zurich has a copy of the Bible printed by Froschover, and also of this Testament, and his autograph signature is on each, with the date 1551 on the Testament, and 1552 on the Bible, but, strange to say, almost every letter of the two signatures is differently shaped, yet any one can see that both are written by the same person.

Froschover's double error.

It is remarkable that Froschover should have stated on the title page of Coverdale's Bible that it was translated into English by "Mayst Thomas Mathew," and on the title of Tyndale's Testament that it was translated by "Miles Couerdal."

Daye and Seres' second edition, 1550.

The second Testament printed by Daye and Seres is dated Feby. 6, 1550. It is small octavo size, and has forty preliminary leaves. It is merely a reprint of their first edition of Octr. 27, 1548.

Cawoode's Tyndale, 1550.

"¶ The new Testament in Englishe after the greeke translation, annexed with the translation of Erasmus in Latin.

"Whereunto is added a Kalendar and an exhortation to the readyng of the holy scriptures, made by the same Erasmus, with the Epistles taken out of the olde testamēt both in Latin and Englyshe, wheruto is added a table necessary to find the Epistles and Gospels for euery sonday and holy day throughout the yere after the use of the Church of England nowe.

"Excusum Londini in officina | Thomæ Gaultier pro I. C.

"Pridie Kalendas Decembris anno Domini MDL."

In the lower panel of the border is the monogram of Edward Whitchurch.

The above is a copy of the title page of an octavo edition of the Testament printed for John Cawoode.

On the back of this title is an almanac dating from 1550 to 1571, at the bottom of which it is stated, "The yeare hath xij. monthes, iij. weekes and one day, and it hath in all three honderth and lxvj. days and vj. houres."

"J. C. *vnto the Christen reders.*

Cawoode's prologue.

"For as muche as it is knowē thorow out all Europa to the great comforte of al them that loue the pure & true religion of Christe, that oure most noble and Christian kynge Edwarde entendeth ernestly to reforme religion in al his gracis Dominions by the holy worde of God, and wolde that his gracis subiectes as in diligent readyng of the holy scripture, so in lyuing and practise of the same shuld be exercised in good workes also, doyng theyr deutye to god and his maiestye, and to theyr neyghboures, to the intent ẏ his maiestis purpose myght the more spedely and easely be brought to passe, I haue caused to be set oute the newe testament in Englishe, translated out of the greeke, with the translation in Latin of Erasmus ryght ouer againste it: for that ende that al men that are learned both in the Englishe and Latin tonge may compare, whether the Englishe texte be faythfully taken out of the greeke or no, by comparyng it with the translatio of Erasmus, whiche was done accordyng vnto the truth of the greeke texte: and that if there be any faute committed eyther by the translatour, or by the Printer, it maye be perceyued and amended by the translation of the moste noble and famouse Clerke Erasmus. They that are learned in the greeke tonge (I graunt) nede none of this labour, but when as there is a very great numbre in this realme which vnderstande well the Latin tonge, and vnderstand not the greeke (which is the tong wherin the newe testament was writé:) it were pytie, (seing the Latin translation is next in goodnes vnto the greke tonge:) for the examinyng of al vulgare and comon translations, of the newe testament, that the learned in Latin shoulde be withoute the Latin text, set ouer against the Englishe. For if they were not set together one againste an other, it wolde be very tedious and werisum to compare them togyther out of two diuerse bookes: therfore to incorage all Englishmen that are sene in the Latin tonge, to the trial of the Englysh translation, as wel for the profyt of their neyghboures, as for their owne learnynge, I haue partely taken this present labor in hande. I reken also that this booke shall be very profytable for yonge scolers of this Realme, whiche are desyrous to learne the

Latin tong. It wyll be also profytable (as I iudge) for all straungers that are learned in the Latin tong, & wold attayne to the knowledge of oure English tong. Besyde all these commodites, whatsoeuer profyt can ensue by the redyng of both the Englishe and Latin translation seuerally, all the same commodites maye be had in this booke alone by it selfe. And these my labours I dedicate vnto you, most Christian reders, desyryng you to take them in good worthe: which, yt I shall perceyue, it shall moue and incorage me to take more suche lyke labor hereafter: almyghty god gyue you as well grace to lyue after your knowledge, as to come vnto the same. Amen."

Then follows a "Kalender" of 6 leaves;

"¶ An exhortacion to the diligent studye of scripture, made by Erasmus Roterodamus," 9 pages;

Collation.

"¶ The summe and content of all the holye scripture." 2 pages.

After the text, 8 pages complete the book.

Sir John Cheke.

Sir John Cheke has been supposed to be the person represented by I. C., but as Sir John had so strong an objection to Tyndale's version that he was at the time engaged in making a translation of the New Testament from the Greek, it is most unlikely that he should become the publisher of an edition of Tyndale's.

On a subsequent page will be found a specimen of the translation Sir John commenced.

More copies of this edition of Tyndale's have been preserved than of any other: no less than five have come into my possession.

John Daye's edition of 1549.

An edition was printed by "John Daye dwellynge ouer Aldersgate, London," in octavo size, about the end of the year 1549, of which no copy is in existence with a title page. In the margins there are references, contents, and notes.

There are a few woodcuts.

The folios are not numbered.

R. Jugge's revision of Tyndale.

Perhaps the best known of all Tyndale's Testaments are the two quartos printed by Richard Jugge in 1552 and 1553, which, although similar in general appearance, may be easily distinguished from each other, as in the 1552 edition Italic type is used for the head lines, and contents in the margins, while in the 1553 edition the references in the margins are in black letter.

The only difference in the title pages is, that the words immediately under the border (Mathewe xiij. f.) in the 1552 title are printed in black ink, and in the 1553 in red.

The title is,

"The Newe Testament of our Saviour Jesus Christe, faythfully tran slated out of the Greke, Wyth the notes and expositions of the darke pla ces therein." Then follows a picture of King Edward within an oval; on the right is "Rex," and on the left "Vivat:" round the border of the oval is, "Edvardvs sextvs Dei gracia, Anglie Francie, et Hibernie Rex. etc. ætatis svæ xv."

Underneath is—

"The pearle, which Christ commanded to be bought
Is here to be founde, not elles to be sought."

On the reverse of title is the formal authorisation, in which the price of the book is fixed, viz., "twenty and two pens for euery boke in papers and vnbounde."

"At Greneviche the x of June MDLij."

Jugge's dedication to Edward VI.

Then the dedication by Jugge,—"to the most puysaunt and mightie Prince Edwarde the syxt," in which Jugge says, "that one vndoubted true impression might be had, wherunto as suche worde debates, men might haue recourse and be resolued. Accordyng to the streyghte charge and commaundemente, that I receaued of your highnesse in that behalfe, I haue endeauoured myselfe accordynge to my duetye and power, to put in print the newe Testament using thaduise and helpe of godly learned men both in reducinge the same to the trueth of the Greke text (appoynting oute also the diuersite where it happeneth) and also in the kepynge of the true ortographie of wordes, as it shall manifestlye appeare vnto them, that will deligently and without affection, conferre this with the other that went forth before."

The Kalendar, 6 leaves.

An Almanac (1552 to 1575), 1 page.

Table of principal matters, 11 pages.

A perfect supputation, 2 pages.

An exhortation, &c., 2 pages.

There are many illustrations in both editions: the most celebrated one is that of the Devil with a wooden leg sowing tares.

Notes of Jugge's revision, 1552.

The notes were specially written for this book, and became so popular that they were continued in various editions, even of the Bishops' version of the New Testament, down to 1619.

Not only were new marginal notes added to this Testament, but the text itself was so much altered in many places that it should be called Jugge's revision of Tyndale.

Extent of Jugge's revision.

In the first fourteen chapters of S. Matthew there are on an average thirty variations from Tyndale's text in each chapter, some chapters having fifty alterations.

In S. Mark i.–iv. the average is ten.

In the xiv. chap. there are eighteen, mostly adopted from the Great Bible, and nearly all, whether agreeing with the Great Bible or not, copied by William Whittingham into the Testament issued at Geneva 1557.

In S. Luke, i.–iii. contain fifty-four variations.

In S. John vii.—ix. there are about eight in each chapter; but from the xivth to the xvith chapter there are double the number of alterations.

Acts i. has fourteen corrections, but the xxviith and xxviiith have only nine each.

Romans x. has twelve, and the next chapter has sixteen, most of which were adopted by Whittingham.

The changes in the latter part of the book are not so many, nor so important.

As a specimen of the notes, I will give a short one at the end of the third chapter of S. Paul's Epistle to Titus: "After that the godly minister hath by the mighty word of God conuinced any man of heresie, if that man will obstinately abide in his erroneous opinion and doctrine, it is lawfull for the godly Magistrate to punish him with the sword. This place (which doeth onely pertaine to the minister, vnto whom the Temporall sword is not delivered) notwithstanding, Paul did smite Bariesu with blindnesse (Acts xiii.). Also the Lord (Deut. xiii.) did command that the false prophet should bee slaine and put to death. This law is not yet abolished." The verses to which this tolerant note refers are the 10th and 11th, which in this version read: "A man that is giuen to heresy after the fyrst and the seconde admonition auoyde, remembering that he that is suche, is perverted, and synneth, euen damned by his own judgement."

The note at the end of Revelation xvij. is,—"The womannes variable garmentes, betokeneth diuers liueries of religious orders, or the rose colour maye sygnyfye a redines to shed Christen bloude. The cupful of abbominations, &c., the pope's decrees, decretalles, bulles, dispensations, suspentions, and cursynges: the beast she sytteth on, is the papall seate."

These notes were drawn up by those who were engaged in preparing the short-lived prayer book of 1552, for a table from that book was inserted in Jugge's New Testament some months before the prayer book of 1552 was issued.

A woodcut on verso of Sig. P p 8 deserves notice, as it was engraved specially for this Testament. It represents the Chancel of a Church; on the Communion table are two lights burning, and an open Office book facing westward.

As this book was published in the darkest days of the Church of England, it proves that even those who revised the Reformation prayer book of 1549 intended the lights on the Lord's table to be retained and be in use, and to make no change in the eastward position of the Celebrant.

About the year 1566, Jugge reprinted the quarto revision of Tyndale of 1552. The editions of 1552, 1553, and 1566 are substantially the same book.

The 1552 edition reprinted by Jugge in 1566.

The 1566 may be known from the other two by the head lines being in Roman type: the head lines of 1552 and 1553 are in Italic.

In addition to the thirty-three Testaments of Tyndale's translation now described, there were two 16mo and five octavos issued without date, mostly reprints of Jugge's revision.

Numerous editions of Jugge's revision of Tyndale.

TYNDALE'S PENTATEUCH.

Tyndale's Pentateuch.

The first portion of the Old Testament Scriptures printed in the English language was the Pentateuch, or Five Books of Moses. These were translated by William Tyndale, printed in different types, and published separately. When bound together they constitute "Tyndale's Pentateuch," but no title page was ever attached to them collectively. Ignorance of this fact might cause a copy to be pronounced imperfect, just as many Latin Bibles printed in the fifteenth century, before title pages were invented, have been set aside as imperfect books because they have no title, but commence with the Epistle of S. Jerome. The book of Genesis was first issued in 1530, and reprinted in 1534, after having undergone revision. The remaining four books were not reprinted. The colophon reads: "Emprented at Malborow in the lande of Hesse, by me Hans Luft, in the yere of our Lorde, MCCCCCXXX. the xvij dayes Ianuarii." Genesis and Numbers (1530) are printed in small black or Gothic letter. Genesis (of 1534), Exodus, Leviticus, and Deuteronomy are printed in a very neat Roman letter.

Tyndale's Pentateuch is a very rare book; the only copy known to be in existence, perfect, as first issued, is in the Grenville Library, at the British Museum.

Hans Luft, "Malborow."

There is considerable difficulty in identifying the locality of "Malborow in the land of Hesse," where the books are stated to have been printed. The general opinion is that Hans Luft had no printing establishment except at Wittenburg: if so, most likely the Pentateuch was printed there, and the word Malborow was put on the imprint for the purpose of deception. It is painful to think that an intentional misstatement should be on the imprint of the first part of the English Bible ever issued.

Collation of Tyndale's Pentateuch.

I will now give a short description of the two editions of the book of Genesis. The first is octavo size, known by the seam wires going down the page. The signatures are in eights (the last is L, having only seven leaves), making eleven sheets, eighty-seven leaves. The title page has a woodcut border, at the bottom of which are two men supporting a shield; the sides are formed of two ornamental pillars, on the summit of each of which is a grotesque figure of a child. On the top is a ring, from which a chain nearly covered by foliage extends to each figure. The words inside the border are: "The fyrst boke of," in large letters, followed by "Moses called Genesis," in small ones. On the reverse is "W. T. to the Reader" — seven pages — beginning: "When I had translated the Newe testament, I added a pistle to the latter ende in which I desyred them that were learned to amend if ought were founde amysse, but our malicious and wylye hypocrytes which are so stubburne and hard-herted in their wicked abominations," &c.

Then a prologue showing the use of Scripture—eight pages. "If a man had a precious juell and a rich, yet if he wiste not the value thereof, nor wherfor it served, he were nother the better nor rycher a straw."

The text begins on folio j to 76. On the reverse of folio 76 begins "a table expoundinge certeyne words"—seven pages. These words are taken in alphabetical order, commencing "Abrech," "Arcke," "Bisse," "Blesse," and finishing thus :—

End of explanatory table.

"That Joseph brought the Egyptians into soch subjection wold seme vnto some a very cruel deade, howbeit it was a very equal waye. For they payde but the fifte part of that that grewe on the grounde and therwith they were qwytt of all duetyes, both of rent, custome, tribute and toll. And the kinge therwith founde them lordes and all ministres, and defended them. We now pay half so mech vnto the prestes only, besyde their other craftie exactions. Then paye we rent yerely, though there grow never so litle on the grounde, and yet when the kinge calleth paye we neuer the lesse. So that if we loke indifferently their condition was easyar than oures, and but euen a very indifferent waye, both for the comen people and the kinge also. Se therfore that thou loke not on the ensamples of the scripture with worldly eyes, lest thou prefer Cain before Abel, Ismael before Isaac, Esau before Jacob, Ruben before Juda, Sara before Pharez, Manases before Ephraim. And euen the worst before the best, as the maner of the worlde is."

Last comes the colophon, as already described. In the margin there are no contents, and there are very few notes. Only this one is repeated in the second edition of 1534 (Genesis, chap. xxxii.) :—

"Prayer is to cleve vnto the promyses of God with a stronge fayth, and to besech God with a fervent desyre that he will fulfyll them for his mercye and truth onlye, as Jacob here doth."

The chapters are not divided into verses. There are no contents before the chapters. There are thirty-one lines on D—a full page—and the page of print measures 3⅝ in. by 2⅜ in., not including the head-line. The head-line is the number of the chapter.

The Second Edition.

[illegible] Tyndale's [illegible] the Pent. teuch.

This consists of the book of Genesis, revised by William Tyndale, and printed in Roman letter, the first edition being in Gothic or black letter, and the remaining books exactly as they were issued in 1530.

[illegible]

The Pentateuch of 1534 is described by Archdeacon Cotton as 12mo. size. It is, nevertheless, an octavo. The title page border is formed of four woodcuts. The one at the top represents Abraham's sacrifice. As it very often occurs in blocks of that period, the figures are repeated twice in the same cut. The right-hand block has the Tables of the Law, and the left the Brazen Serpent. The lower engraving shows Moses stretching out his sacred wand a second time over the Red Sea, and causing the mighty east wind to cease, and the waters to roll together into their former channels, thus overwhelming Pharaoh and all his hosts. The signatures are in eights—A to L—eleven sheets, occupying eighty-eight leaves. The last of A is folio 1, and the last leaf folioed is 81, L 8. These, with the seven leaves not folioed, are eighty-eight leaves.

In the centre of the woodcut title just described are the words: "The firste Boke of Moses called Genesis. Newly correctyd and amendyd by W. T. MDXXXIIII." The reverse of title is blank. On A ij begins: "Vnto the reader, W. T.," eleven pages, ending on recto of A 7. This address differs from that in the first edition. It explains, "Which things moued me (Wm. Tyndale) to translate the New testament." He goes on to say: "Even in bisshope of London's house I intended to haue done it, for when I was so turmoyled in the contre where I was that I could no longer there dwell, I this wyse thought in myselfe this I suffre because the prestes in the contre be vnlerned." Then, after a page of indecent abuse of the clergy of England, he falls foul of the learned and gentle Erasmus. He says: "Erasmus whose tonge maketh of little gnattes, great elephantes, and lifteth upp aboue the starres whosoeur giueth him a litle exhibition;" for

Tyndale's opinions of Erasmus.

Tyndale quarrelled with almost everyone with whom he came in contact, and was most bitter and violent against those who differed from him in opinion.

The text begins on A 7 reverse, ending on the reverse of folio 81 with: "The ende of the first boke of Moses called Genesis." There are notes and contents in the margin throughout the book. The following is a specimen of the notes, Gen. (chapter iv.):—

"Of this place no doute the pope which in all thinges maketh himself equal with God, toke an occasion to marke all his creatures, and to forbid vnder the payne of excommunication, that no man (whether he were kinge or emperoure) be so hardy to punishe them for whatsoeuer myschef they doo."

Difference of the two editions.

The difference in the text of the two editions is not very great, although the changes made were numerous, being not less than 277. Most of them were merely the substitution of a synonymous word, as "covenant" for "bond," "obtayned" for "gotten," or the correction of a printer's error, or omission of an unnecessary word. To give an idea of the revision, I append a short passage from the xvi[th] of Genesis, which in the 1530 edition reads:—

"Than sayd Saria vnto Abram: Thou dost me vnrighte, for I haue geuen my mayde in to thy bosome. And because Saria fared foul with her she fled from her."

The 1534 has:—

"Than sayd Saria vnto Abram: the wronge

I sofre, be on thy heed for I haue geuen my mayde in to thy bosome. And because Sarai was too cruel with her she fled from her."

"Bugge" Bibles.

In the prologue to the book of Exodus is a sentence that explains the meaning of a word that has caused much discussion in times past, viz., the word "Bugges." In the xci[st] Psalm of Matthew's Bible of 1537, and its reprints by Daye and Seres, and Raynalde and Hyll in 1549, as well as in Coverdale's Bible, we read: "So that thou shalt not nede to be afrayd for any Bugges by night." The sentence in the prologue is: "He that hath the spirite of Christ is now no more a childe; he nether learneth or worketh now any longer for payne of the rodde, or for fear of bogges, or pleasure of apples."

The prologue to Leviticus is mainly an attack on the sacraments of the Church and on the clergy, *e.g.*: "But vnder pretence of theer soule health it is a servaunt vnto oure spiritualtyes couetousnesse and an extorcyonar and a bylder of Abayes, Colleges, Chauntryes, and cathedrall churches with false gotten goodes, a pickpurse, a pollar, and a bottom lesse bagge." The prologues to Numbers and Deuteronomy follow in the same strain: one would think Tyndale was trying to create as much opposition to the English Bible as possible. Coverdale, on the other hand, tried to conciliate the clergy and laity of the Church of England by introducing no bitter controversial remarks.

The following is a list showing the alterations made by Tyndale in his second edition of Genesis, drawn up by the late Mr. Fry:

ch.	ver.	Genesis, 1530.	Genesis, 1534.
1.	20.	to flee over the earth	to flee above the earth
	23.	this is once bone	this is one bone
3.	7.	of both them	of both of them
	22.	take also of the tree	take also the tree
	24.	Cherubin	Cherubes
4.	1.	gotten a man	obtained a man
	7.	if thou doest well	if thou do well
		if thou doest evill	if thou do evill
5.	4.	and begat sons	and he begat sons
	8.	and died	and then he died
		Henoch lived a Godly life	Henoch walked with God
	29.	comfort us as concerning	comfort us concerning
6.	7.	and said	and the Lord said
	21.	take unto thee	take to thee
9.	9.	I make my bond	I make my covenant
	11	I make my bond	I make my covenant
	12.	token of my bond	token of my covenant
	24.	as Noe was awaked	as Noe awaked
10.	10.	the beginning of his kingdom	the chief of his kingdom
	14.	from whence came the Philistines & the Caphtorim	from whence the Philistines & the Capterim came
11.	9.	and because that the Lord	and because of that the Lord
12.	15.	so that she was taken	and she was taken
13.	11.	so departed the one brother	so the one brother departed
14.	8.	the King of Zeboim	the king Zeloim
15.	3.	see to me hast	see unto me hast
	4.	shall be thy heir	he shall be thy heir
	5.	and said unto him	and he said unto him
	9.	and a three year old ram	and a ram of three year old
16.	2.	by means of her	by her
	5.	thou doest me unright	the wrong I suffre be on thy head
	6.	fared foul with her	was too cruel with her
17.	2.	make my bond	make my covenant

ch.	ver.	Genesis, 1530.	Genesis, 1534.
17.	4.	my testament is with thee	my covenant is with thee
	7.	make my bond	make my covenant
		to be an everlasting testament	even an everlasting covenant
		so that I will be God	that I will be God
	9.	keep my testament	keep my appointment
	10.	testament	covenant
	11.	bond	covenant
	13.	testament	covenant
	14.	testament	covenant
	19.	bond	covenant
		bond	covenant
	20.	and as concerning	and concerning
	21.	bond	covenant
	22.	God left off talking	God left talking
18.	10.	That heard Sarah	and Sarah harkened
		door which was behind	door behind
	11.	Abraham	and Abraham
	16.	stood up from thence	stod up to depart thence
	30.	if there be found 30 there	if there be found 30
19.	1.	with his face	upon his face
	6.	at doors	at the doors
	8.	for therefore came they	for as much as they are come
	13.	wherefore he	and therefore he
	23.	was uppon the earth	was up upon the earth
20.	4.	and therefore said	and therefore he said
	5.	innocent hands	innocent
	16.	and an excuse	an excuse
21.	9.	a mocking	a mocker
22.	17.	that I will bless thee	I will bless thee
23.	1.	Sarah was 127 year old	Sarah was 122 year old
	2.	died in a head city called Hebron	died at Kirjath arba which is Hebron
24.	9.	to him as concerning	to him concerning
	43.	and when a virgin cometh	now when a virgin cometh
		Isaac was a coming	Isaac was coming
25.	8.	when he had lived enough	when he had lived a full age
26.	4.	and unto thy seed	and to thy seed
	7.	and that men	and the men
	26.	and Ahuzzath	and a certain of Ahuzzath

ch.	ver.	Genesis, 1530.	Genesis, 1534.
20.	26.	his friend	his friends
27.	28.	and plenty of corn	with plenty of corn
28.	4.	(wherein thou art a stranger)	not in brackets
	11.	and took a stone	and he took a stone
29.	2.	at the well mouth	at the wells mouth
	12.	and Rebecca's son	and the son of Rebecca
30.	1.	when Rachel	and when Rachel
	13.	and called his name Asser	and she called his name Asser
	22.	heard her	and heard her
	29.	but he said unto him	and he said unto him
	38.	and he put the staves which he had "pilled"	which he had "pilled"
		when they came to drink	where they came to drink
	42.	the last brode	the last lambing
31.	15.	as strangers for he hath sold us and hath	as strangers for he hath
	21.	over the revers	over the river
	27.	wherefore wentest thou away	wherefore fleest thou away
	42.	sent me away now all empty	sent me now away empty
	44.	make a bond	make appointment
	47.	(therefore is it called "Galeed")	not in brackets
	49.	(said he)	not in brackets
	54.	and they eat bread and tarried	and tarried
32.	8.	may save itself	may escape
33.	3.	until he came	yet he came
	18.	Salem to the city	Salem the city
35.	27.	Mamre a principal city	Mamre the city of Arbah
36.	9.	in mount Seir	in the mount Seir
37.	20.	some wicked beast	some cruel beast
	33.	a wicked beast hath devoured	a cruel beast hath devoured
38.	16.	and turned to	and he turned to
	29.	hast thou rent a rent	hast thou made a rent
40.	8.	tell me yet	tell it me yet
	14.	art in good case	art in a good case

ch. ver.	Genesis, 1530.	Genesis, 1534.
40. 17.	in the uppermost basket	in uppermost basket
21.	and restored the chief	restored the chief
41. 1.	by a river's side	by a lake's side
2.	out of the river	out of the lake
3.	out of the river	out of the lake
	brink of the river	brink of the lake
4.	and he awoke therewith	and therewith Pharaoh awoke
17.	by a river side	by a lake side
18.	out of the river	out of the lake
31.	not be once "asene"	not be once perceived
36.	let them "kepte" it	let them "kepe" it
	and that the land	that the land
39.	nor of wisdom	or of wisdom
51.	(said he)	no brackets
52.	(said he)	no brackets
57.	because that the hanger	because the hanger
42. 28.	and were astonied	and they were astonied
44. 10.	but ye shall be harmless	but yet ye shall be harmless
16.	we say unto my Lord	we say to my Lord
32.	the lad unto my father	the lad to my father
	not unto thee again	not to thee again
45. 9.	come down unto me	come down to me
17.	say unto thy brethren	say to thy brethren
22.	he gave unto each	he gave to each
23.	ten he asses	ten asses
	ten she asses	ten asses
46. 1.	came unto Beersheba	came to Beersheba
	unto the God	to the God
18.	bare unto Jacob	bare to Jacob
	in number 16 souls	in number 21 souls
20.	and unto Joseph	and to Joseph
25.	these unto Jacob	these to Jacob
28.	before him unto Joseph	before him to Joseph
	unto Goshen	to Goshen
29.	unto Goshen	to Goshen
	himself unto him	himself to him
30.	said unto Joseph	said to Joseph
	in so much I have	in as much I have

ch. ver.	Genesis, 1530.	Genesis, 1534.
46. 31.	unto his brethren	to his brethren
	unto his father	to his father
	come unto me	come to me
34.	unto this time	to this time
	unto the Egyptians	to the Egyptians
47. 5.	Pharaoh said unto Joseph	Pharaoh said to Joseph
9.	Jacob said unto Pharaoh	Jacob said to Pharaoh
	unto the years	to the years
15.	came unto Joseph	came to Joseph
17.	their cattle unto Joseph	their cattle to Joseph
18.	they came unto him	they came to him
	said unto him	said to him
19.	give us food	give us seed
21.	the people unto the cities	the people to the cities
	unto the other	to the other
23.	said unto the folk	said to the folk
26.	unto this day	to this day
	bond unto Pharaoh	bond to Pharaoh
29.	and said unto him	and said to him
31.	sweare unto me	sweare to me
	sweare unto him	sweare to him
	unto the bed's head	to the bed's head
48. 2.	cometh unto thee	cometh to thee
4.	land unto thee	land to thee
	and unto thy seed	and to thy seed
5.	born unto thee	born to thee
	be unto me	be to me
11.	said unto Joseph	said to Joseph
17.	unto Manasseh	to Manasseh
21.	unto the land	to the land
22.	give unto thee	give to thee
49. 2.	unto Israel	to Israel
6.	and unto their	and to their
8.	stoop unto thee	stoop to thee
10.	unto whom	to whom
15.	unto tribute	to tribute
17.	so that his rider	that his rider
23.	the shooters have envied him	though the shooters angred him

ch. ver.	Genesis, 1530.	Genesis, 1534.
49. 24.	and yet his bow	yet his bow
	come an herd man a stone	come herd men as stones
28.	spake unto them	spake to them
29.	said unto them	said to them
50. 4.	spake unto	spake to
	speake unto	speake to
12.	did unto him	did to him
16.	unto Joseph	to Joseph
19.	said unto them	said to him
20.	evill unto me	evill to me
	unto good	to good
21.	and for your children	and your children
	kindly unto them	kindly to them
23.	even unto	even to
24.	said unto	said to
	unto the land	to the land
	swear unto	swear to

The only part of the Old Testament which appeared in Tyndale's name besides the Pentateuch, and the chapters ordered by the Church to be read in the Communion Office in place of Epistles on certain days of the year, which were placed at the end of his Testaments, was the book of Jonah.

This, together with a prologue, was known to have been printed in 1531. For a long time it was supposed that every copy had perished, but in 1861 the Bishop of Bath and Wells was fortunate enough to find one in his library.

It consists of 24 leaves, and bears evidence that it was printed by Martin de Keyser at Antwerp.

There are 26 lines on a full page of the prologue, and the print measures 3 ins. by 4½.

Sir John Cheke's Version.

No early English version gave entire satisfaction.

FOR various reasons the early translations of the New Testament into English gave satisfaction only to a very small minority of English people.

Members of the Old learning party thought it an inopportune time for the introduction of a vernacular Testament, as the wave of religious disturbance that was exciting the Continent had already reached this country.

Tyndale's translation was especially objectionable on account of its glosses and of the changes made in the text.

The New learning party received the new translation with disfavour, and in preaching still continued to take their text from the Vulgate.

Hugh Latimer always did so, and his free rendering seldom agreed with Tyndale's translation.

On one occasion, speaking of a particular passage, he said, "I wonder that the English Bible is so translated."

Sir John Cheke, who had been tutor to King Edward VI., and was one of the best Greek scholars of the day, so much disliked all existing English translations that he set about making a new one, but owing to his numerous state engagements his Testament was never completed.

Cheke's dislike to the introduction of new words.

He particularly objected to the introduction of new words formed from foreign roots, as he thought the English language was sufficiently copious, and he urged that the uneducated would be more liable to misunderstand a new word than they would a simple Saxon one.

We now know that our native tongue was much enriched by the formation of words from Latin and Greek sources, and as by use they have become perfectly familiar to all, they sound much sweeter than the harsh words Sir John Cheke proposed to substitute for them.

Comparison of the words used in translating S. Matthew's Gospel in 1550.

The following is a list of words used in Tyndale's Testament (pro I. C.) of 1550, and from Coverdale's 4to. of 1550, published by Hester, with the words Cheke used in place of them in his translation of S. Matthew's Gospel the same year.

S. Matt.	Tyndale has, 1550,	Coverdale has, 1550,	Sir Jno. Cheke substitutes
ch. i.	betrouthed	marryed	ensured
ij.	wise men	wise men	wisards
,,	mocked	deceaued	plaied withal
iij.	locustes	locustes	acrids
,,	vipers	vypers	adders
,,	repentaunce	penaunce	repentans
,,	beare	beare	cari
iv.	mountayne	mountayne	hic hil
,,	dyseases	diseases	feblenes
,,	grinings	grypyngs	torments
,,	lunakike	lunatyke	moond
v.	poore	poore	beggars
,,	mercyful	mercyful	pitiful
,,	publicans	publicans	tollers

S. Matt.	Tyndale has, 1550,	Coverdale has, 1550,	Sir Jno. Cheke substitutes
vj.	euer	euer	ai
,,	gathre	gather	hoord
,,	lyght	lyght	candel
,,	cubite	cubyte	half yard mete
vij.	pearles	parles	margarites
,,	bryers	thystles	briars
viij.	worshypped	worshipped	boud himself
,,	centurion	captaine	hundreder
,,	feuer	feuer	axess
,,	sycke	sycke	il at ease
ix.	lyenge in his bed	lyenge in hys bed	bedrid
,,	receauyng of custome	receauyng of custome	tolbooth
,,	newe cloth	newe cloth	unfulled ragg
x.	gentyls	heithen	heƒen
,,	innocent	innocent	plain
,,	swearde	sweard	war
xi.	glad tidings	gospel	gospeld
,,	violence	violent	extreem
,,	iustified	iustifyed	cleen rid
,,	prudent	prudent	witti
xij.	brethren	brethren	kinsmen
,,	syster	syster	kinsman
xiij.	similitudes	similitudes	biwordes
,,	thornes	thornes	brambels
,,	parabeles	parables	biwordes
,,	secrettes	mistery	misteries
,,	wexed gross	waxed gross	thickend
,,	closed	closed	winked hard
,,	anone	anon	bi and bi
,,	season	season	for while
,,	tares	tares	darnel
,,	thinges that offende	thinges that offende	hindrances
,,	iniquitie	iniquitie	vnlaufulnes
,,	furnes	fornice	chimnej
,,	treasure	treasure	hoord
,,	lande	shore	bank

S. Matt.	Tyndale has, 1550,	Coverdale has, 1550,	Sir Jno. Cheke substitutes
xiij.	scrybe	scribe	lerned man
,,	without honoure	lesse set by	vnesteemed
xiv.	Tetrarche	Tetrarcha	debitee
,,	platter	platter	disch
,,	sprite	sprete	phantasm
,,	tradicions	tradicions	orders saak
,,	evyl thoughtes	evyl thoughtes	il divises
,,	blasphemie	blasphemye	il wordes
,,	sonne of Dauid	sonne of Dauid	Dauids ofspring.
,,	whelpes	dogges	whelpes
xvi.	cloudy	gloometh	darkisch red
,,	congregacion	congregacion	church
,,	fauer	fauer	haue piti
xviij.	pence	pens	grootes
,,	trespasses	trespasses	fautes
xix.	fleshe	flesh	bodi
,,	camel	camel	cable
,,	second generacion	newe byrth	gain birth
xx.	morngyne	morninge	dauning
,,	market place	market place	commun place
,,	ryghte	right	reasonable
,,	steward	stewarde	balie
,,	baptime	baptyme	wasching
,,	dominacion	dominacion	overmaster
,,	exercyse power	exercyse power	overrule
,,	minister	minister	waiter on
,,	immediately	immediately	bi and bi
xxi.	tables	tables	stalles
,,	disdayned	disdayned	miscontented
,,	widdered	wythered	was seered
xxij.	oxen and my fatlynges	oxen and my fed cattell	beves and mi fed waar
xxiij.	resurrection	resurrection	gain rising
,,	philateries	philacteries	brood gardes
,,	bring one to your belefe	proselyte	freschman

S. Matt.	Tyndale has, 1550,	Coverdale has, 1550,	Sir Jno. Cheke substitutes
xxiij.	offendeth	giltie	fauteth
,,	out a gnat	out a gnat	awai the gnat
,,	excesse	excesse	vnstaidnes
xxiv.	fame	noyse	speking
,,	abhomnacion	abhomynacyon	cursednes
,,	generacion	generacion	age
xxv.	harde	harde	sower
,,	chaungers	exchaungers	tablers
,,	gootes	goates	kiddes
,,	begynnyng	beginning	groundworkes
,,	lodged	lodged	harboroud
xxvj.	crucifyed	crucifyed	crossed
,,	thirty peces of sylver	sylver pens	silverlinges
,,	many	many	ye people
,,	temptacion	temptacion	trial
,,	frende	frend	felow
,,	hie prestes place	palace	ye hed bischops court
,,	temple	temple	church of god
,,	wenche	damsell	wench
xxvij.	elders	elders	aldermen
,,	innocent	innocente	giltles bloud man
,,	treasure	Gods cheste	ye Corbon
,,	debite	debite	president
,,	prevailed nothing	could not help	no boot
,,	mocked	mocked	scorned
,,	let be	hold	soft
,,	sepulchre	sepulchre	grave

The chapter following will give an idea of the orthography adopted by Sir John Cheke; from it may be known the pronunciation that obtained at that period.

It will be seen that in all cases in which the letter "a" had a long sound he used the double vowel "aa," and omitted the final "e," and the same with other vowels.

He also substituted a double vowel in place of diphthongs, and omitted all silent letters.

His abbreviations deserve notice, the letter "y" doing duty for "th," "g" for "dg," and "p" for "pri."

In some places a Greek letter is introduced in place of a double vowel.

His notes are chiefly critical and explanatory, and free from the bitter virus which disfigures some other versions.

S. Matthew, chapter xi.

Cheke's translation, S. Matthew, chapter xi.

"And it cam to pass when Jesus had ended his charge to his twelf disciples, he went from yens to tech and preech in yeer citees. Joan being in prison and heering Christs doings sent ij of his disciples with yis word vnto him.

"Art yow he yt is to com, or look we for an oyer, And Jesus answerd on yis soort to yem. Go iour wais to Joan and tel him what ye heer and see. ye blind seeth, and ye laam walketh, ye lepers be clensed, ye deef heereth, ye deed be raised, and ye beggars be gospeld. And happi is he which is not offended with me.

"After yei weer goon Jesus began to sai to ye compaini yeer of Joan. what went ye to see in ye wildernes. A windshaken reed. But what went ye indeed to see. A man appareld in fijn cloying. But yei yt go in fijn apparel be in Kinges houses. But what went ye ovt to see. a ppheet. ye surli I tel yow and moor yen a ppht. For yis is he of whoom it is writin. Lo I send mi messenger afoor ye, which schal prepaar yi wais befoor y coming. Truli I sai vnto yow, among yem yt be born of women, yeer is noon rising greeter yen Joan Baptist.

"Howbeit he yt is lesser in ye kingdoom of heevn is greeter yen he.

"From Joan baptists dais vnto yis tijm is straightli extremli orderd, and extreem men yei catch it.

"For al ye ppheets and ye law did forsai vnto Joans tijm.

"And if ye wil so taak it he is Helias yt is to com. let him heer yt hath ears to heer. To who schal I lijken yis kind. Jt is lijk childern yt sit in ye high streets and speek to yeer felous and sai, We haue blooun our pipes to yow, and ie haue not danced, we haue moornd vnto yow, and ei haue not wailed. For Joan cam noyer eating nor drinking, and yei sai he hath a devel.

"And ye son of man cam eating and drinking. lo ie yis eater and yis wijndrinker, this tollers and sinners freend. And wisdoom is cleen rid from her own childern. yen began Jesus to rebuuk yoos cities in ye which yeer had been doon mani mighti things. yt yei repented not.

"Wo be to ye Corazin wo be vnto ye Beethsaida, for if so be it yoos mighti thinges, which hath been doon among you had been doon in tyrus and Sidon, yei wold haue repent in sackcloth and asches a good while. But I sai vnto you it schal be moor sufferable in yt dai of iugment for tyrus an Sidon yen for iou. And you Capernaum which hast set vp aloft vnto heavn schalt be brought lou vnto hel. For if yoos mighti things which have been doon in ye, had been doon in Sodom, yei wold have remaind to yis dai. But J sai vnto yow it shal be moor sufferabil to ye land of Sodom in ye dai of iugmet yen to ye.

"At yt tijm Jesus answeerd and said. J must needs o fayer acknoulege thanks vnto ye l of heavn and erth, which has hiden yees thinges from wijs and witti men, and hath disclosed ye saam to baabs, ie and yt fayer for sich was thi good pleasur heerin. Al thinges be deliverd me of mi fayer.

"And no man knoueth ye son but ye fayer, nor noon knoueth ye fayer but ye son, and he to whoom ye son wil discloos it. Come to me al yt labor and be burdeind and J wil eas iou. Taak mi iook on iou and learn of me for J am mild and of a lowli hart. And ie schal find quietnes for yourselves. For mi iook is pfitabil, and burden light."

In the year 1556 Cheke was committed to the Tower of London. On the 15th of July 1556, he wrote to Cardinal Pole begging his favour and protection, and on the same day he petitioned Queen Mary for his release. The following is a copy of his letter :—

Sir John Cheke's petition to Queen Mary.

"Pleaseth yt yor matie to vnderstande, that in matters of religion, J haue declared my full mynde vnto yor maiestie by yor virtuous and learned Chaplen Mr. Deane of Paulle:

Trusting that as it is truly myndcd of me, So yor highnes will agreablye receaue it. J besche yor ma^tie therefore, as J haue been and am yor faythfull subiecte, whom J do as gods mynister faithfully honor and serue, that yor highnes will haue that opinion psent of me, that my faithfulnes, J truste, and dutie hereafter shall sheue vnto you. And J truste, amonge many obedient and quiet subiects wch god storeth yor highnes with, J shal be found, though not in trabilitie of other qualities, yet in will and readynes and obedience of yor Lawes, and other orders of religion, as gladd to serue and obeye as any other: Desyering yor maiestie most humblie to fauor suche poore suyte for my Libertie, as Mr. Deane shall make to yor ma^tie on my behalf.

"Almightie god psper and encrease yor maiestie in all honor and godlynes.

"ffrom yor ma^ties Touer of London the 15 of Julie. 1556.

"Yor maiesties moste humble and obedient subiecte

"Jo CHEKE."

On the report of the Dean of S. Paul's to the Queen that Sir John Cheke had changed his opinions he was released from prison; and on the 4th of October 1556 he made a public recantation.

Cheke's recantation.

He died on September 13th, 1557.

Coverdale's Bible.

First complete English Bible printed, 1535.

THE first complete Bible printed in the English language, was issued October 4th 1535.

It professes to be translated out of the "Douche" (*i.e.*, German) and "Latyn" into English by "youre grace's humble subjecte, and daylye oratour Myles Coverdale."

Coverdale's name common in parts of the North Riding.

Coverdale was born at Coverham, in the North Riding of Yorkshire, in the year 1488. The name is still common in that locality. When I made a pilgrimage to the spot I found in the Churchyard many headstones inscribed with the name Coverdale; no doubt all sprung from the same stock as Bishop Myles.

He was educated at the Augustinian house at Cambridge, the head of which at the time was Dr. Robert Barnes, who bore his fagot in 1526.

Coverdale was admitted to Priest's Orders in 1514.

Coverdale one of the most active searchers.

He was active in searching out those who had not, in obedience to King Henry VIII's order, defaced the name of S. Thomas à Beckett in their Office books: so carefully was this done, that the owner of a Prymer in my possession, to be quite safe, scribbled over the name of S. Thomas the Apostle, as well as S. Thomas of Canterbury.

About that date Coverdale wrote to Cromwell, to whom he had been introduced by Sir Thomas More, and solicited his assistance.

After the fall of Cromwell, Coverdale fled to Bergzabern, where he married, although he had taken the vow of celibacy, and there he supported himself by keeping a school.

He returned to England after Edward VI. came to the throne, and was made one of the Royal Chaplains. The King gave him and his wife Elizabeth a license, or dispensation, to eat flesh and white meats in Lent, and other obligatory fasting days.

Coverdale and his wife obtain a dispensation from King Edward to eat flesh meat in Lent.

He accompanied the troops who were sent to suppress the popular rising in Devon and Cornwall, on June 10th, 1549, who were headed by Humphrey Arundel, Governor of S. Michael's Mount.

Coverdale was consecrated August 30th, 1551, and appointed to the See of Exeter during the lifetime of Bishop Veysey.

In Queen Mary's reign he was put into prison, but John Macbee, a Scotch preacher in Denmark, who had married a sister of Coverdale's wife, induced the King of Denmark to intercede with the Queen of England for him, and he was released from confinement and allowed to go abroad.

Coverdale leaves England.

Early in Elizabeth's reign he returned, and assisted at the consecration of Archbishop Parker.

He was appointed to the living of S. Magnus-the-Martyr, London Bridge, but during his stay

Coverdale resigns the living of S. Magnus.

at Geneva he became so impregnated with hostility to the Church, that he resigned his benefice in two years. He died in the year 1569, aged 81, and was buried under the chancel of S. Bartholomew's Church, London, and when that church was destroyed (in 1840) his bones were taken to the Church of S. Magnus.

The difference between the two eminent translators appears to have been that Coverdale was employed on the work of translation by others, while Tyndale acted independently, being urged onwards by his own enthusiasm.

Tyndale's indomitable energy no discouragement nor persecution could daunt. Coverdale, under the wings of powerful protectors, passed prosperously through the major part of his life, content "lowly and faythfully" to follow other "interpreters, and that under correction," and to do his work at "the coste and charges of others."

Coverdale employed by others to translate.

Who it was that, against Coverdale's own wish, induced him to undertake the task of translating the Bible is not known; most likely it was the good Sir Thomas More and those of the new learning party with whom he was associated.

The Vulgate and the German Bible the principal bases of Coverdale's translation.

Internal evidence proves that the first English Bible was not translated from the original tongues, but principally from the Vulgate and Luther's Bible, three volumes of which were printed in 1524, and the remaining two, which complete the edition (the Prophets and Apocrypha), in 1532.

Coverdale tells the reader, "to helpe me herin I have had sodry translacions, not only in Latyn, but also of the Douche interpreters, whom because of their singuler gyftes, and special dilygence in the Bible, I haue ben the more glad to follow for the moste part."

This Bible was printed by Jacob van Meteren at Antwerp, and was sent to Nicolson, of Southwark, in sheets, as an Act of Parliament had been passed a year or two previously for the protection of native industry, prohibiting the introduction of bound books into England. Printed by Jacob van Meteren.

The original Antwerp title, which has the authority of the translator himself, reads,

"Biblia | The Bible/ that | is, the holy Scripture of the | Olde and New Testament, faith fully and truly translated out | of Douche and Latyn in to Englishe. M.D. XXXV." &c.

There was little desire in this country for a Bible in English, and Nicolson had great difficulty in disposing of it.

In order to get the edition off his hands, he removed Coverdale's original title page, which had on the reverse the list of "The bokes of the whole Byble," &c., and substituted the following:

"Biblia | The Bible: that | is/ the holy Scripture of the | Olde and New Testament, | faythfully translated in to Englyshe. | M.D.XXXV. S. Paul. II. Tessal. III. | Praye for vs, that the worde of God maye haue fre passage & be glorified. | S. Paul Colloss. III. | Let the Title page of Nicolson's edition.

worde of Christe dwell in you, | plenteously in all wysdome, &c. | Josue I. | Let not the Boke of this lawe departe | out of thy mouth, but exercyse thy selfe | therein daye and nyghte, y^t thou mayest | kepe and do every thynge accordynge | to it that is wrytten therin."

Reverse of title blank.

Dedication to King Henry VIII.

Jacob van Meteren's preliminary matter was cancelled, and a dedication to Henry VIII. introduced: "Unto the most victorious Prynce, and oure most gracyous soueraigne Lorde, Kynge Henry the eyght, Kynge of Englonde and of Fraunce, lord of Irlonde, &c.

"Defendour of the Fayth, and vnder God the chefe and suppreme heade of the Church of Englonde." After the dedication is "A prologue. Myles Couerdale vnto the Christen reader," then a table of "the bokes of the hole Byble."

Editions in which the blocks bought from van Meteren were used.

James Nicolson not only bought the entire edition from van Meteren, but also the original blocks of the woodcuts, map, and title border; these he used for the edition he printed in 1537; and the edition of Matthew's Bible, printed in 1540 by Petyt and Redman for Thomas Berthelet, has the first and New Testament titles printed from the blocks used for Coverdale's Bible of 1535.

Another edition of Matthew's Bible was published by Daye and Seres in 1549, in which, in the titles, and the text, are forty-nine impressions from the identical woodcuts used in the Bible of 1535.

Richard Jugge used the same woodcuts of the four Evangelists in the New Testaments of 1552 and 1553, and the large map in the Bishops' Version of 1574 is the same as was used in Coverdale's Bible of 1535.

The size of the first English Bible is small folio. There are fifty-seven lines in a page. The type is an angular black letter.

It is divided into six parts:

1. Genesis to Deuteronomy.
2. Josua to Hester.
3. Job to Solomon's balettes.
4. Esay to Malachy.
5. The Apocripha.
6. The new testament.

There are in this version some peculiar renderings:

Gen. viii. 11. "She bare the olive leaf in her nebb."

Judges ix. 53. "Cast a pece of mylstone upon Abimelech's heade & brake his brain panne."

I. Kings xxii. 34. "and shott the King of Israel between the mawe and the lunges."

Psalm lxxiv. 6. "They cutt downe all the sylinge worcke of ye sanctuary with bylles and axes."

Isaiah v. 27. "no one faynte nor feble amonge them, no, not a slogishe nor slepery persone."

I. Timothy vi. 4. "but waysteth his brayne aboute questions and stryuynges of wordes."

In 1537 a second edition of Coverdale's Bible was "¶ Imprynted in Sowthwarke for | James

The first Bible printed in England.

Nycolson." Folio size. Said on the title to be "newly ouersene & corrected."

The first Bible printed in England was like the 1535 dedicated to King Henry in the same words, except the name of "dearest just wyfe and most vertuous Pryncesse Quene Anne" is changed for "Quene Jane."

"¶ The right & just administracyon of the lawes that God gaue vnto Moses, | and vnto Josua: the testimonye of faythfulnes that God gaue of Dauid: the | plenteous abundaunce of wysdome that God gaue vnto Salomon: the lucky | and prosperous age with the multiplicacyon of sede which God gaue vnto A braham and Sara his wyfe, be geven vnto you moost gracyous Prynce, with | your dearest just wyfe, and moost vertuous Pryncesse, Quene Jane, Amen." |

Reprints of Coverdale's Bible.

An edition in quarto also appeared the same year (1537).

"Imprynted in Southwarke in Saynt Thomas Hospitale by James Nycolson."

"Set forth with the Kynges moost gracious licence."

Coverdale had nothing to do with the issue of the reprints of 1537.

Coverdale's Testament in 16mo.

In 1538 was published a 16mo. edition of Coverdale's New Testament, of which only a few copies remain. The title is, "The newe Testament. Faythfully and newly corrected by Myles Couerdale.

"With a true Concordaunce in the margent,

and many necessary Annotacyons after the chapters, declarynge sondry harde places conteyned in the texte.

"Prynted in the yeare of our Lorde M.CCCCC.XXXVIII." (No printer's name or place.) "Set forth wyth the kynges licence."

There are 20 pages of preliminary.

A copy in the British Museum is of interest.

Upon the inside of the cover is the following manuscript note: "This small book was once the property of Q. Elizabeth, and actually presented by her to A. Poynts, who was her maid of Honour. In it are a few lines of the Queen's own hand writing and signing. Likewise a small drawing of King Edward the 6th when very young (of Windsor Castle) and one of the knight in his robes." The view of Windsor measures 3½ in. by 2¾ in., and gives a view of the castle from Windsor Park. Several deer and hares are represented in the foreground, and the grass is of a very bright green colour. The sky and most of the building have become much darkened by discoloration of the paint with which they were depicted; but a red fence skirting the park, a gate with steps down to the park, and the gilt-tipped towers of the castle beyond, are all distinctly visible. The drawing of the knight, about 3 in. by 1½ in. in size, displays greater artistic skill than that of Windsor Castle. Below it is this manuscript note: "This is actually a drawing of King Edward the Sixth. I. W. May, 1768. He likewise drew the Castle of Windsor on the other side of foregoing Leafe." The next leaf bears the following writing:—

> "Amonge good thin" (in Q. Elizabeth's hand-writing)
>
> "Liber Roberti Grove
> ex dono Thomæ Field
> Martii 20mo 1709
>
> Liber Thomæ Gibbon
> ex dono Roberti Grove
> 1714
>
> N.B.
> The Worthy Dr. Gibbon, faithfully
> assured me that the hand writing on
> the other side this Leafe was really
> Queen Elizabeths & I believe it
> having many Letters of her writing
> Jno. Waller."

Upon the other side of the same leaf is the very interesting entry by Queen Elizabeth herself, as follows:

> "Amonge good thinges
> I prove and finde, the quiet
> life doth muche abounde,
> and sure to the contentid
> mynde, ther is no riches
> may be founde
> Your lovinge
> maistres
> Elizabeth."

It appears that the word "friend" had been written after the word "lovinge" in the seventh line of the above, but it has been partially erased, and the word "maistres" in the line below looks very much like an insertion. The writing is in Elizabeth's fine bold hand.

The titles of each book are printed in red, and each page has a red lined border. The cross and half cross, intended to show the beginning and ending of the appointed Epistles and Gospels, the running titles, and initial letters are also printed in red.

There are numerous woodcuts. Gothic type. It has marginal references. Pointing hands are introduced to mark passages on which notes at the end of the chapters are appended.

Matthew Crom's 8vo. New Testament of 1538.

A Testament was also issued in 1538 which measures 6 inches by 4. As the wire lines go down the page it must be an octavo.

The title is,

"The new | Testament of oure | Sauyour Jesu Christ. Faythfully translated & | lately correte: wyth a | true concordaunce in the margent, & many neces | sary annotacions decla | rynge sondry harde pla | ces coteyned in the text. ¶ Emprēt in the yeare of our Lorde M.D. xxxviij."

The colophon is,

"¶ Imprynted at Antwerpe, by Matthew | Crom. In the yeare of oure Lorde M.D. xxxviii."

Copy discovered in a secret drawer.

My copy was found a few years ago in a secret drawer of an old oak cabinet.

The cabinet was bought at a sale near Stratford-on-Avon, and during the process of "restoration" the back was taken out, which disclosed a secret drawer containing Coverdale's Testament in its original binding.

Collation.

It has eight preliminary leaves. At the back of the title is, "¶ An Almanack for xxxij.

yeares"; then four leaves of Kalendar; then five pages of prologue; on reverse of last leaf of preliminary is "A prologe of Saynt Matthew." There is no prologue to S. Mark. The top of the leaf, Sig. K iii., is torn off, but as the preface to S. Luke begins about half-way down the page, perhaps there was a prologue.

"¶ A prologe vpon Saynt Jhon" occupies 31 lines.

The prologues are taken from Tyndale.

Coverdale's summaries are placed before each chapter in smaller black letter type than the text.

There are no objectionable glosses in the book.

The margin contains rather numerous references to parallel passages.

There are about 200 woodcuts; those in Revelation fill the whole page.

This little book very accurately follows Coverdale's 1535; many chapters do not contain a single variation.

Nicolson's 4to, 1538.

The same year (1538) Nicolson issued a quarto reprint of Coverdale's Testament in parallel columns with the Vulgate version.

The title reads,

"The newe tes | tament both in Latine and | Englyshe ech correspondent to | the other after the vulgare texte com | munely called S. Jeroms. Fayth | fully translated by Myles | Couerdale | Anno. | M.CCCCC. XXXVIII. Jeremie xxij. | Is not my worde lyke a fyre sayeth the | Lorde, and lyke an hammer that | breaketh the harde stone? |

Printed in Southwarke | by James Nicolson. | Set forth wyth the Kyn | ges moost gracious licence."

The Latin text introduced by Coverdale is the ordinary Vulgate of S. Jerome, and was inserted to enable the clergy and others to convince themselves that this English translation was an accurate one.

Coverdale was in Paris at the time this book was published: when he had an opportunity of examining it he was much dissatisfied, and at once issued a corrected edition, the title page of which reads as follows:— Regnault's duglot.

"❡ The new testament both in Latin and English after | the vulgare texte: | which is red in the churche. Translated and corrected by My | les Couerdale: and prynted in | Paris, by Fraunces Regnault, | M.CCCCC. XXXVIIJ. | in Novembre."

In the dedication Coverdale thus writes:—

"Trueth it is, that this last lent I dyd with all hũbleness directe an Epistle vnto the kynges most noble grace: trustinge, that the boke (wher vnto it was prefixed) shulde afterwarde haue bene as well correcte, as other bokes be. And because I coulde not be present my selfe (by the reason of sondrye notable impedimẽtes) therfore inasmoch as the new testament, which I had set forth in English before, doth so agree wyth the latyn, I was hartely well contẽt, that the latyn and it shulde be set together: Prouyded allwaye, that the correctour shulde followe the true copye of the latyn in anye Coverdale's address.

wyse, and to kepe the true and right Englishe of the same. And so doynge, I was contẽt to set my name to it. And euen so I dyd: trustinge, though I were absent and out of the lande, yet all shuld be well. And (as God is my recorde) I knew none other, till this last Julye, that it was my chaũce here in these partes at a straungers hande, to come by a copye of the sayde prynte. Which wan I had perused, I founde, that it was disagreable to my former translacion in English, so was not the true copye of the latyn texte obserued, neither the english so correspondent to the same, as it ought to be: but in many places both base, insensyble, and cleane contrary, not onely to the phrase of oure language, but also from the vnderstondyng of the texte in latyn. Wherof though no man to this houre did write ner speake to me, yet for as moch as I am sworne to the trueth, I will favoure no man to the hinderaunce therof, ner to the maynteyning of anyething that is contrary to the ryght and iust furtheraunce of the same. And therefore as my dewtye is to be faythfull, to edifye, and with the vttermost of my power to put awaye all occasions of euell, so haue I (though my businisse be greate ynough besyde) endeuoured my selfe to wede out the fautes that were in the latyn and English afore: trustinge, that this present correction maye be (vnto them that shall prynt it herafter) a copye sufficient."

The cost borne by Bishop Bonner.

There is little doubt but that the "cost and charges" of printing Coverdale's 4to. Testament were borne by Bonner, Archdeacon of

Leicester, then bishop elect of Hereford, for we find he sent copies of this duglot to the King and the principal officers of the Church and State, and his zeal in the cause, and the very important assistance he rendered Grafton and Whitchurch when ambassador at Paris, in publishing the Great Bible of 1539, procured for him his translation from the See of Hereford to that of London.

The "Hollybushe" edition.

At the close of the year 1538, Nicolson reprinted the first Latin-English Testament, but substituted on the title page the name of "Johan Hollybushe" for that of the true translator.

The size of this book is 7 inches by 4⅜ without including margin.

Myles Coverdale's name is retained to the dedication although removed from the title.

Froschover's 4to edition of Coverdale's Bible.

The next time Coverdale's Bible was reprinted was in 1550, when Christopher Froschover, of Zurich, printed an edition in quarto, a copy of which is preserved in the Public Library at Zurich, containing Froschover's autograph signature.

The title page has his device of a tree and frogs, and reads thus: "The whole Byble/ | that is, the Olde and Newe | Testamente, truly and purely translated into Englishe/ by Mayst Thomas Mathewe. | Esaie j. | Hearcken to ye heauens: and thou earth | geaue eare: for the LORD ✠ speaketh. ✠ | Christ. Frosch. Imprinted at Züryeh by Chrystoffer Froshower."

It is most strange that such a mistake should have been made as to attribute the translation to "Mayst Thomas Mathewe;" for although there is difference of opinion as to who was the translator of the Bible of 1535, it is quite certain it was not John Rogers, otherwise Thomas Matthew.

Rogers was engaged, in the years 1536 and 1537, in the work of translation, or rather of compiling a Bible from the translation of others, and correcting proofs; but there is no reason to suppose he took any part in the translation of the Bible of 1535, and it could hardly have been that, because Matthew's Bible, which was edited by Rogers, was the first to have a licence granted by King Henry VIII. Froschover thought that by passing off this quarto as a reprint of the first authorized version, it would be more likely to find favour in England, for in 1550 there was no obstruction put in the way of publishing the Bible in England; the difficulty experienced was to get people to buy copies.

Froschover's preliminary.

The original preliminary matter of this Bible is very interesting, and it was a pity that Andrew Hester cancelled it.

It consists of thirty-six pages, printed in double columns, with the same kind of type and ornamental initial letter as the text. Verso of title is blank. On the next page is an address "To the gentle | Reader."

"Gentle Reader, where as dyuers godly men hath thought it very nedefull and necessary to set before every Chapter in all the bokes of this moost holy Byble, the Summeries or contentes therof, or what euery one of the sayde Chapter containeth, briefly declared, whiche I thinke very comodious. Neuerthelesse (good Reader) I haue considered that euery man hath not at all tymes suche leasure as to reade or to tourne the Byble from one Chapter to another, whan they shall haue a desyre or occasion to seke for any speciall matter conteyned herin (this considered) I thought it mooste nedefull and necessary to prynt and set the Sommaries of ye Chapters of all the bokes contayned in this most sacred Byble together in their order, whereby thou mayste easely finde oute not onely how the bokes stande in order, and how many Chapters euery boke contayneth. But most specyally thou shalt finde therby most spedely how God by the mouth of his most holy Prophetes promised the redemption of the worlde, by oure onely hope and sauioure Jesus Christe by sufferinge in that most perfect fleshe, which it pleased him to take on him in the wombe of that most pure virgin Marie . . . . Thus fare you well."

Then comes :

"Here after follo | weth all the argumentes | vpon the olde and newe Testa ment, euery boke by sonder hys Argumentes, | and how muche and many Chapters they cō | tayneth." |

To give an idea of this condensation of the Bible I append the first thirteen lines :

"Here begynneth the Ar | guments of the fyrst boke of Moses, called Genesis. | What this boke contayneth. |

Summary of the first four chapters of Genesis.

"Chap. j. The creacion of the worlde in sixe | dayes, and of man. |

"Chap. ij. The rest of the seuenth daye, | the tree of knowlege of good and euil is forbid | den, &c. Of the creacion of Eua. |

"Chap. iij. The serpent disceaueth the wo | man: they trãsgresse and are driuen out of Paradyse. |

"Chap. iiij. Abels offering pleaseth God, ther | fore doeth his brother Cain hate him: murthureth | him: and is cursed. Of the children of Cain."

Just as Nicolson bought the entire edition of the 1535 Bible from Jacob Van Meteren, so Hester did of this reprint from Christopher Froschover, and replaced the preliminary matter printed with the text for fresh, printed in small old English letter. Even this did not enable Hester to get the copies off his hands, and Richard Jugge bought up the remainder, and re-issued it in 1553, with another new title and new preliminary leaves, to try to pass the book off as a fresh edition.

I have in my possession a perfect copy of this Bible, as published by Hester, in exceedingly fine condition, and almost uncut.

The size of the book is 9½ in. by 7½ in., and it is 3½ in. thick.

The seam lines of the watermark going across the page prove it to be a quarto.

The title is,

Title page of Hester's re-issue.

"¶ The whole | Byble, | that is the holy scripture | of the Olde and New testament | faythfully translated into | Englyshe by Myles | Couerdale and | newly ouer | sene and correcte. |

(*sic*) M.D.L. Pray for vs that the worde of God maye haue free passage and be glorified. II. Tes. iij. |

"Prynted for Andrewe Hester. dwellynge | in Pauls church yard at the sygne | of the whyte horse and are | there to be solde." |

Within a woodcut architectural border, and under it in large letters: "Set forth with the Kynges mooste gracious licence;" reverse of title blank. Next page is: "¶ The bokes of the hole Byble, how they are named in Englyshe and Latyn, and how longe they are | wrytten in the allegations." | The books are divided into six parts. First part, "Genesis to Deuteronomiō." Second part, "Josue to Hester"; "The Apocripha: Third book of Esdras to II. Machaborum." Third part, "Job to Salomo ballettes"; "The Prophetes—Esay to Malachy." "The New Testament: Math., Mar, Luc, Joh, Acts, Rom, j Cor, ij Cor, Gal, Ephe, Phil, Col, j Tess, ij Tess, j Tim, ij Tim, Tit, Phile, j Pet, ij Pet, j Joh, ij Joh, iij Joh, Heb, Jac, Jud, Apo."

Dedication to King Edward VI.

On the reverse of this leaf is a dedication, of the most fulsome and servile kind, in which the juvenile King is urged to keep the Church under his feet, and to allow no toleration, or religious liberty, but to prevent by the sword any (what Coverdale considers) heresy being preached.

In the most coarse language the Bishop of Rome is called Balaam and Antichrist. This dedication begins as follows:

"✠ Vnto the moost victorious Prince and our moost gracious souerruigne lorde, kynge Edward the sixth, kynge of | Englonde, Fraunce, and of Irlonde, &c., Defoundor of | the Fayth, and under God the chefe | and supreme heade of the | Church of Englande. |

"¶ The right and just administracyon of the lawes that God gaue vnto Moses and | vnto Josua: the testimonye of faythfulnes that God gaue of David: the plenteous | abundaunce of wysdome that God gaue vnto Salomon: the lucky and prosperous | age with the multipliacyon of sede, whiche god gaue vnto Abraham and Sara | his wyfe, be giuen vnto you moost gracious Prynce." |

Eight columns of this sort follow, and the "epistle to the Kynges highnesse" concludes:

"Considering now (moost gracyous prynce) the inestimable treasure, fruit and prosperitie everlasting, that God geueth with his worde, and trusting in his infinite goodnes that he wold bring my simple and rude labour herin to good effect, therfore was I boldened in God sixtene yeares agoo, not only to laboure faythfully in the same, but also in most humble wyse to dedicate this my pore trãslation to your graces moost noble father, as I do now submit this and all other my pore corrections, labours, and interprises, to the gracious spirite of trewe knowledge, vnderstanding, and judgmẽt, which is in your highnesse, most humbly beseching the same that though this volume be small, and not wholly the texte appoynted for the churches, it maye yet be exercised in all other places so long as it is vsed within the compasse of the feare of God, and due obedience vnto your moost excellente maiestie, whome the same eternal god saue and preserue evermore. Amen.

"Your graces moost humble and faithful subiect,

MYLES COUERDALE."

After this epistle there is "A prologue to the reader," of five pages.

The prologue thus begins:

"Myles Couerdale, to the Christen reader. Consyderynge how excellent knowledge and learnyng an interpreter of scripture ought to haue in the tungs, and ponderynge also myne owne insufficiēcy therin, and how weake I am to perfourme the office of a translator, I was the more loth to medle with this worke. Notwithstandynge whan I consydred how great pytie that we shuld wante it so longe, and called to my remembraunce the aduersite of them which were not onely of rype knowlege, but wold also with all theyr hartes haue perfourmed that they began yf they hadde not had impedimentes: consyderynge (I saye) that by reasō of their aduersitie it could not haue so soone haue been broughte to an ende, as our moost prosperous nacyon wolde fayne haue had it: these and other reasonable causes consydered I was ye more bolde to take it in hāde, and to help me herin I haue had sōdry trāslacyons, not only in latyn but also in other lāguages: whō (because of their syngular gyftes and specyall diligence in the Bible) I haue ben glad to follow accordyng as I was requyred. Coverdale's prologue.

"But to say the trueth before God it was nother my labour nor desyre, to haue this worke put in my hande, neuerthelesse it greued me that other nacyons shuld be more plēteously prouyded for with the scripture in theyr mother tunge, thē we in oures, therefore whā I was instantly requyred (though I could not do so well as I wolde) I thought it yet my dewtye to do my best, that the scripture might wholly come forth in englishe."

In the third column he says:

"For the which cause (accordynge as I was desyred anno 1.5.34) I toke the more vpon me, to set forth this specyall translacyon, not as a checker, not as a reprouer, or despiser of other mens translacyons, but lowly and faythfully haue I followed myne interpreters, *and that under correction.*"

It is evident, from the above, that Coverdale was employed and paid for his work; "at the coste and charges of others," are his own words.

Next to the prologue is the "Almanacke." All writers, from Lewis down to Mr. Stevens, say that it commences from the year 1550, but my copy is from M.D. li, to M,D, lxiii.

Coverdale certainly the translator.

It has been the fashion in certain quarters for some years to regard Coverdale merely as the "proof reader and corrector" of the first English Bible, and not as its translator, but I think no one can read this prologue without coming to the conclusion that either Myles Coverdale was the translator, or that he claimed more than his due. Had he been employed solely to see the book through the press, his claim to be the translator thus publicly put forward would have been disputed.

We know that there was not much love lost between Tyndale and his assistants. Tyndale and Joye speak of each other in very plain and no doubt well deserved terms, and had Coverdale dared to take credit for work done by others, we should have heard of it very soon.

Excepting an ambiguous passage in a Dutch biography, which states that Van Meteren was the "begetter" of this "specyall translacyon," and for this purpose "he employed a certain learned scholar, named Miles Coverdale"; and also the fact that a few words in the book imply a foreign parentage, no doubt has ever been thrown on the truthfulness and justice of Coverdale's claims.

It is quite true it has been denied that Coverdale translated the Bible from its original tongues, but this he does not pretend to have done.

The Vulgate was one of the principal bases of his translation, and fortunate it would have been had it been the only source from which his translation was made; but he owns to having consulted "five sundry interpreters," and it is evident that, in many cases, he was led astray by Luther, and by the Swiss Bible.

The Kalendar in this copy begins 1551 and ends 1563. I am puzzled about the Saints' days in it, for it should agree with the Reformation Prayer Book of 1549; but it does not do so exactly, nor does it correspond with the Kalendar in Jugge's revision of Tyndale's New Testament, issued in July 1552, which has the Kalendar of the debased Prayer Book of November 1552.

The Kalendar occupies four pages; then comes the text, printed in the angular German type so often seen in the productions of Froschover's Zurich press, and, although much smaller, resembling the type used in Coverdale's Bible of 1535.

At the top of the page on which the book Genesis begins, is a woodcut of the creation of Eve, the only engraving in the book, excepting the initial letters, some of which are singularly inappropriate—*e.g.*, S. John and the Eagle in the first letter of Genesis. Many of these initial letters contain engravings representing the well-known dance of Death.

Genesis begins on Sig. A, folio I, and Malachi ends on verso of folio CCCXCIX., Sig. D D v.

The Apocrypha begins on folio 400, and is thus prefaced:

Prologue to the Apocrypha.

"Apocripha. |

"The bokes and treatises which | amonge the fathers of olde are not rekened | to be of like authoritie with the other bo | kes of the Byble, neyther are they founde in the | Canon of the Hebrue.

"The translatoure vnto the reader. | These bokes (good reader) which be called Apocrypha, are not judged among the doctours to be of lyke reputacion with the other scripture, as thou mayst perceaue by S. Jeronyme *in Epistola ad Paulinu.* And the chiefe cause therof is this: there be many places in them, that seme to be repugnaunt vnto the open and manyfest trueth in the other bokes of the Byble. Neuertheles, I haue not gathered them together to the intent that I wolde haue them despysed, or little set by, or that I shoulde think them false, for I am not able to proue it.

"Yee, I doubte not verely, if they were equally conferred with the other open Scripture (time, place and circumstance in all thinges consydered) they shoulde neyther seme contrary, nor be vntruly and peruersly aledged.

"Trueth it is a mans face can not be sene so well in a water, as in a fayre glass, neyther cã it be shewed so clearly in a water that is stered or moued, as in styl water.

"These and many other darke places of scripture haue bene sore stired and myxte with blynd and coueteous opinions of mẽ, which haue cast such a myst afore the eyes of the symple, that as longe as they be not conferred with the other places of scripture they shall not seme otherwyse to be understande then as coueteousnes expoundeth them. But whosoever thou be that readeth scripture, let the holy ghoost be thy reader, and let one text expound another vnto the. As for such dreames, visyons and darke sentẽces as be hyd from thy understandynge, commytte them vnto God, and make no articles of them: But let the playne text be thy gyde, and the sperete of God (whiche is the author therof) shall lede the in al trueth.

"As for the prayer of Salomon (which thou findest not herein) the prayer of Azarias, and swete songe that he and his two fellowes songe in the fyre, the fyrst (namely the prayer of Salomon) readest thou in the eight chapter of the thirde boke of the kinges, so that it appeareth not to be Apocryphum: The other prayer and songe (namely of the thre children) haue I not founde amonge any of the interpreters, but onely in the olde latyn texte, whiche reporteth it to be of Theodotions translacion. Neuertheles, both because of those that be weake and scrupulous, and for their sakes also that loue such swete songes of thankesgeuinge I haue not left them out: to the intent that the one shoulde haue no cause to complayne, and that the other also mighte haue the more occasyon to giue thankes vnto God in aduersyte, as the thre chyldren dyd in the fyre. Grace be with the. Amen."

There is no separate title to the New Testament, which begins on folio I, sig. A A, and ends on reverse of folio cxxj., sig. Q Q I.

The New Testament is followed by three leaves of Table of Epistles and Gospels after the use of Salisbury, for Sundays and "diuerse saynctes dayes in the yeare."

The imprint is on the fifth page, and reads thus:

Colophon.

"To the honoure and prayse of God, was this | Byble prynted and fynished in the year of oure | Sauioure Jesu Christ M.D.L. the | xvj daye of the moneth | of August." |

Matthew's Bible.

THE second version of the Bible in English was brought out under the superintendence of John Rogers, a friend of William Tyndale.

It is a composite book, made up of Tyndale's Pentateuch and New Testament of 1535-4, and, from Deuteronomy to the end of the 2nd book of Chronicles, taken from a manuscript translation left behind by Tyndale with Rogers, his literary executor.

Matthew's Version a composite book.

The rest is from Coverdale's Bible, excepting the Prayer of Manasses, which was translated by John Rogers, the editor of this Bible, from the French Bible printed at Neufchastel by Pierre de Wingle in 1535.

Why Rogers did not utilise Tyndale's translation of the Book of Jonah is not known, but there can be no doubt that Jonah in Matthew's version is Coverdale's translation and not Tyndale's.

John Rogers was born about the beginning of the 16th century; he took his B.A. degree at Cambridge in 1525, and, seven years after, obtained a Rectory in London. In 1537 he married Adriana Pratt, by whom he had eight children.

John Rogers Editor of Matthew's Bible.

He left London during the latter part of the reign of Henry VIII., and took up his residence at Antwerp, where he acted as Chaplain to the

Merchant Adventurers, and was also engaged on press work by Jacob van Meteren.

He remained abroad some years after the death of Tyndale.

In 1548 he returned to England, and was, on the 10th of May, presented to the Rectory of S. Margaret Moses, and the Vicarage of S. Sepulchre.

On August 24th, 1551, he obtained the Prebendal Stall of S. Pancras, at S. Paul's Cathedral, where he was Divinity lecturer. He was afterwards preferred to the Rectory of Chigwell, Essex.

In August 1553 the Lords of the Council ordered John Rogers, alias Matthew, to remain in his residence at S. Paul's as a seditious preacher, and on the 4th of February 1555 he was put to death.

In the register of the united parishes of S. Mary Woolnoth and S. Mary Woolchurch Haw, London, is the following entry:

Record of a daughter of John Rogers.

"Suzanna wief of William Shorte, Grocer, and daughter to Mr. Rogers late burned at Smithfield."

Thomas Matthew was either the name assumed by Rogers when at Antwerp, or a pseudonym adopted to conceal the fact that a considerable part of this Bible was the translation of Tyndale, whose writings had been condemned by the English authorities.

Title of Matthew's Bible.

The title, "¶ The Byble, | which is all the holy Scrip | ture: In whych are contayned the | Olde and Newe Testament truly | and purely translated into En | glysh by Thomas | Matthew.

"¶ Essaye j. | Hearken to ye heauens and | thou earth geaue eare:

"For the Lorde speaketh | M,D, XXXVII." |

"Set forth with the Kinges most gracyous lycẽce."

On reverse of title, "These thynges ensuynge are ioyned with thys present volume of the Byble." |

Sig. °ij. has, "The Kalendar and Almanack for xviii yeares," beginning 1538, four pages. Collation of Matthew's Bible of 1537.

Sig. °iiij. begins, "¶ An exhortacyon on to the studye of the holy Scripture," one page, in red and black, and at the bottom the letters I. R., nearly 2½ inches high; on the reverse is, "¶ The summe & content of all the holy | Scripture." The Dedication is on the reverse of the fifth leaf, "¶ To the moost noble and gracyous | Prynce Kyng Henry the eyght," 3 pages, the last signed, "Youre graces faythfull & true subiect Thomas Matthew," and at the bottom H.R. in similar ornamental letters to the previous I.R. Then follows on the next leaf, "¶ To the Chrysten Readers," and "A table of the pryncypall matters conteyned | in the Byble," | 26 pages. Then comes, "¶ The names of all the | bokes of the Byble," and "¶ A brief rehersall of the yeares passed sence the begynnynge of the worlde vnto this yeare of our Lorde M.CCCCC. XXXVII," one page: on the reverse of which is a full page woodcut representing Adam and Eve in the Garden of

Eden, making twenty leaves of preliminary matter.

The text begins on Sig. a, Genesis to Solomon's Ballet, fol. i. to Ccxlvii., reverse of the last being blank.

The second title is in red and black, "The Prophetes | in Englysh," | with a border of sixteen woodcuts. On the upper corners of the reverse are the letters R.G., and on the lower E.W., with a woodcut of "The Prophete Esaye" across the page.

Then follows the text on Sig. A A, fol. i. to xciiij, and at the end the initials W. T. in large capitals. The third title is also in red and black, "¶ The volume of | the bokes called Apocripha: contayned in the comen Transl. in Latyne, whych are not founde in the Hebrue nor in the Chalde," | within a border of 15 woodcuts. On the reverse is an address, "¶ To the Reader," in long lines, fol. ij. to lxxxj., followed by a blank leaf.

The New Testament title is like the first title page, "The newe | Testament of | oure sauyour Jesu Christ, | newly and dylygently translated | into Englyshe with annotacions | in the Mergent to help the | Reader to the vnderstan | dynge of the | Texte | ¶ Prynted in the yere of | oure Lorde God | M.D. XXXVII." Reverse blank.

Text begins on Sig. A ii. "S. Mathew" to "The Reuelacyon," fol. ii. to Cix., ending on the recto. On the reverse is, "This is the Table | wherin ye shall fynde the Epi | stles and the Gospels, after the vse of Salisbury," 5 pages. Next is the colophon. "¶ The ende of the newe Testament | and of the whole | Byble. ¶ To the honoure and prayse of God | was this Byble prynted and fy | nesshed in the yere of oure Lorde God a, | M.D. XXXVII."

A full page has sixty lines beside heading; the printed matter measures 11¼ by 6½ inches, not including marginal notes, which occupy one inch of space on each side.

There are 1110 pages, and nearly 80 woodcuts, those before the Psalms and Proverbs filling the whole breadth of the page.

Three verses of the 14th Psalm, "not being in the Hebrew," are omitted.

There is no printer's name on the colophon, but doubtless it was printed by Jacob van Meteren, Antwerp.

It is folio size, B. L., with marginal notes, the canticles are printed in red and black, the running titles, signatures, marginal notes, &c., are all in black letter. Grafton brought a copy of this Bible into England in the early part of the year 1537, and showed it to Archbishop Cranmer, and begged him to obtain permission for its distribution, and the King allowed it "to be sold and read of every person without danger of any Act, Proclamation, or Ordinance heretofore granted to the contrary." Grafton presented Cromwell with six copies, and petitioned for a license under the Privy Seal, to prevent German printers residing in England from competing with, and underselling

Grafton presents a copy to Cranmer.

him, as he had 1,500 copies to dispose of, which represented considerable capital; but whether he obtained protection or not is not very clear.

Second folio.

The second folio edition of Matthew's Bible was printed in 1538; it is much more rare than the first edition, and a 16mo. in five volumes is said to have been printed by Robert Redman in 1540.

Raynalde and Hyll's Edition of 1549.

A very faithful and accurate reprint of Matthew's Bible of 1537 was issued in 1549, "Imprinted at London By Thomas | Raynalde, and William Hyll, dwelling | in Paules Churche yeard." My copy is absolutely perfect, and as clean as it left the printers' hands.

The woodcut border of the title page of this book is made up of the same blocks as were used for Coverdale's Bible of 1535.

The colophon on recto of last leaf reads, "The ende of the newe testa | ment and the whole | Byble | ¶ To the Honoure and Prayse of God | was this Byble prynted and | fynisshed, in the yeare | of oure | Lorde | God | a | MDXXXVII | and nowe agayne accordyngly imprented, and finy | shed the leaste daye of Octobre. In the yeare | of oure Lord God M.D. xlix. | At London | By William Hyll, and Tho | mas Reynaldes Ty | pographers. | God saue the kynge | Cum priuilegio."

I have not found a single word of difference in the text of the two editions, but in the 1549, Tyndale's prologues to the Pentateuch are inserted as well as to the book of Jonah, and to the Epistle to the Romans.

The initial letters of the prologues to Leviticus and Deuteronomy are very large flourished German text capitals, much like some used in Jugge's revision of Tyndale's New Testament.

A full page generally contains 53 lines, but in some cases 54.

Before Exodus is an explanation of the following words:

Meaning of certain words.

"Albe, a longe garmente of whyte lynen.

"Arcke, a cofer or cheste as oure shrynes, saue it was flatte and thee sample of oure shrynes was taken therof.

"Boothe, an house made of bowes.

"Brestlappe or brestflap, is soche a flap as thou seest in the brest of a cope.

"Consecrate, to appoint a thynge to holye vses.

"Ephod, is a garment somwhat lyke an amyce, saue the armes came thorowe and it was gyrd to.

"Geeras, in weyght as it were an englyshe halfpeny or somwhat more.

"Heue offrynge, because they were houen vp before the Lorde.

"House, he made them houses: yt is he made a kynred or a multitude of people to spring ovt of them, as we saye the house of Dauid for the kynred of Dauid.

"Peace offring, offeringes of thankesgeuinge of deuotion, and not for conscience of synne and trespace.

"Reconcyle, to make at one and to bringe in greace or fauoure.

"Sanctifye, to clense and purifye, to appoynt a thinge vnto holye vses and to seperate from vncleane and vnholy vses.

"Sanctuarye, a place halowed and dedycate vnto God.

"Tabernacle, an house made tentwyse, or as a pauelion.

"Tunicle, moche lyke the vppermost garment of the deaken.

"Waue offring, because they were wauen in the prestes handes of dyuers quarters.

"Worship, by worshippyng whether it be in the old testament or ye newe, vnderstand the boweng of a man's self vpon the ground as we (oftymes we knele in oure prayers) bowe our selues and lye on our armes and handes, wyth our face to the ground."

Daye and Seres' Edition of 1549.

Another folio edition of Matthew's Bible was printed the same year, under the editorship of Edmund Becke, by whom the dedication was written, as well as many objectionable notes which are to be found in no other edition of the Bible.

The title (in red and black) is, "The Byble, that is to say all the holy Scripture: In whych are cõtayned the olde and New Testament, truly and purely trãslated into English, & nowe lately with greate industry and diligẽce recognised. Essaye I. Hearken, &c."

"Imprynted at London by Ihon Daye, dwelling at Aldersgate and William Seres, dwelling in Peter College.

"Cum gratia ad imprimendum solum. xvj daye of August M.D.XLIX."

On reverse is "An Almanack for xxix yeares." Kalendar, 2 leaves.

"An exhortation" and "The summe and content," 1 leaf.

Dedication, in which the Judges, Justices, and Lawyers are very severely dealt with, and which concludes, "geue you honorable & triuphant victory our all your enemies Cyuyl and foren, and in all other your princely affayres, be your guyde, protection and assistance. Your graces faythfull & humble subiect Edmunde Becke," 3 pages.

"¶ A description and successe of the kinges of Juda and Hierusalem declaringe when and vnder what kinges euery Prophet lyued. And what notable thynges happened in theyr tymes, translated out of the Hebrew," finishing with "carried Israel and many of the stocke of Dauid and Jehuda into Spayne," 1 page.

Address to Christian readers.

"A Table of pryncipal matters," &c., and a perfect "supputacion" of the years, by Edmund Becke, 12 leaves.

A prologue and a register, 2 leaves.

Altogether 20 leaves.

Then follows the text.

This Bible has five title pages. It has woodcuts, and before each Gospel is a figure of the Evangelist with his emblem.

In addition to the prologues to the Pentateuch there is an address by W. T. "to the

Christen Reader," of 8½ columns of small type, prefaced to "¶ The boke of | the Prophete Jonas," and after the New Testament title another address by "William Tindale vnto the Christen Reader" of 4½ columns, and one column of explanation of the words "Repentaunce" and "Elders," in which Tyndale tries to prove that Bishops and Elders are all one.

A list of "The bokes conteyned in the new Testament" completes the page.

Ed. Becke's notes.

The notes are very long, and printed in the same type as the text; for instance, those to S. Matthew, chapter vi., occupy nearly 1½ columns, and may be said to be a sermon on the Lord's Prayer.

The notes to S. Matthew, chapter xix., are indecent, and many others are most objectionable, mainly consisting of abuse of the Church, her doctrine, and her Clergy.

The following is the note to I. S. Peter iii.:

"He dwelleth wyth his wyfe according to knowledge, that taketh her as a necessarye healper, and not as a bonde seruaunte or a bonde slaue. And yf she be not obedient and healpfull vnto hym endeuoureth to beate the feare of God into her heade, that therby she maye be compelled to learne her dutie, and to do it."

No doubt such annotations were disapproved of at the time, for they were never reprinted.

Woodcuts in Revelation.

The woodcuts in the Revelation closely resemble those in Flemish and other Bibles printed about the same period; but in this

Bible the woodcuts are explained by the following doggerel, one line being printed on each side the cut:—

1st Figure.

"By the Stars in hys hand we may wel se
What maner of men our preachers should be."

2nd Figure.

"In the middest of his church sytteth God in majestie,
To whom al hys faythfull geue honoure, and glorye."

3rd Figure.

"Pale hypocrytes, enemies to Goddes Gospel,
Bring death in their doctrine and dryue vs to hell."

4th Figure.

"The seinctes that we prayed to, lo, where they lye,
And they that were our spokes men herke how they crye."

6th Figure.

"The Lord hath his numbre, whom he doeth preserue;
Their soules shall not perishe, though theyr bodies sterue."

7th Figure.

"The prayers of godly men that do lyue here,
And they that before God so pleasant appere."

8th Figure.

"Oute of the dark pytte came locustes fell,
To vex them that lyueth not after the Gospell."

9th Figure.

"The doctrine and laws of these beastes cruel
Drawe the thyrde part of men unto hell."

10th Figure.

"Goddes worde is swete in the mouth of the faythful,
But bitter in the bealy, to the flesh it is painful."

11th Figure.

"The Popes parte is caste out and geuen to the sworde
When the Churche is measured wyth Goddes word."

12th Figure.

"Goddes chosen Churche trauayleth here alwaye,
And bringeth forth Christe both nyght and day."

13th Figure.

"The open enemye is most ougly in syghte,
But the wolfe in the Lambes skyne doeth al the spight."

14th Figure.

"The electe of God onely can singe the songe
That soundeth on the herte, and not on the tonge."

15th Figure.

"At the tyme appointed by God's secret wyll,
The sykle shal cut downe boeth good and yll."

16th Figure.

"The seuen trompettes and the seuen seales,
Declare the same thinges that the seuen vialles."

17th Figure.

"The Princes of the earth euerye one
Have with this whore wrought fornicacyon."

18th Figure.

"The Romyshe marchauntes, the Priestes of Bal
Do wepe, houle, and crye, at Babylons fall."

19th Figure.

"All flesh is kylled with the ij edged sworde,
Which after the spirit is called Goddes worde."

20th Figure.

"For euer lyeth Sathan bounds in chayne,
Though in his members he be louse agayne."

21st Figure.

"A beautyfull cytye, most semelye to se
Are the faythfull folowers of Godde's verytye."

N. Hyll's edition of 1551.

The last issue of Matthew's Bible was by Nicholas Hyll in 1551, a certain number of copies being taken by various booksellers, whose names were placed on the copies for which they subscribed.

The names of eight honest booksellers deserve to be recorded; they are: Richard Kele, John and Thomas Petyt, R. Toye, Abraham

Veale, John Whyte, John Walley, L. Harrison. The colophon of this book is as follows:

"Here endeth the whole | Byble after the translation of Thomas Mathew, with all hys Prologues, that is to say, vpon the v bokes of Moses, the pro phet Jonas, and to euery of the four Euangelistes.

"And after euerye Chapter of the boke are there ad ded many playne Annotacions and exposicions of suche places as vnto the symple vnlearned seame heard to vnderstand. With other dyuers notable matters as ye shall fynde no ted nexte vnto the Callender. | Diligentlye perused and corrected.

"¶ Imprinted at London by Nicolas | Hyll, dwelling in Saynt Johns streate, at the coste and charges of certayne honest menne of the occu pacyon whose names be vpon their bokes." |

The following is an extract from the Act of Parliament prohibiting Tyndale's translation at the time Matthew's Bible was authorized by Royal licence, although Matthew's Bible is mainly Tyndale's translation under another name:

"Anno xxxiiij Henrici Octavi.

(1543)

"¶ An acte for the aduauncement of true religion and for the abolishment of the contrary. Cap. j.

"Whereas the kinges most royal maiestie our gracious and natural soueraigne liege lord, supreme head of the churche of Englande, and also of Irelande, and his honourable counsayle, perceiueth the ignoraunce, fonde opinions errours, and blindnes of diuers and sundrye his subiects of this his realme, in abusinge and not obseruinge, nor folowinge the commaundmentes, preceptes and lawes of almyghtie god, nor the verie true and perfecte religion of Christe, notwithstandyng suche holsome doctrines, and documentes as his maiestye hath heretofore caused to be set forth for that purpose beside the great libertie graunted to them in hauing them amonges them and in theyr handes the new and old testament, which notwithstanding many sedicouse people, arrogant and ignorant persons, whereof some pretendinge to be learned and to haue the perfite and true knoweledge, vnderstanding, and iudgment of the sacred and holy scriptures and some other of theyr peruerse, frowarde and malicious mindes, willes and intentes, entending to subuert the veray true and perfect exposicion, doctrine, and declaracion of the saide scripture, after their peruers fantasies: haue taken vpon them, not onely to preache, teach, declare, and set forthe the same by wordes, sermons, disputacions, and argumentes, but also by printed bookes, prynted balades, playes, rimes, songes, & other phantasies subtelly and craftely instructyng his highnes people, and specially the youthe of this hys realme, vntruly, and otherwise than the scripture ought, or should be taught, declared, or expounded, & contrary to the veray sincere, and godly meanyng of the same, wherevpon diuersity of opinions, sayinges, variaunces arguments & tumultes & scismes haue been sprong and arysen amonges his sayd subiects, within this his realme, to the greate inquietacion of his sayd people, and great displeasure of his maiestie, and contrary to his graces true meaninge, good intencion, & moste goodly purpose.

"❡ For reformacion therof, his maiestie most vertuousely, and prudentlye considereth, and thinketh that it is & shalbe most requisite, expedient, and necessarye, not onely by lawes dredful, and penall, to take awaye, purg, and clense this his highnes realme, territories, confines, dominions, and countries, of all such bookes, writinges, sermones, disputacions, argumentes, balades, plaies, rimes, songes, teachinges and instructions, as be pestiferous and noysome, with all the causes instrumentes and meanes of the same: But also to ordeine and establishe a certaine forme of pure and sincere teachinge, agreable with goddes woorde, and the true doctrine of the catholike and Apostolicall churche, whereunto men maie haue recourse for the true desision of some such controuersies as haue in times past & yet do hapen and arise amonges them. And therefore be it enacted, ordeyned and established, by our sayde soueraygne lord the kynge, the lordes spirytuall and temporall, and the commons in this present parliament assembled, and by the authoritie of the same, that all manner of bookes of the old and newe testament in englishe, beinge of the craftie, false, and vntrue translacion of Tindall, and all other bookes and writinges in the englishe tongue, teachinge or comprisinge any matters of christen religion, articles of the faithe, or holy scripture, or any part of them, contrary to that doctrine, which sins the yere of our lorde MDXL. is, or at any time duringe the kinges maiesties lyfe, our saide soueraingе lorde that now is kinge Henry the eyght, whiche our lord longe preserue, shalbe sette forth by his highnes, with such superscription and subscription, as hereafter shalbe declared, shall be by auctoritie of this present acte clerely and vtterlie abolished, extinguished, and forbidden, to be kept or vsed in this realme, or elswhere in anie the kinges dominions.

"¶ And also be it enacted by the auctoritie aforesaid, that if any printer, bokebinder, bokeseller, or anie other person or persons shall after the firste daie of July next ensuinge, printe or cause to be printed, or vtter, sell, gyue, or delyuer within this realme or elswhere within anie the kinges dominions anie of the bookes or writinges afore abolished, or prohibited, or play in enterludes, sing or rime, any matter contrarie to the said doctrine, which sins the said yere of our lorde M.D. xl. is or at anie time (as is aforesaid) shal be set forthe by the kinges maiestie, our saide soueraigne lorde that now is, and be of any the offences aforesaide conuicted, by sufficient witnes, before anie two of the kinges counsaile, or the ordinare of the diocesse, where anie such offence shalbe committed, and two Justices of peace of the same shyre where anie such ordinarie shall sitte within his diocesse, for that purpose, as before anie other person or persons, whome for this purpose the kinges maiestie shall appoint by his highnes commission, shall haue and suffre for the first time, imprisonment of his bodie for three monethes, and also lose and forfaite for euery such booke or writing, printed vttered, and solde, giuen, or delivered (as is aforesaid) the sume of xl. sterling. And for the second time so offending in anie of the said offences, and being therof conuicted, as is aforesaide, shall lose and forfaite all his goodes, and his body, to be committed to perpetuall prison.

"¶ And be further enacted by the auctorite aforesaid, that if any person or persons, after the first day of Julye next comminge, reteine in his handes or custodie, anie englishe bookes or writinges concerning matter against the holy and blessed sacrament of the aulter, or for the maintenaunce of the damnable opinions of the secte of anabaptistes or anie other Englishe bookes or writinges, which heretofore haue been abolished and condemned by the kinges proclamacions, and shalbe therof conuict, in maner and fourme aforesaid, That than euery such offendour shall for euerie such boke or writing so reteined as is aforesaid, lose and forefait the summe of vl. sterlinge. And if any person or persons, after the first daie of Octobre next comminge shall reteine in his handes or custodie, within this realme or elles where within any the kinges dominions, anie other of the said bookes or writinges before prohibited, and shal be therof conuicted, in maner and fourme aforesaid, that the saide person or persons, so being conuicte shall for euery such booke or writinge, conteininge speciall treatie or chapter against anie doctrine, set foorthe or to be set foorthe by the kinges maiestie as is aforesayd, so by him or them retayned, forfait and pay the summe of v*l*. sterling. And if the booke or writing haue onely wordes or sentences enterlaced, contrary to the said doctrine, Then the fine shall be moderate by the discrecion of the iudge: so that it excede not xl*s*.

"¶ Prouided alwayes, that the bibles and newe testament in englishe, not beinge of Tindalles translacions, shall stande in force, and not be comprised in this abolicion or acte. Neuerthelesse if there shal be found in anie such bibles or newe testamentes, any annotacions or preambles, That then euerie person or persons, hauinge anye bibles or newe testamentes with any such annotacions or preambles, shall before the sayd first day of Octobre, cutte or blotte the same, in such wise, as they cannot be perceiued nor red, vpon payne to lose and forfaite for euerie bible and newe testament that any person or person shall have in their handes or custodie, after the sayd first daie of Octobre, with any such annotacions or preambles as is aforesayd, contrary to this acte xl*s*.

"¶ Prouided alway, that this article next

aboue specified, do not extend to the blotting or cutting out of any quotacions or summaries of chapters expressed or conteyned in anye such bibles or newe testamentes any thinge afore mentioned to the contrary notwithstanding.

"¶ Prouided also, that all bookes in englishe, printed before the yere of our lorde M.D. XL. intiteled, the kinges highnes proclamacions, iniunctions, translacions of the Pater nostre, the Aue maria, and the Crede, the psalters, primers, praiers, statutes and lawes of the realme, cronicles, Canterbury tales, Chaucers bookes, Gowers bookes, & stories of mens liues, shall not be comprehended in the prohibicion of this acte, unlesse the kinges sayde maiestie shall hereafter make speciall proclamacion for the condemnacion and reprouing of the same, or any of them.

"¶ Prouided alwaye and be it enacted by the auctoritie aforesayd, that all printers maye lawfully printe all suche bookes conteyninge matters of religion as the kinges maiestie shall by his bill assigned allow, and aproue, wherunto the same printers shall be bound to put the superscripcion and subscripcion in this fourme, that is to saye, by the kinge and his clergie, with adicion in the ende of the printers name, his dwellinge place, the daie and the yere of the printing of the same, which if the said printer do omitte, he shall incurre such penalties, as before is limitted for printing, selling, giuynge, or diliueringe of vnlawfull bookes.

"¶ Prouided alwaies, and be it enacted by

the auctoritie aforesayde, that it shal be lawfull to all and euerie person and persons to sette forthe songes and plaies, and interludes for the rebuking and reproachinge of vices, and the settinge forthe of virtue: So alwayes the said songes, plaies, interludes medle not with interpretacions of scripture, contrary to the doctrine set forth or to be set forth by the kinges maiestie. Anye thing contayned in thys acte to the contrarye notwithstanding.

"¶ And be it further enacted by the auctoritie aforesayde, that no manner of person or persons after the first daye of Octobre next ensuinge, shall take vpon him or them to read preach or teach openly to other, in anye churche or open assembly, within any of the kinges dominions, the bible, or any part of scripture in englishe onlesse he be so appoynted therunto by the kinges maiestie, or by any ordinarye, or by such as haue rule, gouernment and auctoritie vpon peine that euery such offendour, shall suffre imprisonment of one moneth.

"¶ Prouided also that it shall be lawfull to euery noble man and gentleman being a householder, to rede or cause to be reade by anie of his familye servauntes, in his house, orchyardes or gardeine, and to his own familye, any text of the bible or new testament so the same be done quietely and without disturbance of good order. And also that it shal be lawfull for euerye marchanteman, being a housholder and occupiyng the seat of marchaundyse, to read to himself priuately, the bible and new testament, anye thynge in this acte to the contrarye notwithstanding.

"¶ And where the kinges maiestie, of hys moste gracious and blessed dysposicion, hath heretofore caused to be set forth the bible and new testament in the Englyshe tonge, to be read by his louing subiectes, to the intent that they might therby better know theyr dutye to almightie god, and to his maiestie, and also increace in vertue for the welth of their soules. All be it his maiesties said most godly purpose and intent, hath taken good effecte amonges great multitude of his subiectes, and specially amonges the highest and most honest sort, accordynge to hys highnes good expectacion therof, yet for as much as his highnes perceiueth, that a great multitude of his saide subiectes, moste especially of the lower sorte haue so abused the same, that they haue thereby growen and increaced in diuers naughty and erronious opinions, and by occasion therof fallen into great diuision and dissencion among them selves, to the great vnquietnes of the realme and other his maiesties dominions. For remedy wherof be it enacted by the auctoritie aforesayde, that from and after the first day of Julye next commynge no women, nor artificers, prentyses, iorneymen, seruyng men of the degrees of yeoman or vnder husbandmen, nor labourers, shal reade wythin thys realme, or in any other the kinges dominyons the bible or new testament in Englishe to hymself, or to any other priuately or openly, vpon payne of one monthes imprysonment for euery tyme offendyng contrary to thys acte, and beynge therof conuicte in such manner and fourme as is aforesayde, onlesse the kinges maiestie perceiuing such reformacion and amendement in theyr lyues and behauiour, by the diligent and dyscrete readyng and imprinting in their hartes of the most blessed doctrine set forthe, and hereafter to be set forthe by hys sayde maiestie, shal of his clemency thinke good otherwise, to enlarge and giue libertie for the reading of the same.

"¶ Prouided alway, that all maner of persons, other than women, artificers, prentises, iourneymen, seruing men of the degrees of yomen or vnder, husbandmen, and labourers, maye read to themselves, and to none other, any text of the bible and new testament, for theyr own edefieng, and increase of vertue, anything in this acte to the contrary notwythstandyng.

"¶ Prouided alwaies, that euery noble woman and gentelwoman maye reade to themselues alone, and not to others, any textes of the bible or new testament, anything in this act to the contrary notwythstanding.

"¶ And it is also ordeined and enacted by the auctoritie aforesaide, that the one moitie of all the penalties and forfaitures of summes of money aboue specified, shall be to the kinge our soueraine lorde, and the other moitie therof to such person or persons as will detecte and sue for the conuiction of any of the offendours contrary to this acte, in such fourme as is aboue limitted by this acte, and that the moitie of such forfaitures limitted to the partye detectinge and suinge as is aforesayde, shall be leuied of the offendours, that shal be conuicte by auctoritie of this acte as is aforesaid, after such fourme, fashion and order of processe, as shal be deuised by the iudge or iudges afore whome any such conuiction shal be had: and the other moitie of such forfaitures, limitted to the kinges maiestie, shall be estreated by writyng into the kinges escheker, by the said iudge or iudges, within xl dayes next after such conuiction had: if it be in the term tyme, and if it be out of the terme, then within xx dayes nexte after the begininge of the terme following after such conuiction.

"¶ And be it further enacted by the auctoritie aforesaid, that in triall by witnes of any of the matters or offences aboue specified in this acte, the person or persons beinge detecte or complained on, shal be admitted to purge and trie his or theyr innocency by other witnesse, as many or mo in numbre, and of as good honesty and credence as those which be deposed against them or any of them, in whiche case the said iudge or iudges which shall haue auctoritie to examine here and determine the offences aboue saide, by auctoritie of this acte, shall aduisidely and deliberately suruey and consider the witnes brought in by bothe partes, and theyr disposicions and circumstances therof, and there vpon condempne or dismisse from punishment and lose, the person detecte or complained vpon, as to his owne discretion shall seeme best to agree with with conscience and equitie.

"❡ Prouided alwaies and be it enacted, that for the more spedie execution of this act, euery ordinary aforesaid, shall haue full power and auctoritie, by vertue of this act, to giue notice to two iustices of the peace being vnder the degree of barons, and being residaunt and inhabitaunt within such shyre where any such ordinary shall set, for the execucion of this acte, and require them to come to suche place, and at suche time as suche ordinary shall name and assigne, to ioine with the said ordinary in examinacion and determinacion of any offence or offences committed or done against the tenour of this act. And in case any such iustices, being so required, as is aforesayde, hauing conuenient and reasonable warning and knowledge in writinge from and at suche time, of the day and place appointed, do not come to suche place and at such time as shal be appointed, hauing no lawfull and iust impediment to the contrary, shall forfaite and lose to the kinges highnes, for euery such offence xls. to be estreated, as is aforesaide.

Taverner's Bible.

LESS is commonly known of Taverner's version than of any other. It was issued the same year as the Great Bible, folio size. The title is within architectural compartment, surrounded with a double black line.

"The Most Sacred Bible | Whiche is the holy scripture, con teyning the old and new testament, | translated into English, and newly | recognised with great diligence | after most faythful exem | plars, by Rychard Taverner.

"☞ Harken thou heuen, and thou earth gyue eare: for the Lorde speaketh. Esaie i. |

"☞ Prynted at *London* in Flete strete at | the sygne of the sonne by John By | ddell, for Thomas Barthlet. |

"☞ Cvm Privilegio | ad imprimendum solum. | M.D. XXXIX." |

Reverse blank.

Dedication, "To the most noble, most mighty, and most | redoubted prynce, Kinge Henry the viij.," 1 page; on the reverse, "These thynges ensuynge are | joyned with this present vo- | lume of the bible," and "An exhortacion to the diligent studye of the holy scripture | gathered out of the Bible," 1 page. Collation of Taverner's Bible.

The third leaf begins, "The Contentes of the Scriptvre," 2 pages, in long lines. The fourth leaf begins, "The Names of the Bokes of the Byble," 1 page, in two columns; on the reverse,

"A briefe rehersall of the yeres passed," filling about a quarter of the page; then comes, "A Table of the principal maters conteyned in the Bible," filling, in double columns, that and the next twenty-four pages, making in all sixteen preliminary leaves. Text, in double columns, Genesis to Solomon's Ballet, ccxxx. folioed leaves, with signatures A to Z; Aa to Oo in sixes, and Pp in eight leaves.

Then follows, on a separate leaf, the title without any border, "The Boke of | the Pro- | phetes," &c.; reverse blank. Text, beginning on signature A A ij, Esaye to Malachy, LXXXXj folioed leaves, sigs. A A to P P vij; then comes on P P viij a third title, like the second without any border, "The Volume of | the Bokes cal | led Apocripha," &c.; reverse blank. Text—Third book of Esdras to second of "Machabees," LXXV folioed leaves, followed by one blank leaf. Signatures A a a to M m m in sixes, and N n n in four leaves.

Then comes the New Testament title, having a border similar to the first title; reverse blank. Text—S. Matthew to Revelation, folio ij to cj, ending near the centre of the reverse. Signatures, A ij to R v.

At the end of the Testament follows a table, "¶ This is the table wherin ye shall | fynde the Epistles and the Gospels | after the vse of Salisbury," 5 pp. in double columns, ending at the bottom of the fifth page with the Colophon,

"¶ To the honour and prayse of God, was this Byble | printed: and fynyshed, in the yere of | our Lorde God, a M.D. XXXIX." The last page is blank.

Richard Taverner was born in 1505. Of his childhood little is known; there is no doubt he sprang from a good family, and one of considerable fortune. He graduated at Benet College, Cambridge, but attracted by the fame of Cardinal Wolsey's College, he transferred himself to Oxford, where he would find congenial society with men of the "new learning," and the love he afterwards showed for the Greek language and literature no doubt was here implanted in his breast. Richard Taverner.

Foxe says that about this time Taverner recanted his opinions, and publicly bore his fagot.

Anthony à Wood, in his *Athenæ Oxonienses*, says that Taverner "went to an inn of Chancery, near London, and thence to the Inner Temple, where his humour was to quote the law in Greek when he read anything thereof."

Thomas Cromwell, who had a keen eye for all whom he thought would promote his interest and aid his aggrandisement, took Taverner into his employ in the year 1531, and procured him the position of a clerk of the signet. When, in 1540, Cromwell's conduct brought his well-merited doom, Taverner's prosperity was clouded, and he was committed to the Tower of London, from which so many better men than he never returned. Taverner's imprisonment there did not last long; he submitted to the Royal tyrant, Henry VIII., and was restored to the royal favour. This speaks much for his prudence, but shows he was not made of the stuff that Sir Thomas More, and Fisher the good Bishop of Rochester, were.

When King Edward came to the throne, Taverner boldly resumed his principles, and, although he was not in Holy Orders, he was licensed to preach, preaching being then thought more important than anything else. His party very strongly objected to the proper ecclesiastical vestments, but Taverner preached before the King at Court, and at other places, wearing a velvet bonnet, a damask gown, and having a chain of gold about his neck.

During the next reign he prudently retired from public life, and remained unmolested, but as soon as Elizabeth came to the throne, he resumed his self-imposed vocation, and preached at St. Mary's Church, Oxford, in a similar dress and adornments to that worn by him in King Edward's time.

Although not such a favourite with Queen Elizabeth as the Earl of Essex was, Taverner was shown special marks of the royal approval, and was made High Sheriff of the county of Oxford. He died in the year 1575.

Taverner's renderings.

Nearly all the changes Taverner made in his version, appear to be in order to give more vigorous and idiomatic renderings. For instance, in I. S. John, second chapter and first verse, most versions give, "We have an advocate with the Father;" but Taverner renders it, "We have a spokesman with the Father":

again, in the next verse, Tyndale's New Testament and Cranmer's Bible read, "For he it is that obteyneth grace for our sins," the Bishops' Bible has, "For he is the atonement for our sins," the Genevan Bible, "For he is the reconciliation for our sins," the Authorized Version, "For he is the propitiation for our sins," Taverner's translation is, "For he is the mercy-stock for our sins."

In S. Matthew xii. 12, we now have, "and he was speechless:" Taverner reads, "had never a word to say." In S. Luke xii. 19, Tyndale has, "neither climb ye up on high," and King James' version, "neither be ye of doubtful mind:" Taverner has, "and be not carried in the clouds." Taverner's Psalms follow the Vulgate numbering.

Dedication.

Taverner says in his dedication to the King, "This one thyng I dare ful wel affirm, y^t amongst al your Majesties deservings, your highnesse never did any thinge more acceptable to God, more profitable to the advancement of true Christianity, more unpleasant to the enemies of the same and also to your graces enemies, than when your majestie lycenced and wyled, the moost sacred Bible, contaynge the unspotted and lively word of God, to be in the Englyshe tonge set forthe to your highnesse subjects.

"Wherefore the premises well consydered, for as much as the prynters hereof were very dysourous to have this moost sacred volume of the Bible come forthe as faultless and emendably as the shortness of the tyme for the recognising of the same would require, they desired me your moost humble servant, for default of a better learned, dygilently to oversee and peruse the whole copy, and in case I should find any notable default that needed correction, to amende the same, according to the true exemplars, which thing according to my talent I have gladly done."

Two editions of this book were issued the same year (1539), one in folio and the other in quarto, and also two editions of the New Testament by itself, printed by T. Petit for T. Berthelet. The title page of the quarto reads, "The Nevv Testament in Englysshe after the Greke Exemplar: Dilygently translated and corrected by Rycharde Tauerner M.D. xxxix. Cum Privilegio ad Imprimendum solum," surrounded by a border of grotesque and not very decent figures.

In the year 1549, Daye and Seres published an edition of Taverner's Bible in five 12mo. volumes, said to be for the convenience of those who were unable to purchase an entire Bible at one time. I never possessed the whole of the five volumes. I once picked up the Apocrypha part, but a friend having the other four volumes, I gave him mine to complete his set. This Apocrypha was remarkable for having three books of Maccabees. This is the first instance in which the third book of Maccabees appears as a portion of the English Bible.

Daye's Taverner, folio, 1551.

In 1551, John Daye printed a composite Bible

in small folio. It consists of the Old Testament and Apocrypha of Taverner's version, with the New Testament of Matthew's, which substantially was taken from Tyndale's small octavo of 1535 4, known as the "G.H.," from the initials of the publisher, Godfried von der Haghen, on the second title.

The first title reads, "The Byble, | that is to say, al the holy | Scripture conteined in the olde | and newe Testament, faythfully set | furth according to ye Coppy of Thomas | Mathewes translatio, wherunto are | added certaine learned Prologes, and | Annotacios for the better under- | standing of many hard places | thorowout the whole | Bible." Title page.

"Essaye i. ¶ Hearken to ye heuens, and thou earth giue eare, for the Lorde speaketh. | Imprinted at London by Ihon Daye | dwellyng ouer Al dersgate. |

"☞ Cum gracia et priuilegio ad imprimendum solum. Anno a M.D.LI."

At the bottom of the page is the printer's rebus, with the words, "Arise for it is day." This title is very interesting, and shows how careful we ought to be in accepting for facts the statements we find on title pages. It appears as if in many early printed books the publisher, and not the author drew up the title page, and put on them not a true description of the book, but what he thought most likely to cause the volume to be purchased. The various titles to Coverdale's folio of 1535 are instances of this.

Although the above title states that the book is "*faythfully* set furth according to ye coppy of Thomas Mathewes translatiō," the fact is that, excepting from the 31st chapter of Deuteronomy to the 13th of Joshua, and the Psalter, the whole is Taverner's translation, with some verbal alterations by Edmund Becke.

The few chapters referred to above are from Matthew's Bible of 1537. In the Apocrypha, the 3rd book of Esdras, Tobit, and Judith, are an independent translation, unlike any other Bible ever printed, of which I will give a short specimen.

As the preliminary matter in existing copies of this Bible is often defective, it may be useful to give a collation.

Collation.

The reverse of title is said by Cotton to be blank, but mine has on it "¶ An Almanacke for 27 yeares" from 1551 to 1577, in four columns, "The number of the yeares, Easter, The golden numbre or prime, The letter dominical," and the information at the bottom of the page that, "The yeare hath xij monethes, lij wekes and one day, and it hath in al thre hundred and lxvj dayes, and vj houres."

Then a "Calendar," 3 pages, Edmund Becke's dedication to King Edward VI., 3 pages, in which he urges "all from the honourable lord Chanchlar to the honest Constable" to study this book. "Then shuld the ouer long and greate trauayle, the immoderate expences and costes whyth the pore man dayly susteneth in hys endles suites, pearse and moue their stony hertes, wyth pitye and compassion." Next, "To the Christen readers, A table of principall matters" arranged alphabetically. "¶ A gatheryng of certayne harde wordes in the newe Testament with their exposicion," also the following preface. "Because there are in ye newe Testament some wordes which should not of euery body be well understaded because they are not accustomed in common speach, we have made a lytle gathering and an exposiciō of them not thoroughly to treate them as learned men myghte, nor to delaye them with longe circumstance, but only that the rude ignoraunt may knowe what they signifie and so not be troubled in the readinge."

"¶ An exhortacion to the studie of the Holy Scripture gathered out of the Byble."

"¶ The summe and content of al the holy Scrypture, both of the Old and new Testament."

Then, "A perfect supputation of the yeres and tyme from Adam vnto Christe, proued by the Scryptures, after ye colleccion of dyuers Authors, by Edmund Becke," concluding, "And ye whole summe and number of yeares from the begynnyng of the worlde vnto this present yeare of oure Lorde God, a thousand, v hundred. li. are just v thousand v hundreth, and xxv yere vj monethes, and the sayde od x dayes." Next, "The names of al the bookes of the Bible, and the content of the Chapters of euery booke," ending, "¶ Al these thynges are the booke of lyfe, the couenaunt of the hyest and the knowledge of the truth, Ecclesisticus xxiiij c." "A Regyster or a bryefe rehersall of names of the most famous and notable persons mencioned in the old and new Testament," giving the names of the "famous men, the wycked men, the famous wemen, the wycked wemen," the last being "Babilon the great harlot," &c. On reverse of last leaf but one of preliminary is, "A discripcion and successe of the Kynges of Juda and Hierusalem, declarynge when and vnder what Kynges euerye Prophete lyued, and what notable thynges happened in their tymes, translated out of the Hebrew." The last leaf contains the well-known prologue of William Tyndale. These preliminary pieces occupy twenty-two leaves beside the title.

The variation between Tyndale's rendering of the Pentateuch and that of Taverner is not great. As a specimen, I give the opening passage. Taverner has:

Tyndale and Taverner.

"In the begyninge created God heauen and earth. The earth was voyde and emptie, and darcknesse was vppon the depe, and the spiryt of God was borne vppon the waters. And god sayde, lette there be lyghte, and there was lyghte. And God sawe the lyghte that it was good, and deuided the lighte from the darcknes, and called the light the day, and the darknes the night. And the eueninge and morninge was made one daye."

In Genesis iij., where Matthew reads, "Ye shall be as God," Taverner has, "God dothe know that whensoeuer ye shud eate of it, your eyes should be opened, and ye shoulde be as god les and knowe bothe good and euyl."

In Genesis xlix. Matthew reads, "they houghed an oxe:" Taverner has introduced, "Thy brethren Simeon and Leui, wicked instrumentes are their weapons. Into their secretes come not my soule, and vnto their congregacion be my honour not coupled: for in their wrathe they slewe a man and in their luste they threwe downe the walles of the cytye."

In II. Chronicles ii., and also in chapter iv., this book is the last English Bible which gives the name of the artist sent to King Solomon by the King of Tyre as Hiram Abif or Abi.

The xci Psalm varies only in spelling from the early versions. We here have:

"He shal couer the vnder hys wynges that thou maiest be safe vnder hys fethers: hys faythfulnesse and truthe shal be thy shylde and buckler.

"So that thou shalt not nede to be afraied for any bugs by night, nor for the arrowe that flyeth by day."

The last paragraph of the viii[th] chapter of "Jeremy" is,

"The haruest is gone, the sommer hath an ende, and we are not healped, I am sore vexed, bycause of the hurt of my people: I am heauye, and abashed: for there is no more Tryacle at Galaad, and there is no Physycion that can heale the hurte of my people."

In "Exechyel" ix. we have,

"He called the man that had the linnen rayment vpon hym, and the writers ynckhorne by hys syde, and the Lorde said vnto hym, Go thy way thorowe the cytye of Jerusalem, and set this marke, Thau vpon the foreheades of them that mourne and are sorye for all the abbomynacions that be done therein."

Taverner's Apocrypha.

To show that a portion of the Apocrypha in Taverner's version is an entirely new translation a passage is appended from the second chapter of the third book of Esdras.

The 1st and 2nd books of Esdras are now called Ezra and Nehemiah.

Coverdale's, Matthew's, the Great Bible (commonly called Cranmer's), are all alike, and the Bishops' Bible only varies in a few unimportant words, but this Bible will be seen to have an independent translation.

Third Book of Esdras, chapter second. Coverdale's, Matthew's, Cranmer's, and substantially the Bishop's version, read as follows:

"Now when kynge Cyrus raigned over the Persians, and when the Lord would performe the worde that he had promysed by the mouthe of the prophete Jeremy: the lord raysed up the sprete of Cyrus, the kyng of Persians, so that he caused this writinge to be proclaymed thorowoute his whoole realme, sayinge: Thus saythe the kynge of Persians: The lorde of Israell that hygh lorde hathe made me kynge of the Lande, and commaunded me to buylde hym an house at Jerusalem in Jewrye. If there be any now of youre people, the lorde be wyth hym, and go up wyth hym to Hierusalem.

"And all they that dwell roūde aboute that place, shall helpe them whether it be wyth golde, wyth silver, wyth giftes, wyth horses and necessary catel, and all other thynges that are brought wyth a fre wyll to the house of the Lord at Jerusalem."

Third Book of Esdras, chapter second, Taverner's version (numbered iii. in error):

"The first yeare of Cirus kinge of Persians, the lord entending to performe that he had promised bi the mouth of the prophet Jeremi, he stirred up the mind of Cirus king of Persians to make proclamation thorowout all hys realme, writing on this wyse. These things comaundeth Cirus the king of the Persians. The Lord of Israel, that hieste Lorde, hathe made me kynge of the worlde, and hathe commaunded me for to builde uppe hys Temple of Hierusalem, whych is in Jurye, wherefore if there be any of your people the lord be with hym, and let him go to Hierusalem which is in Jury, and buyld the temple to the lord of Israell. This is the Lorde that had a tabernacle at Hierusalem. As manie therefore as dwell there aboute, Lette theym helpe them, whether it be wyth golde, or wyth silver, with giftes, wyth horses, or necessary cattel, and al other thinges that are brought to the house of the Lorde in the temple of Hierusalem."

This Bible has an additional book at the

end of the Apocrypha, viz., the Third Book of Maccabees, consisting of seven chapters. To give some idea of this almost unknown book, I append the table of contents at the head of each chapter:

The first chapter:

The Third Book of Maccabees.

"¶ Philopater overcometh Antiochus. The Jewes declare the joy for hys vyctorye. He desyreth to enter into the holyest place. They denye hym."

The second chapter:

"¶ The Jewes fel to prayer to let the kyng of hys purpose. He was punyshed by God, but he repented not."

The third chapter:

"¶ The kyng maketh a sore decree, and writeth a letter that they shuld be broughte to Egypte as traytoures and there kylled."

The fourth chapter:

"¶ The people had pyty to se them so greuouslye handled, and said they were so many that the names coulde not be wrytten."

The fifth chapter:

"¶ The kyng called for Hermon the Master of hys Elephants and bad hym prepare them that they myght kyll the Jewes, but by the myght of God the kyng fel into such forgetfulnes that he wyst not what he commaunded: and they were saued."

The sixth chapter:

"¶ Eleazarus maketh hys prayer. The kyng commaundeth yet agayne to kyll the Jewes by the force of Elephants. Angels appere and save them. The kyng is tourned to mercye."

The seventh chapter:

"¶ The king wrytteth to all the rulers in Egipte to suffer the Jewes to go home. They take shippynge. They put troubles in wryting, and praise the Lord God of Israel for euer."

The last chapter concludes:

"for al men receyued their goodes, as they were named in the bill of atteindure, so that whosoeuer had anything of theyrs, restored it againe wyth greate feare, the hie God finishing theyr matters to al their healthes. Praysed be God the delyuerer of Israell worlde wythout ende."

The New Testament title is in a border like the first title. The letterpress reads:

"The Newe Testament of oure Sa | uioure Jesu Christe, diligently | translated, accordynge to the Greke | with certayne Notes folowynge | the chapters. Wherin the hardest doutes are | decla red for the better vn | derstandyng of the unlear ned rea der. |

"II Timoth. ij. All Scrypture geuen by inspiracyon of God, is profytable to teache, to improue, to amend, and to instruct in righteousnes, that the man of God maye be perfect and prepared to al good workes."

On reverse of title begins a prologue of "Wyllyam Tyndall vnto the Christyan Reader" of four pages in double columns, then the text, beginning on verso of signature A a a a iij., and headed by a woodcut of S. Matthew, with his usual emblem of a man, on the sides of which are the following lines:

> "A Prince of the Publicans, a taker of tolles,
> Is become a preacher, a feder of soules.—*Math. ix.*"

The text is that of Matthew's Bible, the only difference being that the summary of contents at the head of each chapter is longer.

At the end are "Tables of Epistles, &c., accordyng to the boke of Common Praier," two leaves (*i.e.*, the first book of Edward VI.), and "The Epystles and Gospels for Sayntes dayes."

The Colophon is:

"¶ The ende of the old and newe Testament."

Colophon.

"To the honour and prayse of God was thys Byble prynted and fynyshed in the yeare of our Lord and Sauiour Jesus Christ. M.D.LI. The xxiij daye of Maye. Imprinted at London by Jhon Daye, dwellyng ouer Aldersgate beneth Saynt Martyns. Cvm privilegio ad imprimendvm solvm."

The Great Bible.

BETWEEN April 1539 and December 1541, seven editions of this version were printed, each of which was more or less revised.

There is sufficient difference between the issues to enable any leaf to be recognised, and assigned to the edition to which it belongs, although they all have the same catchwords, excepting the November issues of 1540 and 1541.

The title page of the first edition reads,

"¶ The Byble in | Englyshe, that is to saye the con | tent of all the holy scripture, bothe | of ye olde and newe testament, truly | translated after the veryte of the | Hebrue and Greke textes, by ye dy | lygent studye of dyuerse excellent | learned men, expert in the for- | sayde | tonges. ¶ Prynted by Rychard Grafton | & Edward Whitchurch. | Cum priuilegio ad imprimen | dum solum. 1539." | Title of Great Bible of April 1539.

There are twelve preliminary pages.

The colophon is, "The ende of the new Testamet: | and of the whole Byble, Fynisshed | in Apryll, | Anno M.ccccc. xxxix. | A dno factu est istud." |

Myles Coverdale was the editor and chief translator, but there is no record of the names of the "dyuerse excellent learned men" by whom he was assisted; most likely they were Bishops of the English Church, who did not care to have their names prominently brought forward.

A number of letters from Coverdale to Cromwell are in existence which throw considerable light on the history of the genesis of this book. They are dated from Paris, where Coverdale, accompanied by one of the publishers, had gone to see the book through the press.

Cromwell was evidently paymaster, as Coverdale speaks of the book as "your work."

Cromwell by this time had been raised by King Henry VIII. to the dignity of Vicar-general. His conduct to the bishops was most overbearing, and at length retribution overtook him; for having been proved to have enriched himself by taking bribes to pervert justice, and being found guilty of other malpractices, the disgraced favourite ended his days on the scaffold, July 1540. He enjoyed the earldom of Essex only 102 days. He fell into a pit he had digged for another, for he was condemned under the Act of Attainder, without trial, a process of his own devising.

Cromwell beheaded.

Dean Hook's opinion of Cromwell.

Dr. Hook says: "Cromwell's haughty demeanour when in power contrasted strongly with the abject cowardice of his last letter to the King, which concludes, 'Written at the Tower, with the heavy heart and trembling hand of your Highness most miserable prisoner, and poor slave, I cry for mercy, mercy, mercy.'"

His great friend, Cranmer, voted for his attainder.

The Bible of 1539 was a great improvement on Coverdale's Translation of 1535; the divers excellent learned men who assisted the editor did not slavishly follow the first version. In the 53rd chapter of Isaiah, for example, they made about forty alterations.

Purchase of Bibles ordered by proclamation.

Great efforts were made to induce the people of England to accept this translation, for the majority were hostile to a vernacular Bible, hence the number of injunctions and even penal laws that were required to force it into circulation. Besides the proclamation issued by the King himself, the Archbishop urged the clergy to provide themselves with copies of the Scriptures. The Vicar-general also commanded "that one book of the whole Bible of the largest volume in English should be set up in some convenient place within the church" that "ye have the care of whereat your parisioners may most commodiously resort to the same and read it."

This Bible might well be referred to as "of the largest volume," as its pages are 15 inches in length, and more than 9 inches in breadth. It was without marginal notes, but Coverdale intended to add them to subsequent issues. He promised he would "avoid any private opinions or contentious words, and obtain Bishop Bonner's sanction to each note before it was printed."

Coverdale, with several assistants, was for

some years privately engaged on the translation of this Bible. Early in 1538 it was completed and ready for the press, but the art of printing not being as far advanced in England as in France, and Cromwell being determined that this book should be a typographical wonder, as indeed it proved to be, sent Grafton and Coverdale to Paris, to place the work in the hands of the celebrated French printer, Regnault; having first induced Henry VIII. to enter into direct communication with Francis I., and obtain from him a special licence for Richard Grafton and Edward Whitchurch to have the Scriptures printed in his dominions.

Regnault engaged to print the Great Bible.

Dr. Bonner, Archdeacon of Leicester, then Bishop elect of Hereford, afterwards Bishop of London, rendered most essential service in the issue of this version. Bonner was at that time ambassador from the Court of England, and by his official position, as well as from the high estimation in which he was personally held, was able to afford protection to Coverdale and Grafton, and he did so to the utmost of his power, and they gratefully acknowledged in several letters still extant, his great liberality and kindness to them.

Coverdale and Grafton's acknowledgment of Bp. Bonner's assistance.

Knowing the great efforts that were being made to induce Francis to withdraw the licence he had granted to the printers, and that thus the undertaking was liable to immediate interruption, Bonner conveyed portions of the impression as they issued from the press, to London; an ambassador having the right to

Bp. Bonner conveys portions of the Great Bible to London.

travel without his luggage being examined. On the 13th of December Coverdale writes to Cromwell:

Coverdale's letter to Cromwell.

"Right honorable and my syngular good Lorde (after all dow salutacions) I humbly beseche youre Lordshippe that by my Lorde Electe of Herdforde I maye knowe your pleasure concernyng the Annotacions of this Byble, whether I shall proceade therin or no.

"Pitie it were that the darck places of the text (vpon the which I haue allwaye set a hande) shulde so passe vndeclared. As for anye pryuate opynion or contencious wordes, as I wyll utterly auoyde all suche, so wyll I offre the Annotacions first to my sayde Lorde of Herdforde, to the intent that he shall so examen the same afore they be put in prynte, yf it be your Lordshippes good pleasure, that I shall do so.

"As concernyng the New Testamentes in English and Latyn, wherof your good Lordshippe receaued lately a boke by your seruaunt Sebastian the cooke, I beseche your Lordshippe to consydre the grenesse therof, which (from lack of tyme) can not be so apte to be bounde as it shulde be. And where as my sayde Lord of Herdforde is so good vnto vs as to conuaye thus moche of the Byble to your good Lordshippe, I humbly beseche the same to be the defender and keper therof; to the intent that yf these men proceade in their cruelnesse agaynst vs, and confiscate the rest, yet this at the leest maye be safe by the meanes of your

Lordshippe, whom God the Almightie euermore preserue to His good pleasure. Amen. Written somwhat hastely at Parys the 13 day of Decembre [1538].

"Your Lordshippes humble and faithfull seruitour

MYLES COUERDALE."

Superscribed—"To my most singular good Lorde and Master the Lorde Cromwell. Lorde Preuye Seale. This delyuer."

Regnault forbidden by the French authorities to print the Great Bible.

These gloomy anticipations were fully realised; for four days after the date of this letter, the work was stopped, and by the permission of Francis, an order was issued, dated December 13th, 1538, signed Le Tellier, citing Regnault, and all others it might concern, to answer for what they had already done, and inhibiting the further printing of the Bible, and ordering the sheets already printed to be delivered up. All the printed leaves the authorities could lay their hands on were ordered to be destroyed. Instead of strictly obeying orders, the Lieutenant sold four great dry vats full to a haberdasher, from whom they were rescued and conveyed to England.

Press and type purchased.

Cromwell then sent to Paris and purchased from François Regnault the presses and type, and had them removed to London, where they were used in the production of this and the six succeeding editions.

Title page.

The border of the title page is an elaborate engraving, said to have been designed by Hans Holbein.

It represents our Lord in the clouds, with stretched out arms; underneath is the King sitting on a throne, with Bishops on one side and Nobles on the other. The Bishops stand bareheaded, with their mitres on the ground at the King's feet, a fitting emblem of Henry VIII's supremacy over the Church. The King is represented as holding a book in each hand, which he is presenting to the Bishops and Nobles, and on the cover of each book is inscribed the words "*Verbum Dei.*"

On the right side of the letter press is Cromwell giving a Bible to some laymen, and on the left, Cranmer handing a Bible to a Priest.

Below are represented all sorts and conditions of men, supposed to be shouting "*Vivat Rex.*"

This Bible is without notes; the editor says in his prologue, "We have added many hands in the margent of this Byble vpon which we purposed certen godly annotacyons, but for so moch as yet there hath not bene suffycient tyme mynystored to the Kinges moost honorable councell for the ouersyght and correcyon of the sayde annotacyons, we wyll therfore omyt them tyl their more conuenient leysour." Coverdale's preparation for notes.

This "leysour" never came; for a hint was conveyed to Coverdale from the King that the Bible had better be left without note or comment.

Grafton and Whitchurch took the pecuniary risk of the publication of the various editions of the Great Bible, materially helped by Anthony Anthony Marler provides funds for printing the Great Bible.

Marler, a merchant of London. The price was fixed at 10*s.* unbound, and 12*s.* bound; and a royal proclamation was issued forcing the curates and parishioners of every parish, under a penalty of double the cost of the book per month, to purchase a copy for the common use of the people before the Feast of All Hallows 1540. No version since this one has been formally authorised by the Crown, nor has any authority, excepting that of the Church, been required.

Price paid for the Great Bible.

Although Anthony Marler was authorised to charge the sum of 12*s.* for each bound copy, we find from the Churchwardens' books in various parishes that the price at which the Great Bible was actually sold was much less; for instance, the Ashburton entry is as follows:

"A.D. 1540-1. Paid v*s.* iiij*d.* for a new booke called a Bybyll; Paid viij*d.* for a chaine for fastenynge the sayde booke."

At S. Michael's Church, Bishop Stortford, we have:

"A.D. 1542. For a newe Bybill and ye bryngyng home of it, vj*s.* and j*d.*"

Without dedication.

There is no dedication in this Bible; perhaps the representation on the title page, of the Almighty saying of Henry VIII., in Latin, "I have found a man after my own heart, which shall fulfil all my will," was considered flattery gross enough to gain the King's favour, without making other untruthful statements.

On the colophon is,

Colophon.

"The ende of the new Testamēt, and of the

whole Byble. Fynisshed in Apryll, Anno M.CCCCC. XXXIX.

"A dño factu est istud."

Influenced by his vicegerent, Henry, on the 14th of November 1539, issued a proclamation, of which the following is the substance, "Being desirous to have our people attaining the knowledge of God's word, whereby they will the better honour Him, and keep his commandments, and do their duty better to vs, being their Prince and Sovereign Lord, and considering that this our zeal and desire cannot by any means take so good effect as by the granting to them the free and liberal use of the Bible in our own maternal English tongue; so lest the diversity of translations bring forth manifold inconveniences, we have appointed our well beloved counsellor, the Lord Cromwell, Keeper of our Privy Seal, to take special care that no manner of person within this our realm attempt to print any Bible in the English tongue for five years next ensuing, but such as be deputed, assigned, and admitted, by the said Lord Cromwell." *Per ipsum Regem.*

Cromwell empowered to grant licences for printing Bibles.

No one who had once seen the first edition of the Great Bible could mistake any of the subsequent issues for it, as it varies from them in particulars which at once strike the eye; for instance, the numerous woodcuts are supported by a border or column on each side, while in all other editions the woodcuts are without borders.

Difference between the first and subsequent editions.

The pointing hands in the margins and text,

showing the passages Coverdale considered "dark," and wished to annotate, have ruffles about the wrist, while the hands in other editions have a cuff only.

The stars in the text of the 1539 edition are double trine, or six-pointed, while the stars in other editions are some of them five-pointed.

Even an imperfect copy can be recognised by observing the above three particulars.

If the copy has its title pages complete, this edition will be found to differ from others, in having the Apocrypha title (there called Hagiographa) surrounded by a border like the first title page, and the New Testament title having a border of six woodcuts, which no other edition has.

Cranmer nothing to do with the issue of the Great Bible.

It has been proved most conclusively that Archbishop Cranmer had no share directly or indirectly in the translation, revision, printing, or publication of the Great Bible issued in 1539; therefore the common practice of designating it "Cranmer's Bible" is erroneous and unfair. It was the enterprise of Cromwell; to whom the illuminated copy on vellum, with his coat of arms in colours, now in the library of S. John's College, Cambridge, was presented.

Second edition, with Cranmer's prologue

The second edition of the Great Bible is dated April 1540.

Cranmer wrote a long preface for it, which was re-published not only in almost every subsequent edition of the Great Bible, but also of the version which afterwards took its place, namely, the Bishops' Bible, down to the year

1606; and this was the cause of Cromwell's undertaking becoming popularly known as Cranmer's Bible, and Cranmer having been credited with being its translator.

Cranmer's prologue.

Cranmer begins, "Concernyng two sundry sortes of people it seemeth much necessarie that some thyng be sayde in the entrie of thys booke by way of a Preface or Prologue, whereby hereafter it may be both the better accepted of them whiche hytherto coulde not wel beare it, and also the better vsed of them whiche heretofore haue misused it. For truely some there are that be to slowe, and neede the spurre, some others seeme to quicke, and neede more of the brydle.

"In the former sorte be all they that refuse to read the scripture in the vulgar tongue, much worse they that let also or discourage other from the readyng or hearyng thereof.

"In the latter sorte be they which by their inordinate reading, vndiscrete speaking, contentious disputing, or otherwyse by their licentious living, slaunder and hynder the worde of God most of all other, wherof they woulde seeme to be the greatest furtherers."

Then he quotes, "of a people whiche neuer saw the sunne, by reason that they be situated farre towarde the North pole and be enclosed and overshaddowed with hygh mountaynes: it is credible and lyke yenough, that yf by the power and wyll of God, the mountaynes shoulde syncke downe, and giue place, that the lyght of the sunne myght haue entraunce to them, at the first some of them woulde be offended therewith."

Triacle.

He then states that "out of the most venemous wormes is made triacle, the most soueraingе medicine for the preseruation of mans health in tyme of daunger."

The title of the second edition reads,

"¶ The Byble in | Englyshe, that is to saye the con | tēt of al the holy scrypture, both | of ye olde, and newe testamēt, with | a prologe therinto, made by | the reuerende father in | God, Thomas | archbysshop | of Cantor | bury. | ¶ This is the Byble apoynted | to the vse of the churches.

"¶ Prynted by Edward whytchurche | Cum priuilegio ad imprimendum solum. | M.D. xl."

Collation of second edition.

Title, reverse blank; "The Kalender;" "Almanacke," 4 pages. "An exhortacyon to the studye of the holy Scripture," 1 page. "The summe and content," 2 pages. "A prologue expressynge what is meant by certayn sygnes," 1 page.

"¶ Descripcyon and successe of the kynges," 2 pages. Cranmer's prologue, 6 pages.

"¶ The names of all the bookes of the Byble," 1 page.

In all ten preliminary leaves. One half the edition had the name of "Rychard Grafton" on the title as printer, and the rest "Edward whytchurche." Text, "Genesis to Deuteronomium," folio i to lxxxiiij.

Title to "¶ The seconde parte of the Byble contaynyng these bookes" between 16 woodcuts. "Josua to Hiob," folio ij to cxxiij.

Title to "¶ The thirde parte of the Byble" between 10 different cuts. "Psalmes to Malachy," folio ij to cxxii.

Title to "¶ The Volume of the bokes called Hagiographa" between 16 cuts; on the reverse, "To the Reader." Esdras to II. Mac., fol. ii to lxxx.

Title to "¶ The newe Te | stamet in englyshe translated | after the Greke," exactly like the first title page. "S. Mathew to Reuelacion," folio ii to ciiii, falsely numbered for ciii. "¶ A Table to fynde | the Epistles and Gospels vsually red in the church." On the bottom of the last page is the colophon, "The ende of the newe Testament: and of the whole Byble, Fynisshed in Apryll, | Anno. M.CCCCC. xl. A dño factu est istud."

This edition may be known by large woodcut initials before the books of Ezra, Nehemiah, Esther, Job, S. Matthew, and Romans.

Also by the printer's name being spelled "Whytchurche." This spelling is likewise adopted in the edition of 1553.

Grafton, the printer, describes himself as being a grocer. He became poor towards the latter part of his life, and applied for the situation of Government informer. Grafton.

Whitchurch married the widow of Archbishop Cranmer, and it is to be hoped he treated her with more respect than her first husband did; for, in the words of an eminent writer, "Cranmer's treatment of his second wife shows to what contemptible shifts he could be driven in order to escape the consequences of his own acts." Whytchurche. Cranmer's ill treatment of his wife.

Title of third edition.

The third edition of this version was published in July 1540.

It has a similar title to the previous ones, and bears for the second time the words, "This is the Byble apoynted to the vse of the churches."

The preliminary matter differs from the first and second editions.

It consists of Kalendar, Almanac, 4 pages; Prologue, 6 pages; Names of books, 1 page; all the rest being omitted.

For the first time a translation is given of the Latin motto at the end of the colophon, "This is the Lordes doynge."

S. Mark, in the woodcut at the beginning of the New Testament, is seated behind a table, his hat hanging in the front.

Fourth edition.

The fourth edition is dated November 1540, and bears a remarkable likeness to the edition of November 1541. Both have 65 lines to a full page, while all the other editions have 3 lines less.

They are printed on thinner paper, and were afterwards re-issued with certain sheets reprinted.

Cromwell's arms obliterated.

For the first time the title page is seen with Cromwell's coat of arms obliterated, and the pointing hands are removed from the margins, and also the flourished capitals from the text, excepting one at the beginning of the Old Testament. The title of this edition is:

Title of the November edition.

"¶ The Byble | in Englyshe of the largest and grea | test volume, auctorysed and apoynted |

by the commaundemente of oure moost | redoubted Prynce, and soueraygne Lorde | Kynge Henrye the viii., supreme heade | of this his churche and Realme of | Englande: to be frequented and | vsed in every churche within this his sayd realme, accordynge to the | tenour of his former In iunctions geven in that behalfe.

¶ Oversene and perused at the cō maundemēt of the kynges hyghnes, by the ryghte reuerende fathers in God Cuthbert bysshop of Duresme, and Ni colas bisshop of Rochester." |

Cuthbert Tunstall is described by Sir Thomas More as so "excelling in learning, wit and virtue, that the whole world hath not at this day any more learned, wiser, or better." Bishop Tunstall.

He was consecrated Bishop of London in 1522, and translated to Durham, March 25, 1530.

Nicholas Heath also was a distinguished scholar. The reason the King selected these two Bishops to revise this and the November 1541 edition was to inspire the people of England with confidence in the accuracy of the translation.

Bishop Tunstall has been branded with the accusation of having been one of the greatest opponents of the translation of the Bible, because he tried to prevent the circulation of copies not faithfully representing the original Scriptures, and loaded with notes and annotations, calculated to bring the Church of England and her ministers into contempt.

The colophon of the fifth edition states that it was "Fynysshed in Maye, Anno. M.ccccc. xli."

Fifth edition.

It may be distinguished from all other editions, even if all the title pages and the imprint are wanting, by the woodcut prefixed to S. Matthew's Gospel, in which S. Mark is represented sitting at a writing desk and looking to the left, and having his hat upon his head.

Sixth edition.

The sixth edition corresponds so closely with the fourth that it will not be necessary to say more about it than that it is dated November 1541.

Seventh edition.

The seventh and last of this noble series of Bibles was issued in December 1541.

Bp. Bonner sets up Bibles in S. Paul's for public use.

Bishop Bonner, who, when filling the post of Ambassador at Paris, rendered such important service to Coverdale in conveying portions of the 1539 Bible from France to England, and afterwards assisted in importing from Paris the presses, type, and workmen, by which the Great Bible was so beautifully executed, had been translated to the See of London; he there, in the most practical and unmistakable manner, proved his anxiety that the people should read the Scriptures for themselves, by setting up at his own expense six of these stately folios in certain convenient places in S. Paul's Church, London, for the good of the public. Unfortunately, owing to disregard of the Royal injunction, that the Bible should be read with charity, so much contention, ill-feeling, disturbance, and irreverence was the result of the Bishop's encouragement of biblical research, that he was obliged to threaten the removal of the books, "which," said he, "I should be right loth to do, considering I have been always, and still am, right glad that the Scripture, the Word of God, should be well known, and also set forth accordingly."

Bonner's declaration.

The directions issued by Bonner were,

Bonner's direction.

"The Bible is to be read with all deuocion humilitie, and quyetnesse, the reader leuing behynde hym vayne glorye hypocrisie, and all other carnall and corrupte affection, bring with hym discretion, honeste intente, charytie reuerence, and quyet behauiour, he is not to expound, nor to reade with a lowde voyce, and without disputacion."

On the 11th May 1542, he issued a formal injunction that every clergyman should read a chapter of the Bible a day, with the gloss of some expositor, approved and allowed by the Church of England.

Little desire in England for a vernacular Bible.

The great anxiety on the part of the majority of the people of England to possess a vernacular Bible existed only in the imaginations of Foxe and other party writers; for in spite of all the arbitrary proceedings taken to force the Bible into circulation, we find the printers often complaining of the large stocks remaining on their hands, and begging that persons might be compelled to purchase, and that no fresh editions might be issued. The demands made by Yorkshiremen proved the feeling existing in the North of England: and in less than eighteen months from the accession of Edward VI. the male population of Devonshire and Cornwall were in arms by thousands, and there were popular risings in most parts of England, showing that the hearts of Englishmen revolted from the teaching of Bucer, Peter Martyr, and other foreigners. The Cornishmen objected to have the new translation of the Bible forced upon them, as the Latin Bible was far more intelligible to them than the English.

Convocation desired a revision.

Early in 1542 Convocation made an effort to obtain another revision of the Bible. The Lower House sent to the Bishops a list of those passages that required improved translation. Two companies were formed, the Archbishop of York, the Bishop of Ely, and others, being on the Old Testament, and Bishops Gardyner, Tunstall, Thirlby, and others, being on the New Testament company; but Cranmer got the work taken out of the hands of Convocation, and eventually it came to nothing.

The cause of this unfortunate failure was the objection raised to the introduction of Latin words into a translation of the Bible, many thinking with Sir John Cheke that the English language was already sufficiently copious.

Bishop Gardyner.

Bishop Gardyner was not opposed to the introduction of a properly translated English Bible. A letter of his is still in existence, dated Waltham, June 1, 1535, in which he says, "I have finished the translation of S. Luke and S. John, wherin I bestowed great labour, though I had as great cause as any man to desire rest and quiet for the health of my body."

No edition printed between 1541 and 1549.

No edition of the Great Bible appeared after the end of the year 1541, until 1549. Most likely

Grafton and Whitchurch's seven editions and two reprints, and Berthelet's edition of 1540, were far in excess of the demand.

The King's printer's edition of 1540.

The last-mentioned Bible is interesting from its having its first and New Testament title printed from the very blocks used in printing Coverdale's Bible of 1535.

No one could mistake the woodcuts for a moment. On the top left-hand corner are Adam and Eve; next below, Christ giving the keys to His Apostles; next, The day of Pentecost; on the opposite side, Christ's triumph, Moses receiving the law, The reading of the law; below, David on one side, and S. Peter on the other, and in the middle, Henry VIII. seated on the throne, with the Bishops and Nobles kneeling at his feet.

The title is,

"The Byble | in Englyshe, that is to saye, | the content of all the holye | scrypture, bothe of the olde, | and newe Testament, truly | translated after the veryte | of the Hebrue and Greke | textes, by the diligent stu | dye of dyuers excellent | lerned men, experte | in the foresayde tongues. |

"¶ Prynted at London by Thomas | Petyt and Roberte Redman for | Thomas Berthelet: Prynter vnto the Kinges grace. |

"¶ Cum Priuilegio ad impri | mendum solum. | 1540."

On the reverse, "An Almanac for xxx yeares," beginning 1540.

"The Kalender," 2 leaves.

"The names of all the bokes" and "A Prologue," 1 leaf.

The text, Genesis to Job, i. to ccxiiij.

Apocrypha ends on folio ccxxvij.

The New Testament, said to be "after the last recognicion of Erasmus." The colophon is, "The ende of the newe Testament, and of the whole Byble. Finished in Apryll. Anno. M.CCCCC. XL."

Reprint of the 1539, by authority, in 1540.

This is a reprint of the 1539 Great Bible, and the name of the King's Printer, on the title, shows the issue of this Bible must have had Royal sanction.

New Testament of 1547, 8vo.

In the year 1547 an edition of the New Testament, by itself, was printed, in small octavo size, by Whitchurche.

"The New Testament in Englyshe, according to the translation of the Great Byble," in red and black; reverse, "An Almanache for xxv yeres" (from 1546 to 1560); "Kalendar," 6 pages; "Tables for the foure Euangelists and the Actes," 22 pages; "Rehersall of all the Contents &c.," 2 pages; making 16 leaves of preliminary. S. Matthew begins on A i., and Revelation ends on recto of R iv.; on reverse is, "Table to fynde the Epistles &c."; this ends on recto of R vij.

The last page has the imprint, "Imprinted at Londō | in Flete strete at the sy | gne of the Sune ouer a | gainst the Cōduit, by Ed | warde whytchurche | the first day of De | cember. | M.D. XL vij. cum priuilegio ad impri | mendum solum."

The small folio edition of the Great Bible, printed by "Edwarde Whitchurche" in 1549, presents many peculiarities.

Great Bible of 1549, folio.

The title page border is the well known one used by E. W. in various books, *e.g.*, for the translation of the paraphrase of Erasmus on S. John by "the Princesse Marie;" also for "a treatise by the excellent Clerke Bocatius." This Bible was intended to be a companion to the Reformation Prayer Book issued the same year, as it supplied the Psalms, which were not printed in that volume, as well as enabled the First and Second Lessons, and the Epistles and Gospels, according to the new Calendar, to be read as directed by the table, which for the first time is headed, "The Table to finde the Epistles and Gospels, vsually read in the Churche accordyng vnto the booke of Common prayer," &c.

In this Bible, as well as in the folio editions of 1553 and 1562, this table is not inserted in its usual position at the end of Revelation, but immediately follows the New Testament title page, in fact begins on verso of that page.

The Table follows New Testament title.

It provides for two celebrations on Easter day and Christmas day, and for one on S. Mary Magdalene's day.

This title is shorter than former ones, as they followed the Sarum use, and appointed Epistles and Gospels for Wednesdays and Fridays in Lent and Advent, and also for the Nativity of our Lady, and her Assumption, and for S. George's, All Souls', and other days.

The table in harmony with the Prayer Book.

So closely does the table agree with the Prayer Book, that although the title "Saint" is invariably prefixed to all other names, it is omitted before "Symon and Jude" in both books.

This book printed at two different presses.

A remarkable peculiarity of this edition is that a portion of it appears to have been printed abroad, or from foreign type.

There are five foliations: the first, from Genesis to Deuteronomy; the second, from Joshua to Job; the third, from the Psalms to Malachi; the fourth, the Apocrypha; and the fifth, the New Testament.

The difference in the appearance of the pages is very striking.

The first part, from Genesis to folio 88 inclusive, where sheet L ends, and the Apocrypha, being of one kind, and the rest of the volume being of another.

All the text is printed in ordinary black letter; but the first part has the running titles at the top of the pages, as well as the headings of the contents of the chapters, printed in foreign type, very much resembling that used at Zürich.

Peculiar initial letters.

The initial letters of the chapters with the Zürich type headings are printed with a strange variety of flourished capitals.

There are seven different and most fantastic forms of the letter A, three of the letter T, and two of M and S.

The fifth chapter of I. Chronicles begins with a T in a vignette, and the rest of the capitals not in vignettes are printed in ordinary English type.

The words GOD and LORD are printed in large peculiar Roman capital letters.

In the New Testament the use of larger type for the holy name is rare, and chiefly occurs in S. Luke's Gospel. All the initial letters are in vignettes.

The initials of the books of Leviticus, Joshua, Judges, Kings, and I. Chronicles contain the letters I. R. in white on a black ground.

Printed before the first book of Edward VI. was completed.

The date on the title of this book is Dec. 29, 1540. It was printed before the changes in the Book of Common Prayer had been finally settled: for the passages marked in the text with crosses and half-crosses for the beginnings and endings of the Gospels are more than double the number required by the new table, which was evidently printed after the Bible was finished.

S. Matthew's Gospel begins on fol. 1; this shows the Table of Epistles and Gospels was a subsequent insertion, otherwise the first chapter would have been on folio 3.

In this Bible the fourth chapter of Malachi is separated from the third, whereas in the Great Bible of 1539, and in the edition of April 1540, they form one chapter only.

Worcester Bible.

In the following year the same printer issued a 4to edition of the Great Bible, and Jhon Oswen, of Worcester, printed a quarto New Testament of the Great Bible version, "with notes and expositions of the darke places therein."

The colophon occupies the whole of the last page, "Newly Imprinted | at Worceter by Jhon Oswen, Prynter ap | poynted by the Kynges Maiestie, & his | highnes Honorable Counsaill for | the Principalitye of Wales, | and Marches of the same. |

"¶ They be also to sell at | Shrewesbury. | Cum Gratia et Priuilegio ad imprimendum solum."

The type is a clear black letter. There are 40 lines to a full page. The type (without margins) measures 6 by 3¾ inches. The notes conclude as follows:

Conclusion of the notes in Oswen's Bible.

"☞ Thus haste thou, gentle reader, suche thynges as are darke and hyd from the naturall vnderstandynge briefelye touched, that thou mayste wyth lesse laboure come to the knowledge and vnderstandynge of the whole. Howe be it the study to be bryefe woulde not suffer me to be so playne as I wyshe that I mighte be, wherefore I thynke it necessary that thou playe not the slouggarde folowyng the example of the unprofytable drone be, who liueth onely by honye that the diligent bees gather. But contrarye wyse, be thou a good bee, search for the swete honye of the moost holesome floures of Gods holye worde. And in all this geue ouer thy selfe to the teachynge of Gods holy Spirite, who enstructeth none but the humble spirited & suche as seke reformation of theyr own mysse lyuinge and all suche he enstructeth to the ful makynge theyr hertes a mete temple for hym to dwell in, Yet in the meane tyme, refuse not the gyftes of God, whyche are offered vnto the by the laboures of other men whom God hath endued with the moost excellente gyfte of interpretyng, but vse them as meanes. And yet geue no credence lyghtelye vnto euery enterpretation, but fyrste proue the spirites. And if they confesse not Christe to be comen into the fleshe, that is, that there is no maner saluation besyde hym, beleue them not, for they are the spirite of Antichriste.

"☙ Here endeth the notes of
the newe Testament."

In 1552 the Great Bible was reprinted by Hyll in 4to. The title within an architectural border is, "☙ The Byble in Englishe, that is to saye, The content of al the Holy Scripture, both of the olde, and newe Testament, Accordynge to the translation that is appointed to be reade in the Churches. N. H. Printed at London by Nycholas Hyll. Cum priuilegio ad imprimendum solum." [1552.], in red and black letters. On reverse, "An Almanack for xxvj yeares" (from 1552 to 1577). Hyll's 4to. of 1552.

The running titles, notes, and chapter headings are in black letter. Woodcut initials. A full page has 61 lines.

The last edition of the Great Bible printed by R. Grafton was the small quarto of 1553. Grafton's last quarto of 1553.

This Bible differs from all others in having the name of the month placed at the top of each page containing the chapters appointed by the Church to be read for lessons, so that the Bible is divided into twelve unequal parts.

Although bearing the imprint of R. Grafton, this book was printed abroad, as the type is evidently foreign. The words on the title are, "The Bible in Englishe according to the translation of the Great Byble. 1553"; verso blank. My copy has only one leaf of preliminary, "The names of al the bookes of the Byble, and the content of the chaptres of euery boke with the numbre of the leafe." Then follows the text, without headings of chapters, notes, or woodcuts. Another singular feature in this Bible is that at the end of the "newe Testamente in Englishe" is a "Table to fynd the Epistles and Gospels after Salysbury vse." This looks as if Grafton was aware in 1553, that the second Book of Common Prayer of Edward VI. would not long be used in the Church of England.

Queen Mary's primer.

When Queen Mary's first Prayer Book was issued, care was taken not to offend any reasonable Churchman.

Great prejudice existed against the word "Church," as shown by its omission from all early editions of the New Testament, therefore in the translation of the "Te Deum" (called in Mary's book "the Songe of Austin and Ambrose"), "Te per orbem terrarum: sancta confitetur ecclesia" reads, "The holy cōgregacyō of faithfull throughe all the worlde, magnyfye the."

Whytchurche's last folio of 1553.

The last folio edition of the Great Bible printed by Edward Whytchurche was issued in the year 1553.

The title is entirely in black; the border consists of eleven woodcuts.

It is difficult to make out what they are intended to represent, as the blocks from which they are printed appear almost worn out. Those at the top and bottom of the page are scenes from Old Testament history, as in one of them a man with horns is a prominent figure, and in early prints Moses is always so depicted. The six smaller engravings at the sides had probably been used to illustrate books of devotion, as they portray events in the life of Our Lady.

A considerable portion of this edition is a "remainder" of the 1549 issue.

There are no woodcuts, except in title page and initial letters.

The passage in S. John, known as the "three heavenly witnesses," and also Latin titles of the Psalms, are printed in Roman type. The Epistles and Gospels in this book are not said to be after the "Use of Salisbury," but "accordinge to the boke of Common-prayer."

Cawoode's series of 4to. editions.

John Cawoode printed six editions of the Great Bible, all in quarto. That of 1561 is printed in Gothic type, and has some singular errors. The numbering is regular and continuous to cciiii.; then comes the second title, "The thirde parte of the Byble contaynynge these bokes (from the Psalter to Malachy):" the leaves follow in regular numerical order to 197; then come folios 200, 199, 202, 204, 203, 202, 207, 201, 201, 203, 211, 223. The text is correct, excepting the heading of the 25th, 26th, and 27th chapters of Job is "the boke of Hester." At the Psalter the signature and paging begin afresh, and continue through the books called Hagiographa, which has a separate title and address to the reader. At the end of the Second Book of Maccabees is a woodcut of the Baptism in Jordan, and another of the Good Samaritan. The title page to the New Testament is without the printer's monogram, but it appears on the rest of the titles. The last two leaves of this Bible are not numbered; they contain "A table to fynde the Epystles and Ghospelles usuallye reade in the Churche."

Cawoode's last edition came out in 1569.

The Epistles and Gospels in early Prayer Books do not exactly correspond with any edition of the Bible.

Until the year 1662, when our present Book of Common Prayer came out, the Epistles and Gospels were taken mainly from the Great Bible, but they do not follow with exactness any particular edition of it; like the sentences from Scripture interwoven into various parts of the Church service, they are to some extent independent translations.

Very many instances might be given of verbal differences between the Great Bible and the early Prayer Books.

That glorious version of the Psalms used in the services of the Church, which is endeared to the hearts of the people of England, not only from old association, but from its intrinsic sweetness and beauty, is taken from the November 1540 edition of the Great Bible.

The Prayer Book version of the Decalogue differs from all Bibles.

It is worthy of notice that the ten commandments in the Prayer Book differ in wording from the decalogue in every Bible that has ever been printed.

[illegible] renderings of [illegible] passages.

In comparing the different versions of the Bible no one can fail to be struck with the fact of there being a great deal of force and meaning in some of the old renderings that have been discarded. For instance, in the account of the finding in the Temple, given by S. Luke, the Great Bible reads, "And it fortuned that after thre daies they founde hym in the tempell siteinge in the myddes of ye doctoures hearinge them and posynge them." This gives an idea not conveyed by "asking them questions," the rendering in our present Bible. Matthew's Bible adds to the above, "And all that hearde hym meruaylled at his wit and aunswers."

In S. Luke, ivth chapter, and 5th verse, the Authorized Version has, "And the Devil taking Him up into an high mountain shewed Him all the kingdoms of the world in a moment of time." The Great Bible says, "in the twynklelynge of an eye," thereby intensifying the thought of the rapidity with which the panorama passed before the eyes of our Blessed Lord.

In I. S. Timothy, ivth chapter, and 14th verse, we now have, "Neglect not the gift that is in thee, which was given thee by prophecy, with the laying on of the hands of the presbytery." Matthew's Bible has, "with the laying on of the hands of an Elder." The Great Bible reads, "With the layinge on of handes by the autoritie of priesthode."

In the Great Bible of 1553 and of 1569 the passage in the xixth chapter of Job, so often quoted in support of one of the articles of the

Apostles' Creed, viz., the Resurrection of the Body, is thus rendered, "For I am sure that my redemer liveth, and y^{t} I shal ryse oute of the earth in the latter day, that I shal be clothed again with this skynne and se God in my flesh, yea, I my selfe shal beholde hym, not with other, but wyth these same eyes." The Prayer Book of 1552, the second of Edward VI., gives it, "I know that my redemer liveth, and y^{t} I shal rise out of the earth, in the laste daye, and shal be covered agayne with my skynne, and shal se God in my fleshe, yea, I myselfe shal behold hym not with other, but with these same eyes." The Bishops' Bible reads, "For I am sure that my redeemer liveth, and he shal rayse up at ye latter day, them that lye in the dust, and though after my skin (wormes) destroy this body, yet shal I se God in my fleshe, whom I mee selfe shal se, and mine eyes shal behold and none other for me."

In the Primers, or Prayer Books of the Church of England which immediately preceded Edward VI's book of 1549, this passage reads,

Henry VIII's primer, 1545.

"I knowe that my redemer liueth and that I, the last day shal rise from the yearth, and shal be cladde agayne with myne owne skinne, and in myne own fleshe I shall se God, and myne eyes shall loke vpon, and none other: this hope is layed vp in my bosome."

The rendering in Queen Mary's Prayer Book of 1555 is,

Queen Mary's Prayer Book.

"Who shall warrante me that my dedes shal be wrytten

"Or who can promyse me other that they shall
"Be regysteryd so they shall nat be forgetten
"In yron lede/ or in the stony wall
"But one thing I know that fyrst is of all
"That my redemer shall euer lyue/ this I knowe for trewe
"And in the laste daye that I shall ryse anewe
"And with this skyne agayne tham (*sic*) I shal be clad
"And in my flesshe I shall playnly se
"My sauyour and my god/ whyche hathe me wrought and made
"And as I am now so shall I then be
"I shall nat beholde hym by no depute
"But these same eyes shall se hym manyfeste
"This comforte sure remayneth in my breste."

Harrison's folio of 1562.

In 1562 a folio came out of "The Bible in Englishe, according to the translation that is appointed to be read in Churches.

"Imprinted at London, in White Crosse strete, by Richarde Harrison."

The date on the colophon is, "the yeare of oure Lorde, a thousande fyue hundred thre score and two."

One remarkable feature of this edition is that the Psalter is divided into verses.

The last folio edition of the Great Bible.

The last folio edition of the Great Bible is dated 1566.

It does not resemble any previous issue: the title is in outline; the text is printed with larger and more heavily leaded type.

The title reads, "The Bible. In Englyshe of the largest and greatest volume, that is to saye the contentes of all the holye Scripture, booth of the oulde and newe Testament.

"According to the translation apoynted by the Queene's Maiesties Iniunctions to be read in all churches within her Maiesties Realme.

Collation of the Carmardin folio.

"At Rouen, at the coste and charges of Richard Carmarden. Cum privilegio. 1566." Reverse blank.

Twenty-one leaves of preliminary.

The New Testament title is like the first title, but printed in black ink.

The Latin titles of the Psalms are in Roman capital letters.

The initial letters of the chapters are woodcuts.

There are 58 lines to a full page.

Notes for the months in Calendar of the Rouen Bible.

The Calendar of the last edition of Cranmer's Bible has notes peculiar to it. The note in the middle of January is,

"¶ The xv. daye of January, the daye is encreased an whole houre, and so the sunne aryseth three quarters after seuen, and goeth downe a quarter after foure: and so the daye is nyne howres and a halfe long."

"¶ The xvij. day of Februarye, the sunne aryseth thre quarters after vj. and goeth downe a quarter after fiue, and so the daye is x howres & a halfe long, frõ sunne to sunne."

There are three notes in March:

"¶ The iiij. daye of Marche, the sunne aryseth a quarter after vj. and goeth downe three quarters after fiue, so the day is xj howres and a halfe long, from sunne to sunne."

"¶ The xj. daye of Marche, the sunne ryseth

at vj. and goeth downe at vj. and so the daye is xij howres long, from sunne to sunne."

"❡ The xix. daye of Marche, the sunne aryseth iij. quarters after fiue, and goeth downe a quarter after vj. and so the daye is xij howres and a halfe long."

"❡ The iij. daye Aprÿll, the sunne aryseth a quarter after fiue, and goeth downe thre quarters sixe: and so the daye is xiij. howres and a halfe long."

"❡ The xix. daye of Aprÿll, the sunne aryseth thre quarters after foure and goeth downe a quarter after sixe, and so the daye is xiiij. houres and a halfe long."

"❡ The vij. daye of Maye, the sunne aryseth a quarter after foure, and goeth down thre quarters after seuen: and so the daye is fiftene houres and a halfe long."

"❡ The xij. daye of June, the sunne aryseth iij. quarters after thre, and goeth downe a quarter after viij. and so the daye xvj. houres, and a halfe long."

"❡ The viii. daye Julye the sonne aryseth at foure, and goeth down at eighte: and so the daye is xvj houres long."

"❡ The xix daye of Julye, the sonne aryseth a quarter after foure, and goeth downe three quarters after seuen, and so the day is fiftene houres and a halfe long."

"❡ The vj. of Auguste, the sonne aryseth thre quarters after foure, and goeth downe a quarter after seuen, and so the day is xiiij. houres and a halfe long."

"¶ The xxj. daye of Auguste, the sonne aryseth a quarter after fiue, and goeth downe three quarters after vj. and so the day is fourtene houres and a halfe long."

"¶ The vj. daye of September, the sonne aryseth three quarters after fiue, and goeth downe a quarter after vj. and so the daye is xii. houres and a halfe long."

"¶ The xiiij. daye of September the sonne aryseth at vj. and goeth downe at vj. and so the daye and nyght be lyke long."

"¶ The xxj. daye of September, the sonne aryseth a quarter after vj. and goeth downe three quarters after fyue: and so the daye is x. houres and a halfe long."

"¶ The vj. daye of October the sonne aryseth three quarters after vj. and goeth downe a quarter after v. and so the daye is x. houres and a halfe long."

"¶ The xxij. daye of October the sonne ariseth three quarters after seuen, and goeth downe three quarters after foure: and so the day is ix. houres and a half long."

"¶ The eyght daye of Nouember, the sonne aryseth three quarters after seuen, and goeth downe a quarter after foure: and so the daye is eyghte houres and a halfe long, from Sonne vnto Sonne."

"¶ The xij. daye of Decembre, which is the shortest daye in the yeare, the sonne aryseth a quarter of an houre after viij. and goeth downe iij quarters after three, and so the daye is vij houres long and a halfe from sunne to sunne."

The last edition but one of the Great Bible version is a quarto bearing the imprint of Richard Jugge and John Cawoode, dated 1568.

No edition is known of later date than Cawoode's quarto of 1569.

As a specimen of the translation of the Great Bible I append a few of the first and last verses of the *Benedicite omnia opera* from the Hagiographa, said or sung in churches during Lent and other seasons when the *Te Deum* is not used.

Benedicite in edition of 1566.

It is called in the Great Bible "The songe of the thre chyldren whiche were put into the hote brennynge ouen. The commen translacion readeth thys songe in the thyrde chapter of Danyel."

No doubt by "the common translation" the Vulgate is referred to, as in it the "Benedicite" forms part of the 3rd chapter of Daniel.

"O all ye worckes of the Lorde, speake good of the Lorde: prayse hym and set hym upe for euer.

"O ye Aungeles of the Lorde, speake good of the Lorde: prayse hym, and set hym upe for euer.

"O ye heauens speake good of the Lorde prayse hym and set hym vp for euer.

"O all ye waters y^t be aboue the fyrmament speake good of the Lorde: prayse hym, and set hym up for euer.

o o o o o

"O ye Prestes of ye Lorde, speake good of the Lorde: prayse hym, and sete hym up for euer.

"O ye servauntes of the Lorde speake good of the Lorde: prayse hym, and set hym vp for ever.

"O ye spretes and soules of the ryghteous, speake good of the Lorde, prayse hym, and set Hym up for euer.

"O ye holy and humble men of hert, speake ye good of the Lorde: prayse ye hym, and set hym upp for euer.

"O Ananias, Asarias, and Myseal, speake ye good of the Lorde: prayse ye hym, and set Hym upe for euer.

"Whiche hath delyured vs from the hel, kepte vs from the hande of death, ridde vs from the myddest of the burynge flamme, an saued vs euen in the myddest of the fyre.

"O giue thanckes therfore vnto the Lorde: for he is kynde herted, and hys mercye eduereth for euer.

"O al deuoute men, speake ye good of the Lorde: euen the God of al goddes: O prayse hym and giue hym thanckes for his mercye endureth worlde wythouteende.

"The ende of ye songe of the thre chyldren."

The Douai Bible of 1610 thus renders the chorus,

"Al workes of our Lorde, blesse ye our Lorde, prayse and superexalt him for euer.

o o o o o

"All religious blesse ye our Lorde the God of goddes, prayse and confesse ye to him, because his mercie is vnto al worldes."

Whittingham's New Testament.

ON the 10th of June 1557 there was issued a New Testament from the press of Conrad Badius, of Geneva, the title page of which reads, "The Nevve Testament of ovr Lord Iesus Christ. Conferred diligently with the Greke, and best approued translations *with the argument as wel before the Chapters as for euery boke and Epistle, also diuersities of readings and the most profitable annotations of all harde places, whereunto is added a copious Table.*" Under this is a rude woodcut of Time, with his scythe and hour-glass, drawing a nude female figure out of a well. On the right-hand side of this woodcut are the words, "God by Time restoreth Truth;" and on the left, "and maketh her victorious;" and below, "At Geneva. Printed by Conrad Badius M.D.LVII." Whittingham's Testament, 1557.

On the reverse of the title is a table of "The ordre of the bookes of the Newe testament with the nomber of Chapters."

Next, "The Epistle declaring that Christ is the ende of the Law by Iohn Caluin," 8 leaves; "The Translator to the Reader," 2 leaves; "To the reader mercie and peace through Christ ovr Sauiour," 1 leaf; "The Holy Gospel of Iesus Christe, writ by S. Matthew," signature a.

folio 1. The "Revelation of S Iohn" ends on verso of Sig. H h 7, folio 430. "The table and the supputation of the yeares from Adam to Christe" extends from folio 431 to 455, and thus ends, "The whole sum and number of yeres from the begynnyng of the worlde vnto this presente yere of ovr Lord God 1557, are iust 5531, six monethes and the said odde ten dayes." The colophon is at the foot of the page, "Printed by Conrad Badius M.D.LVII this x of Ivne."

The last leaf has a table of errata, "Fautes committed in the printing." In some copies this table is on verso of colophon. The size of the book is duodecimo. The seam wires go down the leaf. My copy measures $5\frac{1}{4}$ in. by $3\frac{1}{2}$ in., but most copies do not exceed $4\frac{1}{2}$ in. by 3 in., owing to the margins being cut down. It is an excessively rare and very interesting book.

Whittingham, Lay Dean of Durham.

The principal, if not sole, translator of this version was William Whittingham, who was born at Lanchester, near Durham, in 1524, and is said by Lewis to have been made a Fellow of All Souls', and afterwards one of the senior students of Christ Church, Oxford. In May 1550 he had leave to travel for three years; the latter part of the time he resided at Geneva, where his tendency to depart from the teaching of the Church of England developed. He returned home just before Queen Mary came to the throne, but soon after left England again, and we find him settled at Frankfort-on-the-Maine in June 1554. Here, on 15th Nov. 1556,

Whittingham married Catherine Jaquemayne, the sister of John Calvin's wife, and when John Knox left Geneva, in 1559, Whittingham was appointed his successor as "pastor" of the congregation. In 1560 he returned to England, and by the influence of the Earl of Leicester (at that time Queen Elizabeth's favourite) he was made Dean of Durham, although a layman, never having been ordained or admitted to Holy Orders.

Whittingham considered himself a poet, and his doggerel imitation of several Psalms may be found in the old version of Sternhold and Hopkins, and may be recognised by the letters "W. W." appended to them. No second edition of Whittingham's New Testament was ever published, and to this fact, as well as to the circumstance that its convenient size for carriage in the pocket, is due the very few perfect copies of this book now in existence; for of course, a large folio that could only with difficulty be removed from a library was not so likely to be worn out as a 12mo pocket Testament.

Whittingham's version may be considered rather as a revision of Tyndale's than as a new translation.

The Testament that was issued with the 4to Genevan, or "Breeches," Bible, of 1560, has been supposed to be the same as the 12^m of 1557; but a slight examination will show that the two differ on every page. No doubt the translators of the 1560 version were much

1557 issue differs from the Genevan 1560.

indebted to Whittingham and adopted many of his readings.

The fifteenth chapter of S. Luke's Gospel contains a considerable number of renderings, evidently taken from the 1557, still it varies from Whittingham in thirty-eight places.

The most striking innovation made by Whittingham in this version was the division of the chapters into verses, and his use of italics to mark words not in the Greek.

Chapters were first introduced in the year 1248 by Cardinal Hugo de Santa Caro, and in 1528, Pagninus, a Dominican monk, published a Latin Bible at Lyons, in small folio, with the chapters divided into verses; which, however, do not correspond with our present ones, being in most cases three or four times as long.

Coverdale must have been acquainted with this work, as he copied into his Bible of 1535 several notes from it.

Whittingham adopted his verse division from the Testament published by R. Stephens, in 12mo, at Geneva, in 1551. This Testament has three columns: the left, the Vulgate version; the centre, Greek; and the right, Erasmus.

Another respect in which Whittingham's New Testament differed from all that had previously been printed in the English language was the employment of Roman type in the place of black letter or old English. This plan was copied in all the early issues of the Genevan Bible in folio, 4to, and 8vo, and was a cause of their popularity. Still many editions of the

"Breeches" Bible were printed in black letter, even down to the last printed in England by R. Barker in 1615.

No revision was made of the New Testament issued in 1560, except that of L. Tomson in 1576, and this was more the substitution of Beza's notes for those of the Genevan translators, than any very extensive alteration of the text.

The verbal change of the word "child" for "babe" in the 8vo. printed in 1576 by T. Vautroullier for Christopher Barker, which until recently had escaped the notice of all bibliographers, can hardly be classed as a revision.

I will now point out a few of the places in which Whittingham's New Testament of 1557 differs from all other versions.

Readings from Whittingham's Testament of 1557.

S. Matthew, chapter i. verse 19, reads: "Then Joseph her housband beyng a just man, and loth to make her a publike exemple of infamie, was mynded to put her a way secretly."

Tyndale has: "Joseph her husbande beynge a perfect man, and loth to make an ensample of her, was mynded to put her away secretly."

Coverdale (1535) reads: "Joseph her hosband was a perfecte man/ and wold not bringe her to shame/ but was mynded to put her away secretly."

Matthew's Bible (1537) and Taverner's (1539) follow Tyndale.

The Great Bible (1539) and Cranmer's (1540)

read: "Joseph her hosband because he was a righteous man and would not put her to shame, was mynded priuily to departe from her."

The Genevan version (1560) omits "of infamie."

The Bishops' translation (1568) is, "Joseph her husband beying a ryghteous man, and not wyllyng to make her a publique example, was minded priuily to put her awaye."

The Rheims (1582) has, "Joseph for that he was a just man, and would not put her to open shame, was minded secretly to dismisse her."

Whittingham's Testament reads in S. Mark, chapter ii., verse 21: "Also no man soweth a peece of newe and undressed cloth in an olde garment." No other version has the word "undressed:" the nearest to it is the Rheims, "No body soweth a peece of raw cloth to an olde garment."

In S. Luke, chapter ii., verses 7, 12, and 16, both the 1557 and the 1560 have the word "cretche;" all other versions have "manger." This word "cretche" occurs in an old English poem on "le enfaunce ih'u crist." (Bodleian MS. Laud 108):

> "Zwane ih'u crist was i bore
> To saue this worlde that was for loue,
> In one Crachche he was leid
> Bi fore oxe and ass, soth it is said."

The 1557 is the only early English Testament in which the Lord's Prayer concludes with "deliuer vs from the Euyl :" nor has any other the rendering (S. John i. 13). "Which are borne not of bloud, nor of the lust of the fleshe, nor of the lust of man, but of God."

In "The Actes of the Holy Apostles, called the seconde booke of S. Luke, the Euangeliste," chapter i., verse 18, reads, "and he therefore hath now gotten a plat of ground, with the rewarde of iniquitie."

The 1557 thus renders Romans ii., verse 20: "An informer of them which lake discretion, a teacher of vnlearned, which hast the information of knowledge, and of the treweth in the Lawe."

Tyndale's reading is, "Which has the ensample of that which ought to be knowen, and of the treueth in the lawe."

Coverdale's (1550) quarto is, "an enfourmer of the vnwyse: a teacher of the symple which haste the ensample of knowlege and the trueth in the lawe."

Places in which the 1557 differs from all other Testaments.

Matthew, Taverner, and Cranmer follow Tyndale.

The "Breeches" Bible has, "which hast the form of knowledge, and of the trueth in the lawe."

The Rheims, "A teacher of the folish, a maister of infants, hauing the forme of science, and of veritie in the lawe."

I. Cor. ii. 1, 2, in the 1557, reads: "And brethren when I came to you, I came not in gloriousnes of wordes, or of wysdome, shewyng vnto you the testimonie of God. For I dyd not vendicat to my selfe to knowe any thyng among you."

Tyndale has, "Neyther shewed I myselfe that I knewe any thyng among you."

Coverdale: "I came not with high wordes, or high wysdome to show vnto you the preachinge of Christ."

II. Cor. viii. 19: "Chosen by election of the churches."

Galatians v. 1: "Stand faste therfore and not contrarely, wrap yourselves in the yoke of bondage."

Ephesians i. 9: "According to his fre beneuolence."

Philippians ii. 13: "his fre beneuolence."

Col. ii. 2: "In all riches of persuaded vnderstanding."

I. Thes. i. 4: "Because we knowe brethren beloved that ye are elect of God."

II. Thes. i. 5: "fre beneuolence."

I. S. Timothy i. 1: "by the commission of God our Saviour."

Titus i. 5: "That thou shoudest continue to redresse that which resteth."

Philemon 15: "Perchance he therfore departed for a season."

Heb. i. 3: "Sytteth at the right hand of that moste highest maiestie."

Heb. ii. 1: "Lest at any tyme we should not keep them."

S. James i. 20: "For the wrath of man doth execute the righteousnes of God."

I. S. Peter i. 11: "Searchyng when or what time that forwaring Sprite of Christ that was in them should declare the suffrings that shoulde come vnto Christe."

II. S. Peter i. 15: "I will enforce therfore, that ye may be able to haue remembrance of those thyngs after my departing."

I. S. John i. 6: "an yet walke in darkenes, we lye and do not syncerely."

S. Jude 4: "For there are certayne men craftely crepte in which were before euen of olde ordeyned to this condemnation."

Revelation i. 8: "Which is, Which was, and Which is to come, the almyghty I say."

Should the title-page and colophon be lost, Whittingham's Testament may be identified by any of the above passages, which differ from every other version.

It may be noticed that the words Alpha and Omega do not occur in Whittingham's New Testament, the Greek characters being substituted in Revelation i. 8, 11, as well as in the 13th verse of the last chapter. The only other Testament I know in which Greek letters are used for Alpha and Omega is the very rare octavo edition of Laurence Tomson's revision, printed by C. Barker in 1577.

The following is a favourable specimen of Whittingham's poetical talent:

"Nisi Dominus. Psal. Cxxvij. W. W.

"❡ It is not mans witte, power, or labor, but the free goodnesse of God that geueth riches, preserveth townes & cōtreys, grãteth nourishmēt & childrē.

"Sing this as the Lordes prayer.

"Except the Lord the house do make,
And therevnto do let his hand:
What men do build it cannot stand.
Likewise in vaine men vndertake,
Cities and holdes to watch and ward,
Except the Lord be their safegard.

2 Though ye rise early in the morne,
And so at night go late to bed,
Feeding full hardly with browne bread
Yet were your labour lost and worne,
But they whom God doth loue and keepe
Receiue all things with quiet sleepe

3 Therfore marke well when euer you see
That men haue heires to enioy their land
It is the gift of Gods owne hand,
For God him selfe doth multiply,
Of his great liberalitie,
The blessing of posteritie.

4 And when the children come to age,
They grow in strength and actiuenes,
In person and in comelines,
So that a shaft shot with courage
Of one that hath a most strong arme,
Flieth not so swift nor doth like harme.

5 O well is him that hath his quiver
Furnished with such artillerie.
For when in perill he shall be
Such one shall neuer shake nor shiuer,
When that he pleadeth before the iudge.
Against his foes which beare him grudg."

The first edition of Sternhold's Psalms (1548) contained versions of 19 Psalms (1, 2, 3, 4, 5, 20, 25, 27, 29, 32, 33, 41, 49, 73, 78, 103, 120, 122, 138). The first edition of Sternhold and Hopkins' (London, 1549) contained 44 Psalms, 37 by Sternhold and 7 by Hopkins. The next enlarged edition (Geneva, 1556) contained 51 Psalms, 37+7+7, by W. Whittingham. The edition of 1560 contains 65 Psalms, "newly set fourth and allowed according to the order appointed in the Queenes Maiesties Iniunctions:" these are followed by the "Benedictus," "Magnificat," &c. In 1561 the number was increased to 87, with the Song of Simeon, the ten Commandments, &c. In 1562 the first complete English version was issued by Jno. Daye, and again in 1563. The same year, and again in 1565, Daye published "the whole Psalms in foure parts," preceded by the "Veni Creator" and other hymns. This version was adopted by the Church of England, and used until Tate and Brady's version supplanted it.

The Genevan Version.

THIS Bible was translated by Nonconformists who took up their residence at Geneva, soon after the death of Edward VI. William Whittingham acted as editor; his assistants were, Cole, Goodman, Gilby, Sampson, and others. Before the translation was finished Queen Mary died, and most of the party hurried back to England in search of preferment; one or two, however, remained at Geneva until the work was completed.

Translators of the "Breeches" Bible.

Sampson succeeded in obtaining the Deanery of Christ Church, Oxford.

Gilby was made Vicar of Ashby-de-la-Zouch.

Cole became Archdeacon of Essex; he had also the living of High Ongar.

Christopher Goodman was appointed to S. Andrew's.

Christopher Goodman's tractate, 1558.

Just before Goodman returned home he published a tractate intitled, "How superior powers oght to be obey'd of their subiects: and wherein they may lawfully by God's Worde be disobeyed and resisted. Wherin also is declared the cause of all this present misery in England, and the onely way to remedy the same." This was printed by John Crispin (the printer of Whittingham's New Testament), at Geneva, 1558, in small octavo. In it the author says, "If it be treason to defend the Gospel and his countrie from cruel strangers and enemies, then was Wyatt a traytor and rebell, but if this was his duetye, and all others that professed Christe amongst you, then are all such traytours as did deceave him, and such as toke not his parte also: when tyme and occasion by him was justly offered.'

The title of the first edition of the Genevan Bible is, —

"The Bible and Holy Scriptvres. | Conteyned in | the Olde and Newe | Testament. | Translated accor | ding to the Ebrue and Greke, and conferred with the best translations in diuers langages. | with moste profitable annota | tions vpon all the hard places, and other things of great importance as may appeare in the Epistle to the Reader.

Title of the Genevan Bible of 1560.

"Feare not, stand stil, and beholde the saluacion of the Lord, which he wil shewe to you this day. Exod. 14, 13."

Then a woodcut of the Passage of the Red Sea.

"At Geneva | Printed by Rovland Hall | M.D.LX."

Collation of the first Genevan Bible.

On reverse of the title is, "The names and order of all the bo | okes of the olde Testamēt with the nombre of their chapters, and the leafe where thei begyn."

Next, "an Epistle," beginning, "To the Moste Ver | tvovs and Noble Quene Eli | sabet, Quene of England, France & Ireland, &c., Your hum | ble subjects of the English Churche at Geneua wish | grace and peace from God the Father, through | Christ Iesvs our Lord."

Then an address, "To ovr beloued in the Lord."

After these four preliminary leaves comes the text, Genesis to II. Maccabees, 474 folioed leaves. The second title page is, "The | Newe Testament" | &c., with a small woodcut of the Passage through the Red Sea; then, "The description of the holy Lande, conteyning the places mentioned by the foure Euangelists, &c.," and a map. S. Matthew to Revelation, 122 leaves. "A briefe table of the interpretation of the proper names," 7 pages; "A table of the principal things," 17½ pages; "A Perfite Svppvtation of | the yeres and times from Adam vnto | Christ, proued by the Scriptvres, after the collection of diuers Autors."

Collation.

The last leaf contains, "The order of the yeres from Paul's conuersion." Reverse blank.

The book is printed in two columns. A full page has 63 lines.

There is at Numbers xxxiii. a map of the journey of the Israelites.

At Joshua xv. a smaller map of the division of the land of Canaan for the twelve tribes.

At the end of "Ezechiel," a map of the Temple and City restored.

Before "The Acts of the Holy Apostles" a map of the places mentioned therein.

The book is dated April 10, 1560.

The size is a rather larger quarto than the series of the Great Bible issued by J. Cawoode.

First Genevan New Testament, 16mo.

The same year the Genevan Bible came out, a 16mo. edition of the New Testament appeared without printer's name. Most likely it was from the press of Rouland Hall, Geneva.

The notes are shorter, but the text is exactly the same as the first 4to. edition.

The following comparison of three passages will show that the 10mo. is not a reprint of Whittingham's New Testament of 1557, but of the original Genevan version:

1557:	S. Matthew,	chap. i.	v. 19,	"exemple of infamie."
1560:	"	"		"publike example."
1557:	S. Mark,	chap. ii.,	v. 21,	"undressed cloth."
1560:	"	"		"newe cloth."
1557:	Romans,	chap. ii.,	v. 20,	"information of knowledge."
1560:	"	"		"forme of knowledge."

Divided into verses, and printed in Roman letter.

The changes made in the Geneva Bible were the adoption of Roman type instead of the black letter, in which all English Bibles had previously been printed, and the division of the chapters into verses.

These changes were the principal cause of the wonderful popularity of this version, of which about 200 editions are known.

From 1560 to 1616 no year passed without one or more editions issuing from the press, in folio, quarto, or octavo.

In 1599 no less than ten distinct editions were printed, each of which consisted of a large number of copies. The last quarto printed in England is dated 1615, and the last folio 1616. After this time a great many editions were printed at Amsterdam by Joost Broerss and other Dutch printers; the last folio bears the imprint of Thomas Stafford, and the date 1644.

Dutch editions.

It professes to be copied from the Bible printed by Andrew Hart, Edinburgh, in 1610.

The Apocrypha ordered by the Synod of Dort to be omitted.

In the place where the Apocrypha ought to be, there is an address from the Synod of Dort, ordering this portion of Holy Scripture to be omitted, and speaking of it in far less respectful terms than Coverdale did.

150,000 copies were imported from Holland after this version had ceased to be printed in England. On account of the numerous errors in these foreign printed editions, Archbishop Laud prohibited their importation, and the Puritans brought this against him as a crime at the trial which terminated in his martyrdom.

Owing to the vast number of copies in circulation during the three-quarters of a century that this version was the household Bible of England, it is now the most common of all early printed Bibles.

The division into verses, introduced by the Genevan translators, was found to be much more convenient for reference than the old method of placing letters of the alphabet down the sides of the page.

Reason of its common name.

The singular rendering of the 7th verse of the third chapter of Genesis in every edition of the Genevan version, has caused it to be commonly known as the "Breeches" Bible.

This word is peculiar to this version, for in every other English Bible the word "aprons" is employed. No doubt the translators took it from Wycliffe's MS. Bible, which reads, "And whan yei knewen yat ya were naked ya sewiden ye levis of a fige tre and madin brechis."

Voragine's "Golden Legend," printed by William Caxton at Westminster, Nov. 20, 1483, contains a translation of the Pentateuch, and most of the Gospels. In it this verse is thus rendered, Voragine's "Golden Legend."

"And thus theye knewe then that they were naked/ and they toke figge leuis and sewed them to gyder for to couere theyr membres in maner of brechis."

In addition to the word "breeches," every chapter of the Genevan version has some reading by which it may be distinguished from all other Bibles; for instance, the 2nd chapter of S. Luke's Gospel, wherever the word "manger" occurs in other versions, in this "cratch" is substituted. "Cratche" substituted for "manger."

Several duodecimo editions of the Genevan New Testament were published between 1560 and 1575, of which no record exists in any book on the subject. I have two copies of different editions, unfortunately without title pages, but evidently printed soon after the Genevan Bible came out: both unknown at the British Museum.

Strange to say, the annotations, or glosses, in the margin of this version were regarded with favour by many persons of that day, and even as late as 1810 they were added to the text of King James's Bible. Genevan glosses popular

Geneva was so permeated with Calvin's influence, it was almost impossible for the translators of this version to have resided there John Calvin.

without being drawn away from the doctrine and practices of the church of their baptism, consequently we find that almost every chapter has voluminous notes full of Calvinistic doctrine.

Specimens of the German notes.

The note to S. Matthew ii. 12 is, "Promes oght not to be kept when God's honour and the preaching of his trueth is hindered, or els it oght not be broken." This specimen of German ethics was omitted from the 1599 and 1600 editions. The note to Rev. ix. 3 is, "Locusts are false teachers, heretikes, and worldlie suttil prelates, with Monkes, Friars, Cardinals, Patriarkes, Archbishops, Bishops, Doctors, Baschelers, and Masters which forsake Christ to mainteine false doctrine." The note to Romans ix. 15 is, "As the onelie wil and purpose of God is the chief cause of election, and reprobacion: so his fre mercie in Christ is an inferiour cause of saluation, and the hardening of the heart an inferiour cause of damnacion."

Note to II. Chronicles xv. 16.

The note to II. Chronicles xv. 16 is, "Herein he shewed that he lacked zeale, for she oght to have dyed," or, in other words, the mother of King Asa ought to have been murdered. Characteristically enough, the Puritans made allegiance to the monarch depend on the soundness of his or her faith (they being the judges). This feeling culminated in the Puritan persecution of King Charles I., on account of his religion, and his ultimate martyrdom.

Genevan Bible never revised.

Nearly every edition of early printed English Bibles differs from its predecessor, and even the few reprints that appeared professed on the title to be "newly revised and overseen," but nothing of this sort took place with the multitudinous re-issues of the Genevan version.

The edition of 1616 is an accurate reprint of that of 1560, excepting that Tomson's New Testament takes the place of the Genevan. It will not therefore be of any use to trace edition after edition, but will suffice to mention those that from accidental circumstances present some feature of interest.

Second edition, 1562–1, folio.

The second edition of the Genevan version was issued 1562–1, in folio, without printer's name. It is known as the "Whig" Bible, from the beatitude, "Blessed are the peace makers," reading, owing to a typographical error, "Blessed are the place makers."

Third edition, 1568, small 4to.

The third edition was printed at Geneva, by John Crispin.

Like most other early English Bibles, it was found much more easy to print than to sell, there being very little desire on the part of English people, generally, for a vernacular Bible; so the plan resorted to in the case of Coverdale's first Bible of 1535, and also of Coverdale's quarto of 1550, of inserting a new title page, and representing the book to be a fresh edition, was adopted by the publisher of the third edition of the Genevan Bible.

This was a fraud; for the editions of 1568 and of 1569 are, as far as the text is concerned, identical, and were evidently printed from the same setting up of the type; for not only are all errors repeated, but the faults in composition are the same. This could not possibly have been the case had one edition been set up in 1568 and the other the following year. The fact that the date on the New Testament title page is 1568 shows that it is the edition of that year.

I have called this Bible a small quarto, because the wire lines in the water mark go across the page, although to all appearance the size is octavo, the leaves measuring $8\frac{1}{2}$ in. by $5\frac{1}{2}$ in.

The size of a book is no criterion to judge if it is folio, quarto, or octavo; this depends on the size of the paper before it was folded. Whatever the dimension of the book, if the wire-lines go down the page it is folio or octavo; if they go across the page, the size is quarto. This is plain enough if we remember that a folio is a sheet folded once, a quarto four times, and an octavo a sheet folded eight times. I do not now refer to the smaller sizes, such as 12mo, 16mo, and 24mo, &c.

The title-page of the third edition of the "Breeches" Bible reads as follows:

"The Bible | and | Holy Scriptvres con | teyned in the ol | de and newe | Testament. |

"Translated according | to the Ebrue and Greke, and conferred vvith the best | translations in diuers languages. | With moste profitable anno | tations vpon all the hard places, and other things of great im | portance as may appeare in the Epistle to the Reader. | At Geneva, | Printed by John Crispin. | MDLXViij."

On the title page issued in 1569 is added, "There is added in this second edition certeine tables, one for the Explication of the degrees in ma rriage in Leuiticus, with another for the Maccab. and a calender historical, with other things." Title page of re-issue of 1569.

On signature °₀° 2 of preliminary is an address, "To the moste vertvovs and noble Quene Elisabet, Qvene of England, France, and Ireland, &c. Your humble subiects of th English Churche at Geneua, vvish grace and peace from God the Father through Christ Iesus our Lord."

This address begins by comparing the virgin Queen to Zerubbabel, then speaks of "the enemies which labour to stay religion," such as "Papistes," "worldings," and "ambicious prelats," and "The necessitie of gods worde for ye reforming of religion."

"Wherefore great wisdome, not worldelie, but heauenly, is here required, which your grace must earnestly craue of the Lord, as did Salomon, to whom God gaue an vnderstanding heart to iudge his people aright, and to discerne betwene good and bad, For if God for the furnishing of the olde temple gaue ye spirit of wisdome and vnderstanding to them yt shulde be ye workmen thereof, as to Bezaleel, Aholiab and Hiram, how much more will he indewe your grace, and other godly princes, and chefe gouernours, with a principal Spirit that you may procure and commande things necessarie for this moste holy Temple, forese and take hede of things that might hinder it, and abolish and destroy whatsoeuer might impere and ouerthrowe the same."

After this there is about half a page on "what policie must be vsed for the planting of religion." This epistle fills three pages, and is dated, "From Geneua 10. April 1569."

Then comes the address:

"To ovr beloved in the Lord, the brethren of England, Scotland, Ireland, &c. Grace, mercie, and peace through Christ Iesus."

This occupies one page and a half, and is dated, "From Geneua 10. April 1560."

The epistle to Queen Elizabeth is omitted from late issues of this version, but the address, "To ovr beloved," is usually inserted; just as the learned and very valuable address from the translators of King James's Bible of 1611 is omitted from most of the modern editions of the "Authorised" Version, while the fulsome dedication to King James is retained.

The last page of the preliminary matter has "The names and order of all the Bookes of the olde and nevve Testament, vvith the nombre of their chapters, and the leafe where they begyn." It is singular that "the prayer of Manasseth," which in all other Protestant Bibles is placed among the apocryphal books, is here inserted between Chronicles and Ezra.

Preliminary matter.

I must now give an account of four leaves inserted before the title-page. The first contains:

"A svppvtation of the yeares (of the) world

from the creacion thereof vnto this present yeare 1569, according as it is counted by D. M. Luther.

"From the creation to the floode	1656
"From the floode to Moyses	797
"From Moyses to Christ	1514
"From Christ vnto this yeare	1569
"Somme total	5536

"The yeare containeth 365 daies and 6 houres. The day artificial xij houres, the natural xxiv. The Jevves count there (*sic*) houres shart or long as the season maketh the daie and count xij in a daie, thus, 1.2.3.4.5.6.7.8.9.10.11.12. We count owres thus, 7.8.9.10.11.12.1.2.3.4.5.6." On verso is, "A table of the cycle of the Sunne, Letter Dominical, Leape yeare, Easter, golden Nombre, and Indiction, from Anno Domini 1570 to 1594."

Then follow four pages of an almanac, with woodcuts over each month illustrating the season.

Almanac in first small 4to edition.

"Januarie.	This moneth figureth the death of the bodie."
"Feburarie.	This moneth hedges ar closed."
"Marche.	Sowe barly and podware."
"April.	Leade the flockes to fielde."
"Maye.	Walke the liuing fieldes."
"Iune.	Sheare the Shepe."
"Iulie.	Make haye."
"Auguste.	Reape corne."
"September.	Time of vinedage."
"October.	Tille the grounde."
"Nouembre.	The fields make heuy chere."
"Decembre.	This moneth keepeth men in house."

In the middle of each month is a circular woodcut of the signs of the zodiac. One column contains a few of the festivals of the Church, some events in ancient history, the exact dates of which are stated with precision and absence of doubt that must have been most enjoyable.

In addition to others, there are notes of the following events that had then recently occurred:

"Jany. 22. The Duke of Somerset beheded, 1552."
"Feby. 19. Martin Luther the seruant of God died 1546."
"March 7. Martin Bucer a greate clerk and notable godlie man died, 1551."
"May 27. M. Iohn Caluin Gods seruant died, 1564."
"July 6. The Iosiah of oure age Edoward the sixth, King of Englond, died, 1553."
"August 27. Religion reformed, according to Gods expresse trueth in the moste renommed citie of Geneve, 1535."

The text of this Bible is numbered from folio 1 to 410, the Apocrypha from folio 1 to 94, the New Testament from folio 2 to 129. There are seventeen woodcuts, a map of "The situacion of the garden of Eden," "A table of the degrees of consanguinitie and affinitie which do hindre mariage," and a map of the countries mentioned in the Acts of the Apostles.

At the end of II. Maccabees is, "A brief table of the interpretation of the propre names which are chiefly founde in the olde Testament," with the note: "It is placed now in this edition here, because that the most vse of the same is in the old Testament," 8½ pages.

Readers are exhorted to choose names for their children from this list, which is thus headed:

"Whereas the wickednes of time, and the

blindnes of the former age, hathe bene suche that all things altogether bene abused and corrupted, so that the very right names of diuerse of the holie men named in the Scriptures bene forgotten, and now seme strange vnto vs, and the names of infants that shulde euer have some godlie aduertisements in them, and shulde be memorials and marks of the children of God receiued into his housholde, haue bene hereby also changed and made the signes and badges of idolatrie and heathenish impietie, we have now set forthe this table of ye names that be moste vsed in the olde Testament with their interpretation, as the Ebrewe importeth, partly to call back the godlie from that abuse, when they shal know the true names of the godlie fathers and what they signifie, that their children nowe named after them may have testimonies by their verie names that they are within that faithful familie that in all their doings had euer God before their eyes, and that they are bounde by these their names to serue God from their infancie, and haue occasion to praise him for his workes wroght in them and their fathers: but chiefly to restore the names to their integritie, whereby many places of the Scriptures and secret misteries of the holie Gost shall better be vnderstand. We haue medled rarely with the Grekes names, because their interpretation is vncertaine and many of them are corrupted from their original, as we may also se these Ebrewe names set in the margent of this table, which have bene corrupted by the Grecians. Now for the other Ebrewe names that are not here interpretate, let not the diligent reader be carefull: for he shall finde them in places moste conuenient amongs the annotations, at least so many as may seme to make for any edification, and vnderstanding of the Scriptures."

Christian names recommended.

In the list are such charming names as Ahasueros, Artahshaste, Beraiah, Caseluhim, Dositheus, Eleadah, Elichoenai, Gazabar, Hanameel, Jephunneh, Kerentrappuch, Lysimachus, Mahazioth, Noadiah, Orthosias, Pedahel, Retrabeam, Sabteca, Tanhumeth, Vopsi, Zaccur, &c.

The heading of Hebrews, in this and all pure Genevan Testaments, is:

"THE EPISTLE TO
the Ebrewes.

"THE ARGVMENT.

Heading of Epistle to the Hebrews.

"Forasmuche as diuers, bothe of the Greke writers & Latines witnesse, that the writer of this epistle for iuste causes wolde not haue his name knowen, it were curiositie of our parte to labour muche therein. For seing the Spirit of God is the autor thereof, it diminisheth nothing the autoritie, althogh we knowe not with what penne he wrote it. Whether it were Paul (as it is not like) or Luke, or Barnabas, or Clement, or some other, his chief purpose is to persuade vnto the Ebrewes (whereby he principally meaneth them that abode at Ierusalem, and vnder them all the rest of the Iewes) that Christ Iesus was not onely the redemer, but also that at his comming all ceremonies must haue an end: forasmuche as his doctrine was the conclusion of all the prophecies, and therefore not onely Moses was inferior to him, but also the Angels: for they all were seruants, & he the Lord, but so Lord, that he hathe also taken our flesh, & is made our brother to assure vs of our saluation through him self, for he is that eternal Priest, whereof all the Leuitical Priests were but shadowes, & therefore at his comming they oght to cease, & all sacrifices for sinne to be abolished, as he proueth from the seuenth chap. ver. 11. vnto the 12. chap. ver. 18. Also he was that Prophet of whome all ẏ Prophetes in time past witnessed, as is declared from the 12. chap. ver. 18. to the twentie & fiue verse of ẏ same chap. yea, & is the King to whome all things are subiect, as appeareth frō that ver. 25. to the beginning of the last chap. Wherefore according to the examples of the olde fathers we must constantly beleue in him, that being sanctified by his iustice, taught by his wisdome, & gouerned by his power, we may stedfastly & courageously perseuere euen to the end in hope of that ioye that is set before our eyes, occupying our selues in Christian exercises, that we may bothe be thankeful to God, and duetiful to our neighbour."

The heading of Tomson's version is, "The drift and ende of this Epistle is to show that Iesus Christe the Sonne of God both God & man is that true eternall and onely Prophet, King, and high Priest, that was shaddowed by the figures of the old Lawe, and is now indeed exhibited: of whom the whole Church ought to be taught, gouerned, and sanctified."

At the end of the New Testament is, "A table of the principal things that are conteined in the Bible, after the ordre of the alphabet," 62 columns. "A perfite svppvtation of the yeres and times from Adam vnto Christ, proued by the Scriptures after the collection of diuers autors." On the last page of the Bible is, "The order of the yeres from Paul's conuersion shewing the time of his peregrination, and of his Epistles written to the Churches," 1 page.

Psalter

Next follows, "The whole booke of Psalmes, collected into Englishe metre by Sternhod (*sic*) I. Hopkins and others, conferred vvith the Ebrue, vvith apt notes to synge them vvithall. Faithfully perused and allowed, according to thorder appointed in the Quenes maiesties Iniunctions. James v. ℂ If any be afflicted, let hym praye, and if any be mery, let hym sing Psalmes." (Crespin's mark—Anchor and Serpent.) "At Geneva, Printed by John Crespin, M.D.LXIX," 63 leaves. Then 5 pages of prayers, followed by "The Catechisme, or maner to teache children the Christian religion wherin the minister demandeth the question, and the childe maketh answer. Made by the excellent Doctor and Pastor in Christes Churche, Iohn Caluin."

Calvin's Catechism.

The unfortunate child who had to learn this catechism was to be pitied. The following is an example of the answers: "ℂ The minister—

What is the sence of that clause as touching his descendyng into hell? ℂ The childe—The righte meanynge therof is: That Christ dyd not onelye suffre a naturall deathe, which is a departyng and goyng asunder of the body and soule: but also that his soule was in wonderfull dystresse beyng wofully pressed and enduring grieuous tormentes, which Sainct Peter calleth ye sorowes, or pangues of deathe."

In 1568 a quarto Testament was printed by John Crespin at Geneva, and also a quarto Bible, which is dated 1568–70.

The first edition of the Genevan New Testament printed in England appeared in 1575, octavo. Octavo New Testament, 1575.

"The | Newe Te | stament of | ovr Lord Iesvs | Christ. | Conferred with the Greke, | and best approued | translations. | VVith the arguments, as vvel before the | chapters, as for euery Boke and Epistle. | Also diuersities of readings, and | most profitable annotations of all harde places: vvhere | unto is added a co | pious Table. |

"Imprinted at | London by T. V. for | Christopher Barker. | Cum privilegio."

This edition is taken from the 1560, and not from Whittingham's 1557. There is, however, a certain amount of revision peculiar to this edition alone, and by which it may be distinguished from all other Testaments.

For example, the word "babe," which occurs so often in all other versions, is omitted, both in the singular and plural form.

In S. Luke i. 41, King James's version of

1611 has, "the babe leaped in her womb:" the 1575 reads, "the childe sprang in her bellie;" the same in the 44th verse, "the childe sprang in my bellie for joye."

In S. Luke ii. 12 the 1611 has, "Ye shall find the babe wrapped in swaddling clothes, lying in a manger:" the 1575 reads, "Ye shal finde the childe swadled, and layd in a cratch;" the 16th verse the same, "the Child layd in the cratch."

Heb. v. 13: "For every one that useth milke is inexperte in the worde of righteousnes: for he is a childe."

S. Matt. xi. 25: "because thou hast hid these things from the wise and men of understanding and hast opened them unto children."

Rom. ii. 20: "An instructor of them which lacke discretion, a teacher of the unlearned."

1 Cor. iii. 1: "Even as unto Children in Christ."

1 S. Pet. ii. 2: "As newe borne children."

The royal arms are at the top of the title; on the reverse is, "The ordre of the Books," in Italic type; then Calvin's Epistle, 8 leaves; "To the Reader," 5 pages; and on the reverse, "The argvment of the Gospell," 1 page. The text is in Roman type, and on page 813 is the colophon, "Imprinted at London by Thomas Vautroullier, for Christopher Barker."

After this, "A declaration of the Table to the New Testament," 1 page; "A table of the principall thinges," 35 pages; and the volume finishes with "A perfite supputation of the yeres," 3 pages; last page blank.

The declaration and table at the end, and the preface and epistle in the preliminary, are copied from Whittingham's New Testament of 1557.

First folio Genevan Bible printed in England, 1570.

Two distinct issues.

The first folio Genevan Bible printed in England was Christopher Barker's edition of 1570. Of this there were two entirely distinct issues bearing the same date.

The type used for the titles is quite different, and so is the arrangement of the words.

In No. 1, verso of title is blank: in No. 2 is Barker's mark on verso.

In No. 1 the map and explanation reaches to bottom of page: in No. 2 the map, &c. only reaches part way.

The initial letters used in No. 1 are much larger than in No. 2.

In No. 1 the signature is below the notes: in No. 2 it is above the notes.

No. 1 has long running titles: No. 2 has short ones, in different words.

The wood-cut of the royal throne of Solomon, on folio 145, Sig. B b 1, in No. 1, is before the 19th verse: in No. 2 it is at the bottom of the page.

The running title to Ecclesiastes is duplicated in No. 2, but is correct in No. 1.

The two issues read together on every page up to recto of 316; but here in No. 1 a half-page woodcut is introduced, which causes a different setting up of the type, so making the catchwords differ all through Ezekiel.

In No. 1, on page 333, is a large French woodcut, "Le parvis de dedans." On recto of 334 and 335 are woodcuts in No. 1, but not in No. 2. No. 1 only has the double-page French map of the Temple at the end of Ezekiel.

Both editions thus end,

"Then the whole summe and number of yeres from the beginning of the worlde vnto this present yere of our Lord God 1576, are iust 5540, and the said odde sixe moneths and ten dayes.

"The end. Ioshua. Chap. j., verse 8. Let not this Booke of the Lawe depart out of thy mouth, but meditate therein day and night, that thou mayest obserue and do according to al that is written therein: for then shalt thou make thy way prosperous, and then shalt thou haue good successe."

These books were well printed, and have wide margins.

Barker's patent.

Christopher Barker purchased a patent from Queen Elizabeth for the exclusive printing of Bibles, and we find from the year 1576 to 1587 only about 6 editions have any other printer's name; from 1587 to 1599 "Deputies of Christopher Barker" appear, and from 1599 to 1618 seldom is any other name seen but Robert Barker.

Bonham Norton and John Bill obtained from the Barkers permission to print the Bible, and in the year 1635 Robert Barker paid 600*l.* to give his younger sons, Charles and Matthew, a reversionary interest in the patent already held by his two elder sons.

After keeping the patent about 130 years, it passed from the Barkers to the Baskets, who held it for 60 years, and then sold it to John Eyre of Landford, Wilts. It was subsequently taken up and worked by John Eyre's youngest son, Charles Eyre.

C. Eyre took William Strahan into partnership, and they handed it down to the worthy hands of its present possessors, Eyre and Spottiswoode.

The Bassandyne Bible, 1579, folio.

The first Bible printed in Scotland was taken from the folio issued at Geneva, in 1562, without printer's name.

The title page reads: "The Bible and Holy Scriptvres conteined in the Olde & Newe Testament Translated according to the Ebrue & Greke, & conferred with the beste translations in diuers languages (.·.) With moste profitable annotations vpon all the hard places of the Holy Scriptvres, and other things of grete importance mete for the godly Reader. God save the King. Printed in Edinbvrgh Be Alexander Arbuthnot, Printer to the Kingis Maiestie, dwelling at ye Kirke of feild. 1579. Cvm gratia et Privilegio regiæ maiestatis."

Collation.

There are nine preliminary leaves. On the title page is a rough woodcut of the arms of Scotland, and the words, "In defens." On the Lion banner, "Iacob;" on the S. Andrew's cross, "Sextus." On the reverse of title, "The names and order of all the Bookes of the olde & New Testament," one page. The second leaf begins on Sig. (.·.) ij: "To the Richt Excellent Richt heich and Michtie Prince Iames the Sixt King of Scottis," &c., 3½ pages, dated at the end, "From Edinburgh in our general assemblie the tent day off Iulie 1579." The rest of the page blank.

Then comes, "An dovble Calendare to wit, the Romane and the Hebrew Calendare," &c., "Ane Almanake," &c., 7 pages. On reverse of the seventh leaf is, "¶ A table to find out what signe the Moone is at any tyme for euer," half page, under which is, "Rvles for vnderstanding of this double Calendare," &c., occupying that and half the next page, signed "R. Pont;" then follow the verses found in nearly all copies of the Genevan Bible: "Here is the Spring where waters flow," and the usual prayer.

On reverse of eighth leaf is, "A discription and svccesse of the Kinges of Ivda and Ierusalem," 1½ pages; then follows, "An exhortation to the studie of the holie scriptvre." On the reverse, "How to take profite in reading of the holie Scriptvre," signed "T Grashop," 1 page; at the bottom of which is Arbuthnot's device, copied from Richard Jugge's.

Then comes the text, evidently set up from the first Genevan folio, Genesis to II. Maccabees, 503 folioed leaves, ending with: "The Third Boke of the Maccabees newlie translated out of the original Greke;" there is, however, no third book printed, nor does it exist in any English Bible excepting Daye's Taverner of 1551. Then follows the New Testament title: "The | Newe Testament | of ovr Lord Ie | svs

Christ. Conferred diligently with the Greke, and best approued translations in diuers languages." Then the Scottish arms, with "God save the King" at the sides.

The imprint is, "At Edinbvrgh printed by Thomas Bassandyne, MDLXXVJ. cvm privilegio." Reverse of title blank; the text, Sig. A ij, folioed 2 (misprinted 1) to 125, ending on middle of reverse. Then comes, "A briefe Table of the Proper names which are chiefly founde in the Old Testament," in double columns, not paged or folioed, but beginning on the recto of X vj., and ending at the middle of the verso of Y iij. Then follows, "A table of the principal things that are conteined in the Bible," &c., in treble columns, ending on the middle of the reverse of Z vj. The rest of that page and the next are filled with, "A Perfite svppvtation of the yeres and times from Adam vnto Christ," brought down "vnto this present yere of our Lord God 1570." On the reverse is, "The order of the yeres from Paul's conuersion," &c., 1 page.

Seven English Bibles had been printed before this one, in Roman letter, and Bassandyne used the same kind of type, Roman being easier to read than black letter.

The first Scottish printer who obtained license to print the Bible was R. Lekprevik, but he does not appear to have availed himself of the privilege. This license is dated April 14, 1568, and reads as follows:—

Robert Lekprevik's license to print the Bible.

"Ane Letter maid with auice of my Lord Regent, To Robert Lekprevik ovr Souerane

Lordis imprentare Given granted and committed to him ful license priuilege and power To imprent all and haill ane buke callit the Inglis bybill, imprintit before at Geneua, and that continuallie induring the space of tuenty yeires nixt following the dait heirof. Chargeing all and sindrie imprintaris, writtaris, and utheris, his hienes liegis within this realme That nane of thame tak vpoun hand to imprint or caus be imprintit be quhatsumeuer persoun or persounis within this realme in ony tyme heireftir induring the said space vnder the panis of confiscatioun thairof The said buke callit the Inglis bibill viz. samony as salhappin to be imprintit and payment of the soume of twa hundreth pundis money of this realme &c. At Glasgw the fourtene day of Aprile, The yiar of God. 1568."

For the sake of capital to carry on business Bassandyne was obliged to take into partnership a wealthy burgess named Alexander Arbuthnot, as Guttenberg did Fust, and the General Assembly ordered that each parish should purchase a copy of the Bible to be printed by Bassandyne and Arbuthnot, and pay 5*l.* in advance; 4*l.* 13*s.* 4*d.* was fixed as the price of the book, the remaining 6*s.* 8*d.* for expenses. The Bibles were not delivered until about three years after the money was paid. The sureties for the delivery of the book were David Guthrie, of Kilcaldrum; William Guthrie, of Halkerton; William Rynd, of Carse; and James Arnot, of Lentusche, Forfarshire.

The General Assembly appointed certain

persons to "oversee" the printing, and Salomon Kerknett was brought from Flanders to act as "composer," at the weekly wage of 49s.; and a license, dated June 30, 1576, was granted to Bassandyne and Arbuthnot, similar to that previously issued to Lekprevik.

The publication of this Bible was much delayed owing to dissensions between the partners; even the workmen were not paid their wages with regularity. Salomon Kerknett was obliged to complain to the Regent, who ordered the sum agreed on to be paid the "composer" until the work was completed.

Before the printing was finished, the partnership between Bassandyne and Arbuthnot was dissolved, and Bassandyne was compelled to give up the printing-house and plant to Arbuthnot. This accounts for the name of Thomas Bassandyne being on the New Testament title, and that of Alexander Arbuthnot being alone on the first title page.

Bassandyne did not live to see the book issued, and left no record of his version of the dispute.

It seems strange that there should have been so many impediments, and so much difficulty in the production of this Bible, which, from a typographical point of view cannot be compared with the Bibles printed in England at the same period.

The "intense desire" for a vernacular Bible we read about in the works of nearly all writers on the subject, had no existence, and it was only by penal enactments that the Bible could be forced into circulation. The Privy Council were obliged to pass a law "that each householder worth three hundred merks of yearly rent, and all substantious yeomen and burgesses esteemed as worth £500 in land and goods, should have a Bible in the vulgar tongue, under the penalty of £10," double the price at which the book was authorised to be sold, and three or four times the sum at which it could be purchased. To enforce this enactment, searchers were appointed to go from house to house throughout Scotland, and each householder was required to produce a Bible or pay the penalty. As it was found that Bibles were made to do duty for more houses than one, the searcher or inquisitor was furnished with a warrant, under the privy seal, "to require the sicht of their Bible, gif they ony haue, to be marked with their own name for eschewing of fraudful dealing in that behalf."

Searchers appointed.

The magistrates and Town Council of Edinburgh commanded all householders to purchase Bibles under severe pains and penalties, and informed them that Bibles are to be "sauld in the merchant buith of Andrew Williamson on the north side of this burg, besyde the Meill Mercat." In spite of this pressure, we find from the Privy Council Records, that many householders "incurrit the payne of the Act" rather than purchase a Bible.

Sixteen years after the Genevan New Testament was printed, Laurence Tomson, who was in the service of Sir Francis Walsingham, Secretary of State to Queen Elizabeth, undertook to "English" it afresh.

The first edition of Tomson's New Testament was small 8vo size. It is said on the title to be, "The new Testament of our Lord Iesvs Christ, translated out of the Greeke by Theod. Beza. Wherevnto are adjoyned briefe Summeries of doctrine vpon the Euangelistes and Actes of the Apostles, together with the methode of the Epistles of the Apostles: by the said Theod. Beza. L. Tomson's New Testament, 1576.

"And also short expositions on the phrases and hard places, taken ovt of the large annotations of foresayd Author and Ioach. Camerarius, by P. Loseler Villerius. Englished by L. Tomson. Then follows a woodcut of the Angels appearing to the Shepherds, and the words "Beholde I bring you tidings of greate ioy that shalbe to all the people. Luk 2. 10." Below is, "Imprinted at London by Christopher Barkar dwelling in Poules churchyeard at the signe of the Tigres head. 1576. Cum privilegio."

On the back of the title is, "The order of the books." Collation.

"An epistle to the right honorable M. Francis Walsingham Esquier and to the right worshipfull M. Francis Hastings," 12 pages.

This is followed by an address from "Theodorus Beza to the most famous Prince Lewys of Bourbon, Prince of Conde &c and to the rest most famous and noble Dukes, Marqueses, Earles, Barons, and Gentlemen which have embraced the true Gospell of Christ, in the Kingdome of Fraunce." This takes twenty-nine pages, and is dated "at Geneua, the tenth of the Calendes of March 1565."

"The printer to the diligent reader," ending, "this haue I faithfully done for thy commoditie, reape thou the fruite, and giue the praise to God," 2 pages.

"The Description of the holy Lande, conteyning the places mentioned by the foure Euangelistes. &c.," 2 pages.

The text, folio 1 to 460.

On one side of the last leaf is the imprint, and on the other Barker's well-known device, the ribbon bearing the words, "TIGRE: REO. ANIMALE DEL ADAM. VECCHIO. FIGLIVOLO MERCE L'EVANGELIO FATTO. N'ESTAT. AGNELLO;" then follows, "A Table of the principall things that are conteined in the Newe Testament, after the order of the Alphabet," in two columns; lastly, "A perfect supputation," &c.

Popularity of Tomson's revision.

This revision became popular at once, and was re-printed as a separate book twelve times between 1576 and 1587; and in 1587 it supplanted the Genevan translation of 1560 in most editions of the "Breeches" Bible, although the Genevan New Testament continued to be issued also, and was usually printed in black letter, and Tomson's in Roman type.

Tomson's opinion of the marginal readings.

L. Tomson had a very high opinion of Beza's notes. In the preface he says, "I dare avouch it, and whoso readeth shall so find it, that there is not one hard sentence, nor dark speech, nor doubtful word, but is so opened, and hath such light given it, that children may go through with it, and the simplest that are may walk without any guide, without wandering, or going astray."

It is to teaching like that of the Genevan Bible, that no guide is necessary in spiritual matters, that we are indebted for the many different sects that divide the people of England, and embitter our social and political life.

Means of distinguishing different editions.

A New Testament of 1500 may be distinguished from the one "Englyshed by Tomson" by referring to I. Corinthians xvi. 22, which in the former reads, "If any man love not the Lord Jesus Christ, let him be had in execration, yea excommunicate to death," but in the latter, "let him be had in execration, maranatha." It may also be known by the heading of the Epistle to the Hebrews being short in Tomson's, and long in the Genevan.

Rare and edition of Tomson's New Testament.

The second edition of Tomson's Testament is much rarer than the first. Christopher Barker printed it in 1577, and re-issued the same book with fresh printed preliminary matter.

There is no copy of either issue in the British Museum. I have only seen two. One of Barker's first issue is the property of the Rev. Nicholas Pocock, M.A., and a copy of the second is in my collection.

Duodecimo edition of 1580.

An edition of the Genevan Bible in 5 volumes, 12mo (4½ by 3 inches), was printed in London by Christopher Barker in 1580.

No one has a complete set of these volumes.

and it is supposed that only the third part, viz., Job, Psalms, Proverbs, Ecclesiastes and Solomon's Songs, now remains.

The title of this rare book is, "The third of the Bible, conteyning five excellent Bookes, most commodious for all Christians, faithfully translated out of the Ebrew, and expounded with most profitable annotations vpon the harder places."

Questions and answers on predestination.

All pure quarto Genevan Bibles, and one folio, printed in England from the year 1579 have certain questions and answers upon predestination bound up between the Old and New Testament, but they are not in the copies made up of the 1560 Old Testament with Tomson's version of the New.

F. Junius on Revelation.

The editions of 1598 and 1600 have at the end the Revelation repeated, with "copious annotations by Franciscus Junius." This was also published by itself several times. It consists of 22 pages, the last being blank. It has no title page.

The colophon on page 23 is, "Imprinted at London, by Richard Field, for Robert Dexter dwelling in Paules Churchyard at the signe of the Brazen Serpent."

From the year 1599 the title pages of Tomson's version in quarto have the addition of the words, "together with the Annotations of Fr Junius upon the Revelation of S. John."

The Apocrypha is omitted from most of the Bibles printed in 1599, but it is always to be found in pure Genevan Bibles, even in the octavo editions.

The Genevan translators adopted a novel orthography for Hebrew proper names, such as Heuah, Hábel, Iaakob, Izhák, Rahél, &c. *Orthography of the "Breeches" Bible.*

To the quarto of 1578 and to most subsequent issues of the Genevan Bible, and even to some editions of the 1611 Bible, there were added—

"¶ Two right profitable and fruitfull Concordances, or large and ample Tables Alphabeticall. *Concordance.*

The first containing the interpretation of the Hebrew, Caldean, Greeke, and Latine words and names scatteringly dispersed throughout the whole Bible, with their common places following euery of them.

And the second comprehending all such other principall words and matters, as concerne the sense and meaning of the Scriptures, or direct vnto any necessary and good instruction.

¶ *The further contents and vse of both the which Tables* (for breuitie sake) is expressed more at large in the Preface to the Reader: And will serue as well for the Translation called GENEVA, as for the other authorized to be read in Churches.

Collected by R. F. H."

There is a preface of two pages beginning, "Good Christian Reader, because thou mayest enioy and reape the profite of these two Alphabets of directions vnto Common places hereafter following, which I haue in maner of a briefe Concordance, or large & ample Index, collected, digested, and caused to be imprinted for thy cōmoditie: I thought it not amisse to aduertise thee somewhat touching the principall contents, vse, and commoditie of them," and ending,

"And so beseeching Almightie God to giue vs
his grace to be studious of vnitie, and bringing forth such fruites, as may declare
our vndoubted election in Christ
Iesus, I take my leaue of thee,
this xxij of December.
Anno Domini.
1578.

"*Thine in the Lord, Robert F. Herrey.*"

This Robert Fitz Herry was the Norfolk Brownist, Robert Harrison: and he thus formed his name,—Harrison=Henry-son=Fitz-Herry.

Description of title page.

During the long series of years the Genevan Bible continued to be printed, very few changes were made in its title pages. Nearly always on the left side may be seen the standards of the twelve tribes of Israel, and on the right the twelve apostles; over the letterpress is a dove, and at the foot the Agnus Dei; representations of the four Evangelists are at the corners of the letterpress; and in the centre of the bottom of the page are the initials of the reigning monarch. The same title page, with different letterpress, was used for the early quarto editions of the

Authorised Version. Next to the title page of most "Breeches" Bibles will be found the following doggerel lines:

"Of the incomparable treasure of the holy scriptures, with a prayer for the true use of the same.

Isa. 12. 3. and 49. 10. Revel. 21. 6. and 22. 17 — "HEre is the spring where waters flow,
to quench our heat of sin:
Jerem. 23. 15. Psal. 119. 160. — Here is the tree where truth doth grow,
to lead our lives therein:
Revel. 2. 7. and 22. 2. — Here is the judge that stints the strife,
when mens devices fail:
Psal. 119. 142, 144. — Here is the bread that feeds the life,
John 6. 35. — that death cannot assail.
Luke 2. 10. — The tidings of salvation dear:
comes to our ears from hence;
Ephes. 6. 16. — The fortress of our faith is here,
and shield of our defence.
Matth. 7. 6. — Then be not like the hog that hath
a pearl at his desire,
2 Pet. 2. 22. — And take more pleasure in the trough,
Matth. 6. 22. — and wallowing in the myre.
Ps. 119. 27, 73. — Read not this book in any case
but with a single eye,
Read not but first desire Gods grace,
to understand thereby,
Jude 1. — Pray still in faith with this respect
to fructifie therein.
Psal. 119. 11. — That knowledge may bring this effect,
to mortifie thy sin.
Joshua 1. 8. Psal. 1. 1, 2. — Then happie thou in all thy life,
what so to thee befalls;
Psal. 94. 12, [illegible] — Yea, double happy shall thou be,
when God by death thee calls."

and this prayer,

"O Gracious God, and most merciful father, which hast vouchsafed us the rich and precious jewel of thy holy word, assist us with thy spirit, that it may be written in our hearts to our everlasting comfort, to reform us, to renew us, according to thine own image; to build us up, and edifie us into the perfect building of thy Christ, sanctifying and increasing in us all heavenly vertues. Grant this O heavenly Father, for Jesus Christs sake. Amen."

4to Genevan Bible, dated 1495.

A quarto Genevan Bible was issued in 1594, on the New Testament title page of which two figures in the date were transposed. Frequently the first title with the true date is lost, and the book is exhibited as an English black letter Bible of the fifteenth century.

Genevan and Tomson's New Testaments.

A very large number of editions of the Genevan New Testament, and of Tomson's version, were published separately in all sizes, from the extra large quarto of 1583, to the minute 48mo. printed at Cambridge in 1589.

Some of them are re-issues of old editions with new title pages.

Booksellers' frauds.

We find that in the year 1596 Monsieur Adam d'Orival, minister of the congregation at Sancerre, was ordered by the Protestant Synod of Saumur, to acquaint the authorities at Geneva with the frauds practised by their booksellers, who vended New Testaments of the old translation prefixed by new title pages, to pass off the books as new impressions and translations.

The first edition of the Genevan New Testament by itself was the 16mo. of 1560.

The first quarto was printed by J. Crespin, Geneva, in 1568.

The quarto of 1583 is the finest edition of the

Genevan New Testament ever issued; the 1595 much resembles it, but can be distinguished by the absence of the two black lines at the head of each page, which are so conspicuous in the 1583.

The first Testament printed in Cambridge was by John Legate.

First New Testament printed at Cambridge.

My copy measures 2½ inches by 1½ inch. It has no preliminary matter, contents, nor marginal references; it is printed in very small Roman type, and capitals are used for the heads of chapters.

No Testament was printed at Cambridge for 30 years after this one was issued.

I have copies of the octavo Tomson, 1580; the 12mo of 1581; the octavos of 1582, 1602, 1610 and 1616. The 1616 is the last edition that was published.

The Bishops' Bible.

Reading of the Bible confined to certain classes.

THERE was no prohibition of the circulation or reading of the Bible during the reigns of Edward VI. or of Mary, but no new version was made. In 1543 Parliament restricted the use of the Bible to certain grades of society, forbidding the lower classes to read it to themselves, or to others, under pain of imprisonment for one month. Tyndale's New Testament was specially condemned, as "crafty, false, and untrue," and ordered to be destroyed, and forbidden to be kept or used in any of the King's dominions. This Act was introduced and passed by the influence of Cranmer, who, not satisfied with having been indirectly a party to the death of Tyndale, vented his spite against the translation of Tyndale, even after the translator's body had been burnt. Soon after Edward's accession to the throne this Act was repealed, and during the next six-and-a-half years, although no new translation was issued, yet many editions of previous versions found ready sale.

Repeal of this prohibition.

Thirty-one out of 57 English printers were engaged in the work of printing Bibles or Testaments, each selecting the version he thought most likely to sell.

New version required.

Soon after Elizabeth ascended the throne it was felt to be necessary that another translation of the Bible should be undertaken.

The Genevan version had obtained a large circulation, and its mischievous glosses were undermining the Church of England.

Archbishop Parker at first favoured the use of this Bible, but becoming aware of its animus he decided to introduce a translation which should be free from party spirit and fairly represent the Biblical knowledge of the day.

Archbishop Parker's letter to Lord Burleigh.

It was not his wish to confine the work to Bishops, but his efforts to obtain lay assistance failed. In a letter to Cecil, Lord Burleigh, dated November 20th, 1566, he says, "I haue distributed the Bible to diuers men, and I am desirous if you could spare so much leasure either in morning or euening, we had one Epistle of SS. Paul, Peter, or James, perused by you, that ye may be one of the builders of this good work in Christes Churche."

Being unable to obtain the assistance of laymen, he entrusted the work to the following clergymen, whose initials may be seen at the end of their contributions.

Translators of the Bishops' version.

The initials and places at which they occur are as follows: At the end of the Pentateuch, "W. E." (W. Exon, William Alley, Bishop of Exeter); II. Samuel, "R. M." (R. Meneven, Richard Davies, Bishop of S. David's); II. Chronicles, "E. W." (E. Wigornen, Edwyn Sandys, Bishop of Worcester); Job and Proverbs, "A. P., *C.*" (Andrew Pearson, Canon of Canterbury); Song of Solomon, "A. P., *E.*" (Andrew Perne, Canon of Ely); Lamentations, "R. W." (R. Winton, Robert Horne, Bishop of Winchester); Daniel, "T. C., L." (Thomas Cole, Bishop of Lichfield and Coventry); Malachi, "E. L." (E. Londin, Edmund Grindal, Bishop of London); II. Maccabees, "J. N." (J. Norvic. John Parkhurst, Bishop of Norwich); Acts and Romans, "R. E." (R. Elien, Richard Cox, Bishop of Ely); I. Corinthians, "G. G." (Gabriel Goodman, Dean of Westminster). As these initials are only in Bishops' Bibles of folio size, to identify smaller sized copies we have to rely on peculiarity of translation.

This was the second attempt made by the heads of the English Church to translate the Bible for the use of all English-speaking people. The first, in Henry VIII's time, failed, from their being unable to decide how many Latin words should be retained. But that the Bishops at both periods should be equal to such a task, one requiring biblical research, and accurate critical scholarship, is a proof that in those days the sees were filled by the Bishop of Rome, and afterwards by the Crown, not from favouritism, and political motives only, as has often been represented, but by men of the highest attainments. Although initials were affixed by most of the translators to their work, it was the desire of Parker that the translation should be regarded as the work of the Church, and not of private men. As each translator finished the parcel (as it was called) assigned to him, he returned it to the Primate, who supervised it. In addition he translated Genesis and Exodus, the Gospels of SS. Matthew and Mark, and

The Bishops the best scholars of their day.

Parker's share in the translation.

most of the Epistles of S. Paul, and also wrote the prefaces.

When complete it was properly and formally sanctioned by Convocation, and a copy was presented to Queen Elizabeth on Oct. 5, 1568. Nineteen editions of this version were printed (12 folio, 6 quarto, and 1 octavo), all of which bear marks of having been more or less revised.

The dates of publication are: 1st edition, 1568, folio; 2nd edition, 1569, quarto; 3rd edition, 1572, folio; 4th edition, 1573, quarto; 5th edition, 1574, folio; 6th edition, 1575, folio; 7th edition, 1575, quarto; 8th edition, 1576, quarto; 9th edition, 1577, quarto; 10th edition, 1577, octavo; 11th edition, 1578, folio; 12th edition, 1584, folio; 13th edition, 1584, quarto; 14th edition, 1585, folio; 15th edition, 1588, folio; 16th edition, 1591, folio; 17th edition, 1595, folio; 18th edition, 1602, folio; 19th edition, 1606, folio.

The following is a collation of the Bishops' Bible of 1568: Title, within a border, "The holi Bible conteynyng the Olde Testament and the newe," with a copperplate engraving of Queen Elizabeth. At the bottom is a lion and a dragon, with the motto, "Non me pudet Evangelii Christi," &c.; reverse blank. "The summe of the whole Scripture of the bookes of the Old and New Testament," 1 leaf. Collation of first edition of 1568, folio.

"A table of the genealogie from Adam to Christ," 11 pages. The running title of this is, "Christ's line." In the initial T are Archbishop Parker's paternal arms, empaled with those of Christ Church, Canterbury, also M [atthew] P [arker], with the date 1568 at the bottom, and underneath a cypher. Through the stem of the T is run the crosier-staff, the head of which appears above in the place of the crest, and round the arms, within a double circle, is the motto: "Mvndvs transit et concvpiscentia eivs." The recognition of the crosier is interesting at this moment.

"A table of the books of the Old Testament: the Newe in lyke manner," two pages; then follows one blank page; "Proper lessons for Sundays, and for holydayes," two pages.

"Proper psalms for certayne days;" "The order howe the reste of holy Scripture is to be read;" "A brief declaration when every terme beginneth and endeth;" "An almanacke for xxix. years," beginning 1561; "To fynde Easter for euer;" "These to be obserued for holy dayes;" "A table for the order of the Psalmes." These pieces occupy four pages.

"A calendar," 12 pages. In the inner margin are notes of the sun's rising and setting.

At the bottom of January is this: "Admonition to the Reader. Where in this Calendar be appointed almost to all the dayes of euery moneth names of Saintes, this we have done gentle reader, not for that we accompte them all for saintes, of whom we repute some not good, or yet for that eyther, howe holy soever they be, we judge any divine worship or honour to be referred to them, but rather that they should be as notes and markes of some certayne matters, whose appoynted tymes to knowe, as it maye do much good: so to be ignoraunt of the same, may do to men much hurt. And this is the reason of this fact and purpose. Farewell."

Parker's preface, in Roman letter, six pages; Cranmer's prologue, in black letter, five pages; "A description of the yeeres from the creation of the world until this present yere, 1568," one page; "The order of the bookes of the Old Testament: and of the Newe Testament," one page; reverse blank.

Then comes the text, paged, Genesis, fol. 1 to 128. There is a woodcut at the beginning, representing the history of the Creation. After the second chapter is a map of the Garden of Eden. To some verses, in various places, are placed inverted commas, that the public reader may know what verses may be omitted if desirable.

After the 10th verse of the 18th chapter of Leviticus is a table of the kindred or affinity within which marriage is unlawful, *i.e.*, by the laws of God—human laws change.

After "Deuteronomium" comes the second title: "The seconde part of the Byble conteyning these bookes," &c., with an engraving of the reigning favourite of Queen Elizabeth, the profligate Earl of Leicester, within an oval. In a panel of the border are the figures,—

123
456
789

This part is paged from folio 2 to 185, one blank.

The third title has a woodcut of King David, and on the reverse: "A prologue of S. Basill the great upon the Psalmes:" the paging is from folio 2 to 204. At the beginning is an engraved portrait of Cecil, Lord Burleigh, with a Hebrew psalter, and his motto, "Cor vnvm via vna." At the end of the Psalms is a table of how the Psalms are numbered according to the Hebrews.

The fourth title is, "The volume of the bookes called Apocrypha;" underneath is the woodcut of the rebuilding of Jerusalem. The Apocrypha is numbered from folio 2 to 118. There are only three woodcuts in the Apocrypha—one in the book of Tobit, one of Judith and Holophernes, and the last on L 8 verso.

The fifth and last title is that of "The newe Testament of our Sauiour Iesus Christe;" text, folio 2 to 156. On the reverse of the New Testament title is a preface in Roman letter by Archbishop Parker. Prefixed to each of the Gospels is a representation of its author, with the usual emblems of a man, a lion, an ox, and an eagle. Before S. Paul's Epistles is, "The Cart Cosmographie, of the peregrination or iourney of Saint Paul, with the distaunce of the myles."

In the book of the Revelation are figures of remarkable things, twenty in number.

After the word "Finis" is, "A Table to fynde the Epistles and Gospels read in the Church of Englande VVherof, &c.," continued to the next leaf, and erroneously numbered 159 for 157.

The whole number of engravings, woodcuts, maps, &c., is 143. The imprint is: "Imprinted at London in powles Church-yarde, by Richarde Jugge, printer to the Queenes Maiestie. Cum priuilegio Regiae Maiestatis."

The second edition of the Bishops' Bible was published in the year 1569, in quarto (about 8 in. by 6 in.), by the Queen's printer, R. Jugge. Second edition, 1569, 4to.

This book is interesting for many reasons: the first is, that it shows the transition from the old plan of continuous chapters, merely broken by paragraphs, to the new system of verses.

In it the letters of the alphabet still continue in their old place, down the margin of the text, which is not separated into verses, but the figures are intermixed with the letterpress. In the Psalter the verses are separated.

The Psalms are the Bishops' translation, and not those of the Great Bible of Nov. 1540, usually known as the Prayer Book version. The collation is as follows: Title—On the upper part is an engraving of Queen Elizabeth on a throne, with two of the cardinal virtues, viz., Justice and Mercy, one on each side of the Queen, holding a crown over her head; a little lower down are Fortitude and Prudence, reaching out their hands to uphold her throne. The words, "The holi bible," are below the Queen's feet. At the bottom of the title is represented a preacher habited in a chimere, facing an audience, and the words, "God save the QVEENE," are at the bottom of the page; reverse blank; "The preface," five pages; Collation.

"The Prayer," one page; "The whole Scripture of the Bible is divided," &c., three pages; "The newe Testament in lyke manner," &c., two pages; "A Kalender," in black and red, twelve pages; "The order howe the rest of holy Scripture," &c., and "Proper Lessons," &c., altogether eight pages; "The order of Morning and Euening prayer," eight pages.

Genesis to Deuteronomy, folio 1 to 105. A representation of the Creation is over the first chapter of Genesis, and the initial letter has Archbishop Parker's arms. With the next chapter is a map of the Garden of Eden, giving the exact position of the four rivers, but evidently not drawn to scale. Between the 27th and 28th chapters of Exodus is a plan of the encampment of the children of Israel in the wilderness, with the Tabernacle in the centre (situated due east and west), and the tents of the twelve tribes in proper position, and the standards of the four divisions of the army of Israel at the corners, bearing respectively the emblematic devices of a man, a lion, an ox, and an eagle.

At the end of Numbers (chap. 33) is a chart or map:

"¶ This Charte sheweth the way that the people of Israel passed the space of fourtie yeres, from Egypt (through the desertes of Arabia) tyll they entred into the lande of Chanaan, it contayneth also the fourtie and two iourneyes or stations, with the obseruations of the degrees, as well of the longitude, as of the latitude of the places of the saide iourneyes, and also the order of the numbers of them."

At "the ende of the fifth booke of Moyses, called in the Hebrewe Ellehaddebarim, and in the Latine Deuteronomium," is Jugge's well-known device,—an oval picture of a pelican feeding her young; no doubt an allusion to the sacrament of the altar. The space at the top is blank.

Inside the oval is the motto, "Pro lege rege et grege," and outside, "Love kepyth the lawe, obeyeth the kynge, and is good to the commenwelthe."

R. Jugge's device.

On the right of the oval is a female figure representing Prudence, and on the left Justice; beneath are the following lines—

"Matris vt haec proprio stirps est saciata cruore:
Pascis item proprio Christe cruore tuos."

This leaf must be intended as a second title page, for although the numbering of the leaves is continuous from Genesis to Job (1 to 261), yet the title before the Psalter is said to be "The thirde part of the Bible contayning these bookes;" but there are actually only four parts and not five.

At the end of the Second Book of Chronicles is, "A very profitable declaration for the vnderstanding of the Histories of Esdras, Nehemias, Ester, Daniel, and diuers other places of scripture, very darke by reason of the discorde that is among Historiographers, and expositours of the holy scriptures touchyng the successiue order of the kinges," &c.

After the Psalter title page is "a prologue of saint Basil the great;" then, after a short quotation from S. Austen, follows this excuse for a new translation of the Psalms:—

Address to the reader.

"Nowe let the gentle reader have this christian consideration within hym selfe that though he findeth the psalmes of this translation following, not so to sounde agreeably to his ears in his wonted wordes and phrases, as he is accustomed with, yet let hym not be to muche offended with the worke, which was wrought for his owne commoditie and comfort. And if he be learned, let hym correct the worde or sentence (whiche may dislike hym) with the better, and whether his note ryseth eyther of good wyll and charitie, eyther of enuie and contention not purely, yet his reprehension, if it may turne to the finding out of the trueth, shall not be repelled with greefe, but applauded to in gladnesse, that Christe may euer haue the prayse. To whom with the father and the holy spirite, be all glory and prayse for euer. Amen."

The Apocrypha title, like that of the third part, is in plain Roman type. At the end is "A Table to make playne the difficultie that is founde in S. Matthewe and S. Luke, &c."

The New Testament title has only the words, "¶ The newe | Testament of our | Lorde and saui | our Iesus | Christ. | 1569, | Cum priuilegio," within a woodcut border. Page 1 (incorrectly numbered 2) to 127.

On page 74 is, "¶ The Cart Cosmographie

of the peregrination or iourney of Saint Paul, with the distaunce of the myles," and then, "the order of times," reprinted from the first edition of the previous year, 1568.

After the New Testament are six columns of table "to fynde the Epistles and Gospels read in the Churche of Englande," and then Richard Jugge's imprint, who does not seem to have had the right to print the Metrical Psalms, for they are printed by John Daye, Aldersgate, "cum privilegio regiae maiestatis per Decennium." They have the usual title page: "The whole booke of psalmes, collected into Englishe metre by Thom Sternh (*sic*), John Hopkins and others, conferred with the Ebrue, with apt Notes to sing them withall."

Metrical Psalms printed by John Daye.

This Bible is printed in black letter, with all the headings in Roman type, except the heading of page 89 of the New Testament, which is in Italic; the marginal references are also in black letter, but the notes are in Roman. It is an improvement on the first edition, for not only are many printer's errors corrected, but a thorough revision of that edition had been made, hundreds of passages having been altered. It is true that whole books, *e.g.*, the prophet Hosea, remained nearly unaltered, but many of the historical books are considerably revised; in one instance twenty alterations were made in one chapter.

The New Testament was revised to a less extent than the Old; generally the alteration consisted of the substitution of a different word in the text, while the reading of the first edition was preserved in the margin.

Headings of chapters shortened.

As the 1569 edition was in small quarto, it was necessary, to save space, to abridge the headings of the chapters. This apparently was done by the printer to suit his own convenience. For the same reason for which the headings were abbreviated, all the woodcuts so liberally used in 1568, were now omitted, though one would have thought they would be more appropriate for a Bible intended for family use and private study than in the large edition issued for use in the church. Perhaps it was thought the explanatory tables and maps were sufficient.

To give an idea of the Bishops' version of the Psalms, I will insert a short one, which the reader can compare with the same Psalm as given in the Authorised Version and in the Prayer Book:

Psalm xix., Bishops' version.

The argument of the xix Psalme.

¶ Gods glorie wherby he may be knowen, appeareth sufficiently in all his workes, in heaven, ayre, and earth; but especially to his chyldren in his holy worde, which therefore ought to be of more value and commendation then all other worldly thynges. Vpon consideration hereof, Dauid confesseth his secrete and presumptuous sinnes, he craueth pardon and mercie at gods handes.

COELI ENARRANT.

To the cheefe musition a Psalme of Dauid.

A The heauens declare the glorie of god: and the firmament sheweth his handie worke

"powreth out wordes
"discloseth

2. A day "occasioneth talke thereof vnto a day: and a nyght "teacheth knowledge vnto a nyght,

(a) rule or lyne
3. No language, no wordes, no voyce of
theyrs is hearde, yet theyr (a) sounde goeth into
all landes and theyr sayinges vnto the endes
of the worlde.
[illegible]
4. (In) In them he hath set a tabernacle
for the sunne, which commeth forth as a brydgrome
out of his chamber and rejoyceth as a
giaunt to run his course
5. His settyng foorth is from the vtmost
part of heauen, and his circuite vnto the vtmost
part thereof, and there is nothing hyd
from his heate.
(b) [illegible]
6. The law of God is perfect, conuerting
the soule: the testimony of God is (b) sure
and geueth wysdome vnto the simple.
B 7. The statutes of god are right, and reioyce
the heart: the commaundement of
God is pure, and geueth light vnto the eyes.
8. The feare of god is sincere and endureth
for euer, the iudgementes of god are trueth,
they be iuste at all poyntes.
9. They are more to be desired then golde
yea then muche fine golde, they are sweeter
then honye, and the honycombe
C 10 Moreouer, by them thy seruant is
well advertised: and in kepyng of them
there is a great (c) rewarde
(c) [illegible]
(d) [illegible]
11. Who can knowe his owne (d) errours?
Oh clense thou me from those that I am not
priuie of.
(e) [illegible]
12. Kepe Thy seruaunt also from (e) presumteous
(sinnes) let them not raigne ouer
me: so I shall be perfect and voyde from
all heynous offence.
13. Let the wordes of my mouth, and the
meditation of my heart be acceptable in thy
sight: O God my strength and my redeemer.

Some of the marginal notes in the first quarto edition of the Bishops' Version must have been

Marginal notes.

written for it, as they occur in no other Bible, but some are taken from the folio of 1568; for instance, the ninth verse of the 45th Psalm reads, "Kinges daughters are among thy honourable women: vpon thy ryght hande standeth the queene in a vesture of golde of Ophir." The note is, "Ophir is thought to be the Ilande in the vvest coast, of late founde by Christopher Columbo, from whence at this day is brought most fine golde."

The note to the word "Leviathan" in the 104th Psalm is, "A whale or a ballan, a beast that is King of the sea, for his greatnes and strength: he appeareth aboue the top of the sea as bigge as a Ilande, or a greate huge mountayne."

At the 5th verse of the 103rd Psalm it is said that "An Egle of all birdes liueth a long tyme without all kind of feeblenesse: dying neuer of age, but of famine. Plin. lib. 10. cap. 3."

The third edition of 1572, folio.

The third edition of the Bishops' Bible was issued in 1572, printed on better paper than the first edition of 1568, large folio size. It is commonly spoken of as the second folio Bishops' Version, or the "Leda" Bible.

As it very much resembles the first edition, to avoid repetition, I will mention only the points in which it differs from it.

First comes the title page, with copperplate engraving of Queen Elizabeth below the words, "The holi Bible conteynyng the Olde Testament and the Newe."

The almanac begins with 1572 and ends

with 1010. I will just say that the date at which the almanac in a Bible begins is no proof whatever of the date of the book: generally the almanac commences about three or four years before the book was issued: sometimes the almanac does not begin until one or two years after the issue of the book, but in the case of this Bible the two dates agree. The Calendar has the signs of the Zodiac in little circles on the inner margin. The description of the years is brought down to 1572. At the beginning of Genesis there is a woodcut, placed in a sort of frame composed of another woodcut.

Date in almanac not always date of issue.

There are thirty illustrations in this Bible, including portraits, maps, and titles, 113 less than appeared in the first folio. The first part is numbered from folio 1 to 112, the second part from 113 to 270. The map at the 21st chapter of Joshua is a copper engraving, with Lord Burleigh's arms, on detached paper. Before the Book of Ezra is "a very profitable declaration for the understanding of the histories of Esdras, Nehemias, and divers other places of Scripture."

The third part is numbered from folio 2 to 190, by mistake paged clxxxix. On the title is a portrait of Cecil, Lord Burleigh. This portrait differs in many respects from that in the first edition. There are two versions of the Psalter. On the right-hand column is the Bishops' translation in Roman type, on the left the Great Bible version in black letter. In the initial letter of Jeremiah is Lord Burleigh's coat of arms within the garter.

The fourth part is numbered from folio 2 to 105, and contains the Apocrypha. Prefixed to the first book of Maccabees is, "A necessary table for the knowledge of the state of Juda, from the beginning of the monarchy of the Greeks until the death and passion of Jesus Christe;" and at the end of the Apocrypha, "A table to make plain the difficultie . . . . because the difficultie is only in his posteritie."

The fifth part (the New Testament) is numbered from folio 2 to 138, two more leaves of Table of Epistles and Gospels, &c., unnumbered. There are woodcuts of SS. James and Peter before their epistles. The colophon, "Imprinted at London in Powles Churche-yarde, by Richard Jugge, Printer to the Queene's Majestie 1572. Cum privilegio Regiæ Majestatis," is on the recto of the last. The portraits of SS. Matthew, Mark, Luke, and John are not the same as appeared in 1568. The woodcuts to the Revelation are all brought together instead of being dispersed through the book.

"Leda" Bible.

The reason this book is sometimes called the "Leda" Bible is that several of the initial letters used in the New Testament contain woodcuts prepared to illustrate an edition of Ovid's Metamorphoses, and the initial at the Epistle to the Hebrews represents Jupiter appearing to Leda under the form of a swan. These incongruous figures were severely commented on at the time, and were never afterwards used.

It is remarkable that the great improvements made in the translation when the Bishops' Bible was revised in 1569, should have been so completely ignored in the issue of 1572; and that errors in the first edition of 1568 should be re-introduced, although they had been corrected in the preceding quarto.

Printer's error.

A strange printer's error is to be found in all copies of the Bishops' Bible which contain the Prayer-Book Psalms. The 29th verse of the 37th Psalm reads: "The righteous shall be punished; as for the seed of the ungodly, it shall be rooted out," instead of the "unrighteous shall be punished." It is only fair to say that this error occurs not only in the Bishops' version, but in every Prayer Book, either bound up with the Genevan Bible or published separately, down to the time of King Charles II., *i.e.*, 1661.

Fourth edition, 4to.

The next issue of Parker's version was the quarto of 1573. After the title page comes "The order how the rest of holy Scripture (besyde the Psalter) is appoynted to be read," 1 page. On verso begins "Proper Lessons," which fills 7 pages. "The booke of common prayer," &c., 48 unnumbered pages, sig. A to C 8. On first page of text is a woodcut of Adam. The initial I is surrounded by Archbishop Parker's arms and motto. The second title has a border, with royal arms at head and pelican at foot. The fourth and fifth titles have similar borders. Jugge's device at the end 4¼ inches long. The copy in the Lambeth collection is said to be a presentation one from Queen Elizabeth to Archbishop Parker: it is richly bound in five volumes, and illuminated by hand, in gold and colours. This edition has the letters A, B, C, &c., down the margins, in addition to verse numbers.

The quarto of 1573 has the long note on folio 2 anent the Garden of Eden.

Fifth edition, 1574, folio.

The Bishops' Bible, in folio, of 1574, is very interesting, from the fact of its containing a large map, printed from the same block as was used in the first English Bible of 1535.

Another point of interest the 1574 edition possesses is that it is the first Bishops' Bible with authorisation. On the title page may be seen the words, "Set foorth by aucthoritee," which was repeated on the folio and quarto published the following year (1575). It is not stated by what authority, but as we have no account of the Queen or Parliament having interfered in the matter, no doubt Episcopal authority is referred to, and as the Church is Divinely appointed the witness and keeper of Holy Writ, no other authority should be needed.

In my copy of the 1574, after the title page comes, "Proper lessons to be read for the first lessons both at Mornyng and Euenyng prayer, on the Sundayes throughout the yeere, and for some also the seconde lessons," 2 pages: "Proper Psalmes on certayne dayes;" "The order howe the rest of holy scripture besyde the Psalter, is appoynted to be read;" "¶ A briefe declaration when euery Tearme beginneth and endeth," 1 page: "An Almanacke," beginning 1572 and ending 1610, with this note at the end, "❡ Note, that the supputation of the yeere of our Lorde, in the Churche of Englande, beginneth the xxv. day of Marche, the same day supposed to be the first day vpon whiche the worlde was created, and the daye when Christe was conceiued in the wombe of the virgin Marie," 1 page: "To finde Easter for euer," "These to be obserued for holy dayes, and none other," 1 page: "A table for the order of the Psalmes, to be sayde at Mornyng and Euenyng prayer," 1 page: The Kalendar, 8 pages: "❡ A preface to the Byble folowing," by Archbishop Parker, with his arms in the initial O, and around it the motto, "*Concupiscentia eius mundus transit et*," concluding with a prayer, 5 pages: "A prologue or preface, made by Thomas Cranmer late Archbyshop of Canterburie," in Italic, ending with "❡ Prayse be to God," 5 pages: "A description of the yeeres from the creation of the worlde, vntyll this present yeere of 1574, drawen for the most part out of the holy scripture, with declaration of certayne places, wherin is certayne difference of the reckonyng of the yeeres," 1 page: Queen Elizabeth's prayer book of 1550, 16 pages: "The order of the bookes," 1 page; verso blank: "The first booke of Moses, called in Hebrewe, of the first worde of the booke, Bereschith, and in Greeke Genesis," folio 1 to 102. At the top of the page is a large woodcut representing Adam in the Garden of Eden, giving names to the various animals, and around it twelve pictures of events recorded in Genesis, concluding with the removal of the bones of Jacob.

On the title page to the second part of the Bible is an engraving filling about half the page, of the children of Israel passing into Canaan, and other events mentioned in the book of Joshua. Folio 2 to verso of 142.

The third part, from the Psalter to Malachi, has a rather smaller engraving of David sending Uriah to the battle, and Bathsheba placidly looking out of a window at them, folio 2 to verso of 156. The title to the Apocrypha has a woodcut of Judith and Holophernes in the centre, and several circumstances described in Esdras, Tobit, and the Maccabees around it.

The New Testament (folio 2 to 132) has a full-page title, similar to the first title. Before each of the Gospels is a large woodcut of the Evangelist by whom it was written, and at the end of S. John is a large map of the Holy Land, with a note, "The places specified in this mappe, with their situation by the obseruation of the degrees, concernyng their length and breadth."

The Revelation of S. John the Divine is faced by a page containing eighteen woodcuts. My copy has no colophon, nor is there any date on the New Testament title.

Sixth edition, 1575, folio.

The folio that succeeded the 1574 is a very inferior looking book, printed on worse paper, and with much worn type. Its size is 10½ in. by 7½ in. by 2½ in. It was produced as a trade speculation by a number of booksellers as cheaply as possible. On the title of my copy is, "The holy Byble, conteynyng the olde Testament and the newe" "Set foorth by auctoritie" "Searche the Scriptures, for in them ye thinke ye haue eternall lyfe: and they are they whiche testifie of me." S. John v. 39. "Imprinted at London by Iohn Harison." Other copies of the same book have the names of Richard Jugge, Richard Kele, John Walley, Lucas Harrison, John Judson, William Norton, Francis Coldock. There is a woodcut at the bottom of the title page representing a mermaid regarding herself in a hand looking-glass, and under it, "God saue the Queene." The date (1575) is at the top of the page. Collation as follows: Bishops' preface, 7 pages: Cranmer's prologue, 5 pages, in Roman type; all the rest of the book in black letter: "The summe of the whole Scripture," 2 pages: "The division of the books"—Legal, Historical, Sapiental, and Prophetical, 4 pages: "A discription of the yeeres from the creation of the worlde, vntil this present yeere 1575," 1½ page: "The order of the books," ½ a page.

Part 1, folio 1 to 102; second title, folio 2 to 151 verso; third title, folio 2 to 156 verso. On back of third title is, "A Prologue of S. Basill the great vpon the Psalmes." The Psalms of the Great Bible are inserted instead of those properly belonging to the book, and have the usual mistake in the 37th Psalm. Fourth title, The Apocrypha, folio 2 to 103 recto. Fifth title, "The New Testament," which in most old Bibles differs from other titles, in this edition is like the rest. It has the emblems of the four Evangelists in the corners of the cartouche. On verso of the New Testament title is, "A preface to the nevve Testament." The text, folio 2 to 135 verso.

On the last leaf is, "A Table to finde the Epistles and Gospels" for the Sundays, &c.

It was not an uncommon circumstance for several booksellers to share in the pecuniary responsibility of bringing out an edition of the Bible.

Seventh edition, 1575, 4to.

The only thing noteworthy about the quarto edition of 1575 is, that the initial letter of the first chapter of Genesis contains Archbishop Parker's arms, and the date 1570.

It has the letters A, B, C, &c. in the margins as well as verse numbers.

Eighth edition, 1576, 4to.

The edition of 1576 was the first quarto printed with verses numbered and without the A, B, C, &c. in margins. It has on title page, "Whereunto is adioined the whole service vsed in Church of England." "Set foorth by aucthoritie."

The New Testament title has the same border as the 1575, excepting the date and "Cum privilegio," &c. are in smaller type, and has no "¶" before it.

Ninth edition, 1577, 4to.

The quarto Bishops' Bible of 1577 has on its title the words, "Whereunto is adioined the whole service used in the Church of England." "Set foorth by auctoritie."

The size of the book is 9in. by 6in.; the seam line of the watermark goes across the page.

Like other Prayer Books the "order for Euenyng prayer throughout the yeere" begins with the Lord's Prayer; but prefixed to "An order for Mornyng Prayer dayly throughout the yeere" is a rubric directing the Sentences, Address, Confession, and Absolution, to be said at Evensong before the Lord's Prayer.

The first book of Moses is said to be "called in Hebrue Bereschith, and in Greeke Genesis;" then follows a half-page woodcut of Adam in the Garden of Eden. The note to the 14th verse of the 1st chapter informs us: "These lights were not made to serue astronomers phantasies, but for signes in natural thynges, and tokens of gods mercy or wrath."

On verso of folio 2 is a map of "God's garden," with the following note: "If there be any kingdome under heaun that is excellent in beautie, in abundance of fruites, in plenteousnesse, in delytes, and other gyftes; they vvhiche haue vvritten of countreyes, doo prayse above al, the same that this figure representeth, VVherefore with the prayses of those vvryters, Moses exalteth this paradise, as duely belongyng vnto it. And it is very vvel lyke, that the region or kingdome of Eden hath ben situated in that countrey, as it appeareth in the xxxvii Chapter of Esaias, the xii verse, and in the xxvii of Ezechiel, the xxiii verse. Moreouer, vvhereas Moses sayde, that a floodde dyd proceede from

Note on the Garden of Eden.

that place : I doo enterprete it, from the course of the waters ; as yshe shoulde have sayde, that Adam dyd inhabite in the flooddes side, or in the lande vvhich vvas vvatered on both sides. Howebeit, there is no great matter in that, eyther that Adam hath inhabited vnder the place where both flooddes came togeather towards Babylon and Seleucia, or aboue : It is sufficient that he hath ben in a place watered of waters. But the thyng is not darke nor harde to understande, howe this floodde hath ben diuided in foure heades. For they be two flooddes whiche be geathered in one, then they separate themselves in dyvers partes. So in theyr ioynying and flowing togeather, it is but a floodde, whereof there is two heades, into two chanels from aboue, and two towarde the sea, when it beginneth to separate it selfe abrode. But to declare vnto you the diversities of the ryvers names, besides theyr vsual and principal appellations, and howe they be called as they passe through eche prouince, with the interpretations of the same, I thynke it rather tedious and combersome, then profitable. Wherefore the simple sense of Moses is, that the garden whereof Adam was the owner, was watered with waters, because that the course of this floodde was there, whiche was divided into foure heades."

On folio 84 is another map of the "desertes of Arabia."

The first part is from folio 1 to 103 verso ; the second part from folio 106 to 252 verso. A note on page 252 states that "some write that when men purpose to take the Elephant, they make a hollowe place in the grounde where he vseth to haunt, and couereth the same with hay, or prouender, whiche so soone as the Elephant espieth, he runneth hastyly vnto it, and falleth into the pitte, and then the Hunter thrusteth him through the nose, because it is the tenderest part of hym."

The third part is paged from folio 254 to 411 verso. The "Bishops'" Psalms are omitted, and the Great Bible version inserted in their place.

The Apocrypha is paged from folio 414 to 501, a blank leaf and the Apocrypha title being counted 412 and 413. On page 592 is a large map of the Holy Land, with the "Table to make playne the difficultie," on the other side.

The New Testament has fresh signatures and fresh paging from folio 2 to 126 verso. On verso of page 17, "A Table for the better vnderstandyng of the xxvj. chapter of S. Matthewe, the xiiii of S. Marke, the xxij of S. Luke, and the xix of Saint Iohn." On verso of page 73 is a full-paged "Chart Cosmographie," printed from two blocks. Both sides of page 74 are filled with "The order of tymes." At the end of the New Testament is Jugge's mark, varied by the words "Cogita mori" placed above it, and followed by Jugge's imprint.

The Metrical Psalms at the end were "Printed by John Daye, dwelling ouer Aldersgate, An. 1577." This Bible is frequently referred to by

This edition critirised by Father Martin.

the clergy who were driven into exile on account of their religion, not only in the marginal notes to the New Testament, published at Rheims in the year 1582, but also in several controversial works printed about that time, notably, the book written by Father Martin, entitled, "Discovery of the manifold corruptions of the Holy Scriptures by the Heretics, &c." This was answered by Dr. Fulke in 1589, and in 1601 a second edition came out, "perused and enlarged by the Author's own hand, more amply than in the former edition."

Last Bible printed by Richard Jugge.

This Bible is also particularly interesting from its being the last Bible ever printed by Richard Jugge. This makes the words placed over his mark on the last page of the book so significant.

R. Jugge appears to have had a University education, and to have engaged in what was then called "the art of printing," as the best means of propagating his theological views, which were those of the dominant party of the day in which he lived, and we find that in the quarto New Testament of Tyndale's version, revised by or for him in 1552, and reprinted the following year, that the worst passages that could be culled from the writings of S. Austin are placed at the heads of the chapters. These notes were very popular, and in many editions of the Bishops' New Testament, published separately, they were substituted for the "Bishops'" notes.

Richard Jugge's shop was at the north door

of S. Paul's Churchyard, London, "the sign of the Bible," but his residence was in Newgate Market, next to Christ Church. He was one of the original members of the Stationers' Company, of which he was Warden in the years 1560, 1563, and 1566, and Worshipful Master in 1568, 1569, 1573, and 1574, the years in which he printed the principal editions of the Bishops' Bible—books that reflect the greatest credit upon him as a typographer.

On the 15th of Nov. 1558, he printed the proclamation of Queen Elizabeth's accession to the throne, and on the 24th March 1560, he in conjunction with Cawoode, Queen Mary's printer, obtained a patent by which they were appointed printers to Queen Elizabeth, with a salary of 6*l.* 13*s.* 4*d.* per annum.

J. Cawoode died 1st April 1572, after which privileged books were printed with Jugge's name only. After the death of Richard Jugge the business was carried on by his son John, who did not long survive his father; for in 1579 we find a book on Navigation "Imprinted at London, by Joan, the widowe of Richarde Jugge, late printer to the Queene's Maiestie, 1579. *Cum privilegio.*" John Cawoode.

This is the only edition of Parker's Bible ever printed in octavo size. It is an exceedingly rare book, only two or three copies are known to be in existence. Tenth edition, 1577, 8vo.

My copy is imperfect, as it wants the preliminary matter. The only woodcut it has is a large one on sig. A 1; the subject is, Adam in the Garden of Eden giving names to all creatures.

The type is minute black letter. The book is divided into five parts, but there are only two title pages.

Great Bible Psalter substituted for the "Bishops'."

The Great Bible Psalms are inserted in place of the "Bishops'." Instead of the usual heading, over each psalm is, in Italics, "Moneth the j day." "Mornyng prayer." The Latin titles are in small Roman type.

As usual, Solomon's songs are entitled, "The Ballet of Ballettes of Solomon, called in Latine, Canticum Canticorum."

The title of the next book is, "The booke of the preacher, otherwyse called Ecclesiastes, which is Solomon the king.

Explanation of King Solomon's titles.

"For Solomon is called in scripture by three sundry names. The one, Solomon, that is, the maker of peace. The seconde Idida, that is, beloued of God. The thyrde, Ecclesiastes, that is, a preacher, teachyng that true felicitie consisteth in a whole ioynyng our selues to God by pure religion."

The 1st verse of the 11th chapter of this book reads, "Lay thy bread vpon wet faces, and so shalt thou find it after many dayes." This rendering is not peculiar to this Bible.

The New Testament title has a peculiar border, in which are birds eating fruit. Below is the Tree of Life, and the words, "OMNE◆ BONV̄◆ SVPERNÆ."

At the end is the imprint, with Jugge's mark, filling three parts of the page. The space at the top being vacant shows the book must have been printed very early in 1577; for in that year the words "Cogita mori" were inserted in the space.

Eleventh edition, 1578, folio.

The next edition of the Bishops' Version that was issued, viz., the folio of 1578, is a much handsomer book than the 1575, but not equal as a specimen of typography to the editions of 1568 or 1572. It reads with the 1574 book. The collation is as follows: Copper plate title, "The holy Bible, conteynyng the Olde Testament and ye New. Set foorth by auctorite;" 1 blank page; "The summe of the whole Scripture," 4 pages; a preface, 7 pages; "A prologue by T. Cranmer, late Archbyshop of Canterburie," 4 pages; "A Description of the Yeeres from the Creation," 1 page; "The Order of the Bookes," 1 page; one blank page; "Proper Lessons," 2 pages; "Psalmes on Certayne Dayes," 1 page; "An Almanake," "To find Easter," 1 page; "A Table of the Order of the Psalmes," 1 page; "A Kalendar," 12 pages; a blank leaf; "Mattins and Euensong," 5 pages; "Letanie," 3 pages; Collects, 5 pages. Then the Bible interspersed with a number of tables, maps, woodcuts, &c.; and at the end, "A table to find the Epistles and Gospels," 3 pages.

From the year 1578 to the year 1584 no edition was printed that I am aware of, but long experience has taught one not to speak very positively of the non-existence of a Bible of any particular year. There is no doubt that many editions were printed of which no copy is known.

Twelfth edition, 1584, folio.

In 1584 two editions came out, one in folio and the other in quarto. On the title page of the folio are the words, "Of that translation authorised to be read in churches."

It has many more marginal notes than the edition of 1573. The alternative readings, which in the 1573 are printed in large black letter, are here in small Roman type.

The five parts are not paged separately; but the pagination is continuous from Genesis to Revelation, folio 1 to 560 recto.

Large engraving of the royal arms.

There is no title page to "Jehosua." At the end of Job is a woodcut of the royal arms, supported on one side by a dragon and on the other by a lion. The cut measures 4½ by 3½ inches. The next title is not the usual one to "The thirde part of the Bible conteynyng these bookes," but reads as follows: "The Psalter or Psalmes | of Dauid, after the transla | tion of the great | Bible, Appointed as it shall be sung or said in Churches. Anno Domini 1584." The woodcut border to the Psalter is different to the other title pages in the book.

The books in the Apocrypha are not named. The title reads, "The | volvme | of the bookes | called Apocry | pha | Anno Domini | 1584." |

The New Testament title is signed M m m iiii; verso blank. On the next page is a map of the Holy Land, at the foot of which is the following note:

Note to map of the Holy Land.

"Mount Oliuet is two mile from Jerusalem,

East by South. Gethsemani a village, lieth at the foote of the mount, betwixt the same and Ierusalem. Bethpage a village, lieth not farre from it. Also in the vale, betwixt the mount and Ierusalem, Golgotha, or the mount of Caluarie lieth, hard by Ierusalem, West and by North."

At the end of the Acts is a full page map of S. Paul's journeys, followed by two pages of "The order of times."

The woodcut of the royal arms is repeated at the end of Revelation; below it is Christopher Barker's imprint; verso blank.

At the end of my copy is the Metrical Psalter, printed by John Day, 1583.

Thirteenth edition, 1584, quarto.

There are no "parts" in the 1584 quarto. Deuteronomy ends and Joshua begins in the middle of folio 87 recto. It is without the map of Eden and long note, nor has it the map of Arabia, or the "Cart cosmographie." At the end is a colophon after folio 111 of the New Testament, and a leaf with the royal arms and Christopher Barker's imprint, filling the whole page; reverse blank.

The New Testament title has no printer's name, but merely the words, "Anno 1584."

Fourteenth edition, 1585, folio.

In my opinion, the most beautiful of all the editions of the Bishops' Bible is the folio of 1585. It measures 16½ in. by 11 in., and is a marvel of typography, equalled only by the glorious Vulgates printed by Koberger, Nürnberg.

The title page is printed in red and black.

On the upper part of the border is an engraving of a clasped quarto-shaped book, with the following words on the cover: "Verbum Dei manet in æterna," and at the bottom are two verses from Proverbs viii.:

> "All the wordes of my mouth are righteous
> there is no lewdnesse nor frowardnesse in them
> They are all plaine to him that will understand
> and straight to them that would finde knowledge."

In the centre, "The Holy Bible, conteining the Olde Testament and the Newe. Authorised and appointed to be read in Churches. Imprinted at London by Christopher Barker, Printer to the Queenes most excellent maiestie. Anno 1585. Cum gratia et priuilegio." Then comes Cranmer's prologue, 4 pages. On signature B begin 11 pages of tables, quite different to those of J[ohn] S[peed] (but really drawn up by Hugh Broughton), which may be found in the early editions of King James's Bible of 1611. They are headed, "This Table setteth out to the eye the Genealogie of Adam, so passing by the Patriarches, Judges, Kings, Prophetes, and Priestes, and the Fathers of their time, continuing in lineall discent to Christ our Sauiour." At the commencement is a circular woodcut of Adam and Eve, and from them Christ's line is traced in a most interesting and instructive manner. The world is divided into eight ages—

Genealogical Table and 8 ages.

> "The first age was from Adam to Noe,
> the second from Noe to Abraham,
> the thirde from Abraham to David,

the fourth from David to the transmigration of Babylon.

the fifth from thence to Christ,

the sixth from Christ to the end of the world.

the seventh may be added as of them that be in rest,

which may be accompted from Christ's passion

to the day of judgement.

the eyght age, as of them which shall rise againe, from the day of judgement for euer. And these ages be not so called for the distinct number of certaine thousande yeeres, but for certaine notable actes which were wrought in the beginning of euery one of them, for in the beginning of the first age the worlde was created,

"In the beginning of the second age the worlde was purged by the flood,

"In the beginning of the third, circumcision was giuen against originall sinne,

"In the beginning of the fourth, was the anoynting of the Kings of Israel,

"In the beginning of the fifth was the transmigration of God's people into Babylon.

"In the beginning of the sixth was the incarnation of the Sonne of God.

"In the beginning of the seuenth, were the gates of heauen opened,

"In the beginning of the eyght, shal be the resurrection of the bodies, and the rewarde of good and euill."

It is not positively known by whom this genealogical table was compiled, but it is attributed to the Archbishop.

Hugh Broughton.

Hugh Broughton, than whom a better Hebrew scholar modern times has never produced, except perhaps the saintly Dr. Pusey, found many faults in it: his words are, "The cockles of the Sea shores and the leaves of a Forest, and the granes of the Popy, may as well be numbered as the grosse errours of this Table, disgracing the ground of our own hope."

On verso of the last leaf is, "An Almanacke" from 1580 to 1611. On sig. ¶ i is a beautifully printed calendar, in red and black, of 12 pages. On sig. ¶ ¶ is, "The Division of the Books," 3 pages; and facing the text is a full-page engraving of Adam and Eve, one on each side the Tree of Knowledge, with fifty animals around them. Under the neck of Adam are the words, "In Christs death," and under that of Eve, "Throughe faithe," and in the tree and other places,

> "Created good and faire
> By breache of lawe a snare
> Desire to knowe hath wrovght ovr woe,
> By tastinge this thexile of blisse.
> By promis made restored we be
> To pleasvres of eternyte;"

and around the serpent,

> "Duste for to eate, mvst be my meate."

This edition is not divided into parts, as most Bishops' Bibles are, but the leaves are numbered consecutively, from 1 to 536 (the end of the Apocrypha). The New Testament is paged from 3 to 137. There are four title-pages. The first, that at the Psalter, and the New Testament title are from the same blocks, but the Apocrypha title is one Barker used in some of his folio Genevan Bibles. In this edition the Psalms are of the Bishops' translation, and not those of the Great Bible. On verso of the last leaf of the New Testament are the royal arms and Christopher Barker's imprint. On the New Testament title are the words, "Perused and diligently corrected," so often met with on early versions. They would have been more appropriate on the title-page of the second folio of 1572, or even the first quarto of 1569. This edition (1585) mainly follows that of 1572: there are no important changes.

I must pass over the next two editions, viz., the folios of 1588 and 1591, both of which correspond with the 1585, and have the same title.

The title of the folio of 1595 is, "The Holy Bible; conteyning the Old Testament and the New. All the wordes of my mouth are righteous, there is no frowardnesse nor falshoode in them. Seventeenth edition, folio.

"They are all plaine to such as wil understand, and right to them that find knowledge. Prov. viij. 8, 9. Imprinted at London by the deputies of Christopher Barker, Printer to the Queenes Maiestie. Anno 1595."

Cranmer's Prologue; "An Almanacke," from 1580 to 1611; "Of the Golden number, &c.;" "The Kalendar."

The text has the Great Bible Psalms only.

After the New Testament title come several tables, &c.

Eighteenth edition, 1602, folio.

The preliminary of the 1602 is the same as in the 1585, but printed on inferior paper, and with worn type,

It has only three title-pages, the Old Testament, the Apocrypha, and the New Testament, all of which are from the blocks used for the 1585, with the name of "R. Barker" substituted for "C. Barker."

The Psalms are the Great Bible translation.

The colophon is at the bottom of the last page of the New Testament; verso blank.

Reprint of the Eighteenth edition,

The 1602 edition was twice issued; the second time with a woodcut border like that of the New Testament title.

1602 edition, the basis of King James's Bible.

The 1602 edition was the basis of our present version, and does not differ more from the Bible of 1611 than it does from the first edition of the Bishops' Version. Improvements were introduced into one edition after another, so that it is not easy to give the exact date of any change. Many fresh readings that long have been credited to the revision published in 1602 may be found in earlier issues.

The Bishops' Bible never acknowledged by the Puritans.

Parker's Bible took the place of the Great Bible in the public services of the Church, but for private use it never displaced the Genevan; and we find that the Puritans, who held so many livings in the Church of England, often in defiance of all authority took their texts from the "Breeches" Bible, even though Convocation had directed the Bishops' Version to be used, and as early as 1571 had ordered that a folio copy should be placed in the hall, or dining room, of every Bishop, for the use of their servants or visitors, and also that each Church should be supplied with this version.

One of the changes made in the 1573 edition was the substitution of the word "charity" in place of "love," introduced by Tyndale.

Parker's [illegible] to the revisers.

The first rule laid down by Archbishop Parker for the revisers of the Bishops' Bible was, "To follow the common translation used in the Churches (*i.e.*, the Great Bible), and not to recede from it but where it varieth manifestly from the Hebrew or Greek original;" therefore few novelties were introduced: for example, at the end of the 8th chapter of Jeremiah, the Bishops follow the early versions in reading, "Is there no tryacle in Gilead, is there no phisition there?" The Douai has, "Is there no rosin in Galaad?" The word translated "tryacle," "triacle," or "balme," or "rosin," frequently occurs in the Bible. Although the A.V. has adopted "balm" in the text, it gives "rosin" in the margin, as the alternative reading, King James's translators being doubtful which word more exactly represented the original.

"Tryacle" Bibles.

In their preface to the readers, they say, "There be many wordes in the Scriptures which be neuer found there but once, (hauing neither brother nor neighbour, as the Hebrewes speake) so that we cannot be holpen by conference of places."

The quartos of 1573 and 1575 have "triacle," but the 1576, 1577, and 1584 have "tryacle."

In Acts xxi. 15, all editions of Parker's Bible follow the Great Bible in reading, "we took up our burdens."

Readings which differentiate versions.

Matthew's Bible has, "we made ourselves ready."

Wm. Whittingham, in 1557, translated the passage, "And after those dayes we trussed vp our fardeles and went vp to Ierusalem," a rendering copied by the Genevan translators.

The Douai rendering is, "being prepared."

Any of these translations are less likely to be misunderstood than that of King James's Bible; as certainly the first Bishops did not travel in carriages.

The last edition of the Bishops' Bible, viz., the folio of 1606, is exceedingly rare. I have never met with a copy in any library, and should doubt its ever having existed were it not for the fact that in the *Bibliotheca Sussesiana* (vol. ii., page 327), Dr. T. J. Pettigrew makes the following entry: "62. The Holy Bible. *R. Barker*, London. 1606. Folio. The Bishops' Bible. Last leaf wanting."

THE NEW TESTAMENT OF THE BISHOPS' VERSION.

The Bishops' New Testament.

The Bishops' translation of the New Testament was printed many times by itself.

Two editions were issued by Jugge in the year 1570, one in quarto, the other a very small size; and copies exist of quarto editions dated 1575 and 1576.

Bishops' Testament without verses.

A very interesting one came out, undated, in 1577, printed in long lines, and not divided into verses; black letter type.

Of this edition only two copies are known to exist; neither of them are perfect. One is in the Chetham Library, Hunts Court, Manchester, and the other is in the Lambeth Palace Library.

The size of the book is small octavo. It was printed by Richard Jugge, but the date has always been a puzzle to bibliographers. The late Francis Fry, of Cotham, Bristol, tried to solve the problem, but failed to do so. His opinion was that it was printed between the years 1568 and 1572.

In Mr. Fry's great work on Tyndale's New Testaments, in which he gives a description of this book with his characteristic accuracy, he states that the date of issue is unknown.

The key to the difficulty about the date is furnished by the colophon. R. Jugge's device or trade mark is well known—A pelican feeding her young, supported at the sides by two of the cardinal virtues, Prudence and Justice.

The inside of the oval has the motto, "Pro lege, rege, et grege," and the outside, in rather smaller letters, "Love kepyth the lawe, obeyeth the kynge, and is good to the commonwelthe." At the upper part of the oval is a small compartment left blank in the first edition of Parker's Bible of 1568, and all editions I have seen down to 1577. In that year Rd. Jugge inserted in this space the words "Cogita mori," no doubt having a premonition of his own death, which occurred the following year, the quarto Bishop's Version of 1577 being his last work.

"Cogita mori."

It is very remarkable that the problem as to the date of this book, which has puzzled so many eminent bibliographers, should have such a simple and plain solution.

The Chetham librarian assisted me to compare the summaries heading the chapters, the notes, and the prefaces to the Gospels, with Jugge's revision of Tyndale of 1552, and we found them to be almost exactly the same.

The book is labeled on the back, and catalogued as "Tyndale's New Testament."

All Souls', Oxford, Bishops' Testament.

Another Bishops' Testament printed in long lines, black letter type, and not divided into verses, resembling some of the issues of Tyndale, for which it has been mistaken, exists in several libraries.

A very early date has been assigned to this book, but as it has the words "Cogita mori" in the upper part of Jugge's mark, it cannot be earlier than 1577.

The title is, "The newe | Testament of our Sauiour Iesu Christe. Faythfully translated out of the | Greke, with the Notes and expositions of the darke | places therein.

Under Edward VI's likeness, in a frame, is, "Mat. 13.

The pearle which Christe commaunded to be bought,
Is here to be founde, not els to be sought."

At the end is, "Imprinted at London in | Powles Churchyarde by Richarde Iugge, | Printer to the Queenes | Maiestie.

"Forbidding all other men to print, or cause to be printed, this, or any other Testament in Englishe.

"¶ Cum priuilegio Regiæ Maiestatis."

Then R. Jugge's mark, with the words "Cogita mori" in the upper compartment.

"¶ A Preface into the newe Testament," 2 pages; "A Kalendar," 12 pages; "An Almanack for twenty-four yeares" (1561 to 1584), 1 page; "A Table of principall matters," 41 pages; "A true and perfect reckenyng," &c., 1 page; "An exhortation," 2 pages; Life of S. Matthew, by Eusebius Hieronimus Sophronius.

Then follows the text on A 1. As in all other editions of the Bishops' New Testament, after the Acts comes, "The order of tymes &c."

The text ends on T t 2. On the reverse begin, "¶ The Epistles of the olde Testament," 5 pages. The book concludes with "A Table to finde the Epistles and Gospels," and the colophon.

The text was taken from the second folio of Parker's Bible of 1572. The leaves are not numbered.

Various other editions.

A $16^{mo.}$ edition in ordinary type was printed in 1579, and another rather larger in 1581, by Christopher Barker.

The deputies of Christopher Barker printed a $12^{mo.}$ Bishops' New Testament in 1596.

Three editions were issued by Robert Barker; the last is dated 1617; and the following year (1618) a $12^{mo.}$ bears the imprint of the deputies and assignes of R. Barker.

All these editions are a revision of the text of the Bishops' New Testament made early in the year 1570, and that revision was taken as "copy" for all subsequent editions of the book.

Here and there words differ in spelling, and occasionally a printer's alteration may be met with, but practically all editions from 1570 to 1619 are alike.

Only two of them read together, therefore imperfect copies cannot be completed from other editions.

Most of them are printed from different fonts of type, and as the spacing varies, some editions are much thicker than others.

Edition of 1613.

The edition printed by Robert Barker in 1613 begins with the Great Bible version of the Psalms, in large black letter, filling 188 unnumbered pages; then a calendar of 12 pages; an almanac for 32 years (1603 to 1634); followed by the Bishops' Testament, word for word like the 1619 edition. After this comes the Metrical Psalter,—

"Set forth and allowed to be sung in all churches of al the people togither before and after Morning and Euening prayer, as also before & after sermons: and moreouer, in priuate houses, for their godly solace & comfort, laying apart al vngodly songs and Ballads, which tend only to the norishing of vice, and corrupting of youth.

Printed for the Company of Stationers. 1618.

The Testament from which the notes in this book were taken was the "Authorized Version" of 1552, having in it the King's licence and privilege, forbidding any other version to be printed. Jugge's version authorised.

This authority extends to the notes, which plainly show the religious bias of the dominant party at the close of Edward VI's reign, and their intense hostility to the Sacramental teaching of the Church of England, which ultimately culminated in their separation from the Church.

I have copies of five distinct editions, and a description of the last edition will apply to the rest. Last edition, 1619.

The size of the book is 5½ inches by 3½ inches.

The seam wires of the water mark go down the page.

The signatures are in eights, beginning on the first leaf of the text. The preliminary matter is numbered independently, but the title-page is not included. The signatures end on Nn4. The book is without pagination. There are sixteen pages of preliminary matter after the title, which reads as follows :—

Title of the last edition of the Bishops' New Testament.

"The New Testament of our Saviour Jesus Christ, faithfully translated out of the Greeke, with the Notes and Expositions of the darke places therein, Mat. 13.

"The Pearle which Christ commaunded to be bought,
Is here to be found, not else to be sought."

"¶ Imprinted at London, by Bonham Norton and John Bill, Printers to the King's most excellent Maiestie MDC. XIX."

At the corners of the title are woodcuts of the four Evangelists with their emblems (a man, a lion, an ox, and an eagle). Supporting the sides are two female figures, and at the bottom the royal arms and crown.

Then comes "A Preface vnto the New Testament," four pages, in Roman type. On sig. A 3 is, "The Pith or Contents of the New Testaments," in which the books are divided into—Legal, SS. Matthew, Mark, Luke, and John; Historical, The Acts of the Apostles; Sapiental, The Epistles; Prophetical, The Apocalypse, seven pages, in black letter. Then an address, "By the Booke of the New Testament, wee be taught also that Christ afore promised, etc.," two pages; "A true and perfect reckoning of the yeeres and times from Adam vnto Christ, gathered out of the holy Scriptures;" "An exhortation to the diligent studie of the holy Scriptures gathered out of the Bible." On the last page of the preliminary matter is. "¶ The order of the bookes of the New Testament with the proper names and number of chapters."

The text is a revision of the Bishops' Version. I have almost every edition except the 1600 in my collection of Bibles, and I find that the 1619 does not agree with any of them. The edition it comes nearest to is the folio of 1602; but in spite of all that has been said about the revision made in the 1602 edition, there are comparatively few alterations in it that cannot be found in the edition of 1572, or in some edition between that date and 1602. An examination of the Second Epistle to the Corinthians gives the following results:—

The 1619 reads with the quarto of 1569, and not with any subsequent edition, in chaps. i. 13; ii. 7; iii. 10; iv. 1; vi. 7, 14, 17; viii. 3; xii. 7; xiii. 5 (*bis*), 7; and also in putting verse 20 of chap. 1 in brackets, and omitting the brackets in verse 5 of chap. 2.

In the following places the 1619 does not agree with any version: chaps. i. 4, 23; iii. 3, 7, 11, 13; iv. 2, 3; v. 5, 7, 13, 18, 20; vi. 2; viii 2, 8, 11, 17; ix. 1, 4 (*bis*); x. 5, 12; xi. 12; xii. 4, 13, 16; xiii. 1, 12. None of the changes made are of any great importance.

There are notes at the end of most chapters. These notes are not taken from the Bishops' Version, nor from the Genevan or "Breeches" Bible, nor from any of the numerous editions of Matthew's Version, but from the quarto Jugge's Tyndale's New Testament, revised in 1552 by the persons who brought out the happily short-lived Book of Common Prayer known as "The Second Book of Edward VI."

The notes are very copious, in some cases nearly as long as the chapters to which they are appended: *e.g.*, S. Matthew ii. has 23 verses and 34 lines of notes; chapter iii. has 17 verses and 27 lines of notes; chapter ix. has 30 verses and 38 lines of notes. Towards the end of the book the notes are shorter. I give two or three specimens of these annotations.

The note to S. Timothy, chap. v. is: "S. Paul doth not here speake of the euerlasting damnation, but by this word damnation, doeth rather vnderstand the shame that those wanton widowes shall haue in the world for breaking their promise. Ambr. Eras.

"If this place be well vnderstood, it is able to ouerthrow all the Monkish vowes."

That vows were not binding, and that "promise ought not to be kept" were articles of Martin Luther's creed.

Notes to Revelation, chap. xviii.: "This chapter intreateth moost principallye againste the seconde regimente of Rome, that is the papisticall kingdome, which vnder the pretence of the name of Chryste, hath dealte so cruelly against all faythfull Christians, and the euangelicall Kyngdome of God."

Notes to Revelation, chap. xiii.: "Thys beast is the kingdome of Rome, the cat of the mountayne is the errours and blasphemos vices of the whole worlde gotten in battayl, the bears fete tiranny, the mouth of a lion is spoylfull and gredy to deuour: wouded by insurrections and ciuil warre, vntil dominion and gouernaunce came in one mans hand. This other beast yt cometh cvt of the earth, is the pompe of the romish bishops. He pretendeth to be a lambe. This is the second kingdom of Rome."

The note to Hebrews vi. 6 is:—

"This is Pauls meaning, They that doe beleeue truely and vnfainedly, do continue & abide stedfast in the knowen trueth. If any therefore fall away from Christ, it is a plaine token that they were dissembling hypocrites, and that they neuer beleeued truely: as Iudas, Simon Magus, Demas, Hymeneus, and Philetus were, which all fell away from the knowen verity, and made a mocke of Christ, which Paul doeth call here to crucifie Christ anew, because that they turning to their olde vomit againe, doe most blasphemously tread the benefites of Christs passion vnder their feete. They that are such can in no wise be renewed by repentance: for they are not of the number of the elect, as S. John doeth say, They went from vs, because they were not of vs, for if they had beene of vs, they would have remained with vs, vnto the end. If such men doe repent, their repentance is as Iudas and Cain's repentance was."

The note to St. Matthew ii. 12 is: "Promise ought not to be kept, where God's honour and the preaching of the trueth is hindered, the wise men, notwithstanding their promise made vnto Herode, returned home into their owne countrey, by another way."

This doctrine was so convenient that the note was adopted at Geneva by William Whittingham, afterwards Lay Dean of Durham, and the compilers of the "Breeches" Bible.

No doubt King Herod requested the Magi to bring him word when they had found the young Child, but there is no evidence that they promised to do so.

The very people who complained of the dictum that "faith should not be kept with heretics," were ready to insert in the New Testament itself that faith was not to be kept with anyone if "the preaching of the word" was hindered thereby.

S. Matthew xii. 3. *Note.*—"Charity, faith, and necessity may alwayes dispence with the Law." This also is exceedingly convenient.

S. Luke xix. 8 reads: "And Zachee stood forth, and said vnto the Lord, Behold Lord the halfe of my goods I giue to the poore, and if I haue taken from any man by forged cauillation I restore him fourefold." *Note.*—"We learne in Zaccheus what be the true fruites of repentance: He doeth not build vp Abbies, not yet Chantries, with his ill-gotten goods, but maketh restitution according to the law of God."

Considering that the building of religious houses had ceased a hundred years before the date of this New Testament, the introduction of such a note was unnecessary.

One of the shortest notes is at the end of Heb. i.: "Angels are ministering spirits, created for the elects sake, therefore they ought in no wise to be worshipped or prayed to."

Before each book is a prologue or argument: the one preceding St. Matthew's Gospel reads:

S. Jerome's Prologue.

"¶ The life of the blessed Euangelist S. Matthew, written and set foorth by that moost holy Doctor S. Hierome. Matthew, who also was called Leui, being of a Publican made an Apostle, did first in Iurie write the Gospel of Christ in the Hebrew tongue for their sakes which beleeued of the circumcision.

"It is vncertaine who afterwards did translate it into the Greeke tongue. Howbeit the copy of the Hebrew is kept vnto this day in the library of Cesarea, which library one Pamphilus Martyr did gather together most diligently. And the Nazarenes, which in Berea a city of Syria, did vse the same booke, gaue vs leaue to copie it out. Where yee shall note, that wheresoeuer the Euangelist either in his owne person, or in the person of our Lord Iesus Christ, doeth alledge the testimony of the olde Testament, he followeth not the authority of the seuenty Interpreters, but the authority of the Hebrew. Among the which these two testimonies are, I haue called my sonne out of Egypt, and, He shall be called a Nazarene."

The Rev. W. J. Loftie, in his excellent and most trustworthy book, *A Century of Bibles* (published by B. M. Pickering, Piccadilly, 1872), states that the quarto was the first Bible on which Norton and Bill's names are to be found; but with all respect to Mr. Loftie, I venture to claim for the Bishops' New Testament the position of being the first issue after the name of Robert Barker ceased to appear on the title page. The ground on which I make this claim is, that the date 1618 is on the colophon, and 1619 on the title, showing the book was printed the year before 1619, and the title-page only added that year. It is true that some copies of the octavo Authorised Version have 1618 on the colophon; but other copies have 1619 at the beginning and end, and so far as I am aware no copy of the Bishops' New Testament has the date 1619 at the end.

It would be interesting to know by what authority Norton and Bill, following the example of the Barkers, omitted the Bishops' notes, which properly belong to this book, and inserted in place of them notes taken from a Testament issued the last year but one of the reign of Edward VI. The change was certainly not a desirable one, for the Bishops' notes, if not very sound, are comparatively free from controversial points, and contain nothing opposed to the teaching of the Church, which cannot be said of the notes of Jugge's revision of Tyndale.

Following the Testament is a table of "The Epistles of the Old Testament according as they be now read" (*i.e.*, in the Church service), when certain chapters from the Old Testament are ordered to be read as Epistles in the Communion Office. The days on which these chapters are substituted for Epistles are Ash Wednesday (Joel ii. c), the Monday before Easter (Esay lxiii. a), the Tuesday before Easter (Esay l. b), the 25th Sunday after Trinity (Jere. xxiii. a), the Annunciation of S. Mary (Esay vii. to), S. John the Baptist's Day (Esay xl. a).

It might naturally be expected that as these chapters are at the end of a Bishops' New Testament, they would be taken from the Bishops Bible: but, singular to say, not one of them follows the rendering of any edition of the Bishops' Version. The next idea that presents itself is, that they are taken from the version that preceded the Bishops'—viz., the Great Bible, erroneously called Cranmer's Bible and the fact that to this day the Prayer-Book Psalms are taken from the November 1540 edition of the Great Bible strengthens this probability, but it is not the case. They are taken from the first authorised version, printed by Jacob van Meteren, Antwerp, in 1537, known as Matthew's Bible.

Epistles from Matthew's Bible of 1537.

They do not follow the text with absolute accuracy, but only four words are different. The greatest variation is in the portion read for the Epistle on the Monday before Easter (Esay lxiii. a):—

"What is hee this that commeth from Edom, with stained red clothes of Bosra, which is so costly cloth, and commeth in so mightily with all his strength? I am he that teacheth righteousnesse, and am of power to helpe. Wherefore then is thy clothing red, and thy raiment like his that treadeth in the Wine presse? I haue trodden the presse myselfe alone, and of all people there is not one with me. Thus will I tread downe mine enemies in my wrath, & set my feete vpon them in mine indignation, and their blood sprang vpon my clothes, and so haue I stained all my raiment. For the day of vengeance is assigned in mine heart, and the yeere of my deliuerance is come. I looked about mee, and there was no man to show me any helpe, I fell downe and no man held me vp. Then I held me by mine owne arme, and my ferventnesse sustained me. And thus haue I troden downe the people in my wrath, and bathed them in my displeasure, insomuch that I haue shed their blood vpon the earth."

The portion for S. John the Baptist's Day (Esay xl. *a*) begins: "Be of good cheare, my people, be of good cheare (saith your God)." Coverdale and Matthew are the same; but the 1535 reads very differently to the 1537 and 1619. A few lines further on the Great Bible has: "Comforte my people (O ye prophetes) comfort my people, sayth your God, comfort Jerusalem at the herte." The Bishops' agrees with the Great Bible. The Douai (1610) has: "Be comforted, be comforted my people, saith your God. Speake to the hart of Jerusalem and cal to her, because her malice is accomplished." The Genevan rendering is almost the same as that of our present version: "Comfort ye, comfort ye my people will your God say."

On the last two leaves of the book are Tables "to finde the Epistles and Gospels read in the Church of England, whereof the first line is the Epistle and the other the Gospel," and "The Epistles and Gospels for the Saints dayes." I have not yet made out from what Prayer Book they are taken. I have compared them with the Reformation Prayer Book of 1549 and the books of 1559 and 1604 without success.

"¶ A Table to finde the Epistles and Gospels read in the Church of England, whereof the first line is the Epistle, and the other the Gospel.

Portion of the table in the Bishops' New Testament of 1[illegible]

¶ First Sunday in Advent.

Owe nothing .	Rom. xiii. *b.*
When the . .	Matt xxi. *a.*

¶ Second Sunday.

Whatsoever . .	Rom. xv. *a.*
And there shall .	Luke xxi. *d.*

¶ Third Sunday.

Let a man . .	1 Cor. iiii. *a.*
When John . .	Mat. xi. *a.*

¶ Fourth Sunday.

Rejoyce in .	Phil. iiii. *a.*
And this is . .	John i. *c.*

¶ On Christmas Day.

God in times	Heb. i. *a*
In the beginning	John i. *a.*

¶ On S. Steuens Day.

But he being .	Acts vii. *h.*
Wherefore . .	Mat. xxiii. *c.*

¶ On St. John's Day.

That which . .	1 John i. *a.*
And when . .	John xxi. *c.*

¶ On Childermas Day.

And I looked .	Apoc. xiiii. *a.*
Behold the angel	Mat. ii. *b.*

¶ Sunday after Christmas.

And I say . .	Gal. iiii. *a.*
The booke of .	Mat. i. *a.*

¶ On New yeeres Day.

Blessed is that .	Rom. iiii. *b.*
And it fortuned	Luc. ii. *c.*

¶ On twelfth day.

For this . . .	Eph. iii. *a.*
When Jesus . .	Mat. ii. *a.*

¶ First Sunday after twelfth day.

I beseech you .	Rom xii. *a.*
And his father .	Luc. ii. *g.*"

It is most remarkable that so late as the year 1619, chapters from Matthew's Bible of 1537 should be printed, and stated "to be now read" at the Sacrament of the Altar, and still more strange that this book should never have been before noticed by any writer on the subject.

The Rheims and Douai Version.

THE RHEIMS NEW TESTAMENT.

THE New Testament was translated into English from the Vulgate, at the English Roman Catholic College at Rheims, in 1582, by Gregory Martin, Fellow of S. John's College, Oxford, assisted by other men of eminent learning.

Roman Catholic New Testament of 1582.

One of the translators was William Allen, the founder of the College. He was born in Lancashire in 1532; entered Oxford at the age of 15; was elected Fellow of Oriel in 1550; became Principal of S. Mary's Hall, and Canon of York; was afterwards consecrated Archbishop of Mechlin; and in 1578 was made Cardinal by Pope Sixtus V.

Cardinal Allen.

Early in 1561 he went to Louvain to study theology.

He resided in England from 1562 to 1565, in which year he finally quitted his native land, and opened the College of Douai on Michaelmas day, 1568.

The success of the Prince of Orange led to the expulsion of the students from Douai in 1578, and they took refuge in Rheims, where they remained until the year 1593, when they returned to Douai.

Many copies confiscated.

This translation and the annotations attached to this version excited great opposition; many copies were seized by Queen Elizabeth's searchers and confiscated. If a priest was found with a copy in his possession, he was at once imprisoned.

Clergy tortured on the rack.

Cecil, Lord Burleigh, in a black letter tract of 39 pages, the second edition of which was printed in London, January 1583, entitled, "The Execution of Justice in England, for maintenaunce of publique and Christian peace, against certeine stirrers of sedition, and adherents to the traytors and enemies of the Realme, without any Persecution of them for questions of Religion, as it is falsely reported and published by the faurors and fosterers of their treasons;" and in another, entitled, "A declaration of the favourable dealing of Her Majesty's Commissioners," denies that the rack was used unmercifully. Speaking of a certain priest, he says, "he was charitably used, and never so racked but that he was presently able to walke," and "that the warders whose office it is to handle the racke, were charged to use it in as charitable maner as such a thing might be."

So that there is no doubt that torture was applied to those who circulated this translation of the Testament, and inflicted by those who most zealously advocated the unlimited right of private judgment.

Thomas Cartwright, Divinity reader at Trinity College, Cambridge, was requested by Sir Francis Walsingham, Secretary of State, to refute it, but after some progress had been made, Archbishop Whitgift prohibited his proceeding further, judging a Puritan an unsuitable person to defend the doctrine of the Church of England.

The Archbishop appointed Dr. Fulke, Master of Pembroke Hall, Cambridge, in Cartwright's place.

Fulke's Refutation.

Fulke's Refutation was printed at London by the deputies of Christopher Barker, 1589, folio. It has the Bishops' New Testament and the Rhemish in parallel columns, and has the annotations and refutations after each chapter.

Title of Fulke's Refutation.

The title is, "The text of the New Testament of Jesus Christ, translated out of the vulgar Latine by the papists of the Traiterous Seminarie at Rhemes, with arguments of books, chapters and annotations, pretending to discover the corruptions of divers translations, and to cleare the controversies of these dayes.

"Thereunto is added the translation out of the original Greeke, commonly used in the Church of England, with a confutation of all such arguments, glosses, and annotations, as containe manifest impietie, of heresie, treason and slander against the Catholike Church of God, and the true teachers thereof, or the translations used in the Church of England; both by auctoritie of the Holy Scriptures, and by the testimonie of the ancient fathers."

Four editions of Fulke's Refutation.

An enlarged edition of this book was printed by Robert Barker in 1601; a third edition for Thomas Adams, London, in 1617; and a fourth folio, by Augustine Matthews, London, in 1633.

Title of Rhemish Testament of 1582.

The title of the Rhemish New Testament is, "The | Nevv Testament | of Jesvs Christ, trans | lated faithfvlly into English, | out of the authentical Latin, according to the best cor | rected copies of the same, diligently conferred vvith | the Greeke and other editions in diuers languages: VVith | Argvments of bookes and chapters, Annota | tions, and other necessarie helpes, for the better vnder | standing of the text, and specially for the discouerie of the | Corrvptions of diuers late translations, and for | cleering the Controuersies in Religion, of these daies: | In the English College of Rhemes. |

Psal. 118.

Da mihi intellectum, & scrutabor legem tuam & custodiam | illam in toto corde meo.

That is,

Giue me vnderstanding and I vvill searche thy lavve, and | vvill keepe it vvith my vvhole hart. |

S. Aug. tract. 2. in Epist Ioan. | Omnia quæ leguntur in Scripturis sanctis, ad instructionem & salutem nostram intentè oportet | audire: maxime tamen memoriæ commendanda sunt quæ aduersus Hæreticos valent plu | rimùm: quorum insidiæ, infirmiores quosque & negligentiores circumuenire non cessant. | That is, | Al things that are readde in holy Scriptures, vve must heare vvith great attention, to our instruction and saluation: but those things specially must be commended to me | morie which make most against Heretikes: vvhose deceites cease not to cir cumuent and beguile al the vveaker sort and the more neligent persons. Printed at Rhemes, | by Iohn Fogny. | 1582. Cvm privilegio."

Collation of the Rheims Testament.

On reverse of title is, "The censvre and approbation," Signed, "Petrus Remigivs," "Hvbertvs Morvs," "Ioannes le Besgve," "Gvlielmvs Balbvs;"

"The Preface to the Reader treating of these three points: of the translation of Holy Scriptvres into the vulgar tongues, and namely into English: of the causes vvhy this nevv Testament is translated according to the auncient vulgar Latin text: & of the maner of translating the same." 22 pages;

"The signification or meaning of the Nvmbers and Markes vsed in this Nevv Testament," 1 page;

"The bookes of the nevv Testament, according to the counte of the Catholike Churche," 3 pages;

"The svmme of the New Testament," 1½ page;

"The argument of S. Matthewes Gospel," ½ page;

The text, page 3 to 745;

"A table of the Epistles and Gospels, after the Romane vse, vpon Svndaies, Holidaies, and other principal daies of the yere, for such as are desirous to knovv and reade them according to this translation. And therfore the Epistles taken out of the old Testament are omitted, till the edition thereof," 4 pages;

"An Ample and particvlar table directing the reader to al Catholike truthes, deduced out of the holy Scriptures, and impugned by the Aduersaries;"

"The explication of certaine vvordes in this translation, not familiar to the vulgar reader, vvhich might not conueniently be vttered other-vvise;" errata, altogether, 27 pages.

In the preface the translators say that the Scriptures have been translated into the vulgar tongue of divers nations from the time of S. Chrysostom and S. Jerome, and that at the provincial Council holden at Oxford, by Thomas Arundel, Archbishop of Canterbury, versions approved and allowed by the Diocesan were not forbidden to be read.

Reason why translated from the Vulgate.

The following reasons are given why this Testament was translated from the Vulgate:

1. Because the Vulgate is the most ancient.

2. It was corrected by S. Jerome.

3. It was commended by S. Augustine.

4. It was used and expounded by the Fathers.

5. It was declared authentic by the Council of Trent.

6. It is the most grave and majestic of all versions.

7. It is exact and precise according to the oldest Greek.

8. That even Beza preferred it to all the rest.

9. That all other translations are acknowledged to be imperfect.

10. That it is purer than the modern Greek text, which has been corrupted, and Beza bears testimony that the Vulgate was taken from more ancient and purer Greek copies than were known to be extant in his day.

11. The Vulgate agrees with the earliest quotations from Holy Scriptures in the writings of the primitive Fathers.

The translators then defend the use of certain words not then in ordinary use; for instance the word "Amen" at the beginning of a solemn sentence, they say that, - "Verily, verily, doth not expresse the asseueration and assurance signified by this Hebrue word, besides that it is the solemne and vsual word of our Saviour to expresse a vehement asseueration, and therefore is not changed, neither in the Syriake nor Greeke, nor vulgar Latin Testament, but is preserued and vsed of the Euangelistes and Apostles themselues euen as Christ spake it."

They also prefer to keep "Hosanna," "Alleluia," "pascha," "neophite," &c., and justify themselves by showing that while in English Bibles words like "Pentecost," "raca," "phylacteries," and other words are left untranslated, they cannot be blamed. Untranslatable words.

They say that the full signification of many words is lost by translation; for example, that to "evangelize" means more than the English translation, "to bring good tidings."

They conclude by admitting that they sometimes take a word that is in the Latin margin, instead of that in the text, when it agrees better with quotations in the Fathers and the best Greek MSS.

Second edition, 1600, quarto.

The title of the second edition is as follows: "The | Nevv Testament | of Iesus Christ faith- | fvlly translated into English, | out of the authentical Latin, diligently conferred with the | Greeke, and other Editions in diuers languages: VVith Ar | gvments of bookes and chapters: Annotations, | and other helpes, for the better vnderstanding of the text, | and specially for the discouerie of Corrvptions in di | uers late translations: and for cleering Controver | sies in Religion of these daies: By the English | College then Resident in Rhemes. | Set Forth the second time, by the same College novv | returned to Dovvay. VVith addition to one nevv Table of Heretical Cor | rvptions, and other Tables and Annotations somevvhat augmented. |

Search the Scriptures, *Ioan* 5.

Giue me vnderstanding, and I wil search thy Law: and | wil kepe it with my whole hart. *Psalm* 118, *v.* 34. |

S. Augustin, Tract 2, in Epist. Ioan.

Al things that are readde in holie Scriptures &c.

Printed at Antvverp
by Daniel Vervliet
1600.
VVith Privilege."

On the reverse is the "Approbation" of both editions; that of the second is dated, "Duaci, 2 Nouemb. 1590," and signed "Gvilielmvs Estivs," "Bartholomævs Petrvs," "Ivdocvs Heylens"; Collation of second edition.

"The Preface to the Reader treating of these three points," &c., 22 pages;

"A Table of cer | taine places of the Nevv Testament corrvptly translated in favovr of heresies of these daies in the English Editions: especially of the yeares 1562 77. 79. and 80 by order of the Bookes, Chapters, | and Verses of the same.

"VVherein vve do not charge our Aduersaries for disagreeing from the authentical Latin text (vvherof much is saide in the Preface) but for corrupting the Greeke it selfe, vvhich they pretende to translate."

Concluding, "The blessed Confessour, Bishop Tonstal noted no lesse than two thousand corruptions in Tindals translation, in the Nevv Testament only. VVherby, as by these fevv here cited for examples, the indifferent reader may see, hovv vntruly the English Bibles are commended to the people, for the pure vvord of God," 5½ pages; Bishop Tunstal.

"The explication of certaine vvordes in this translation, not familiar to the vulgar reader, vvhich might not conueniently be vttered othervvise," 1½ page;

"The bookes of the Nevv Testament, according to the counte of the Catholike Church;"

Followed by 2½ pages of quotations from

"S. Augstin" (*sic*), "Turtellian," "S. Hierom," "Vincentius Lirinensis," and "S. Basil," in five divisions :—

"1. The infallible authoritie and excellencie of the Scriptures, aboue all other writings.

"2. The discerning of Canonical from not Canonical, and of their infallible truth, and sense, commeth unto vs, only by the credite we give vnto the Catholike Chvrch : through whose commendation we belieue both the Gospel and Christ himself, whereas the Sectaries measure the matter by their fantasies and opinions.

"3. No heretics haue right to the Scriptures, but are vsurpers : the Catholike Church, being the true owner, and faithful keeper of them. Heretics abuse them, corrupt them, and vtterly seeke to abolish them, though they pretend to the contrarie.

"4. Yet do they vaunt themselves of Scripture exceedingly, but they are neuer the more to be trusted for that.

"5. The cause why, the Scriptures being perfit, yet we use other Ecclesiastical writings and traditions," 3 pages ;

"The summe of the | Nevv Testament," and "The Argument of S. Matthewes Gospel," 2 pages ;

The text, from page 3, sig. A ij, to page 744, sig. A a a a iiij verso ;

"A Table of the Epistles and Gospels," 4½ pages ;

"An ample and particular table, &c.," concluding, "The faultes escaped in printing, vve trust the gentle reader vvil of his curtisie easily amend and pardon. Lavs Deo." 33 pages.

Quotations from the Old Testament in Italics.

This edition is well printed in good Roman type, but with all quotations from the Old Testament in Italic letters, which shows clearly how much more of the Old Testament is contained in the New than we imagine.

Not divided into verses.

The text is not broken up into verses, but the verse numbers are placed on the inner margin, within a black line, outside of which are references to parallel passages.

The notes are on the opposite margin; for instance, S. Matthew, chap. xvij. v. 27, reads, "Iesvs said to him, then the children are free.† But that we may not scandalize them, goe thy waies to the sea, and cast a hooke: and that fish which shal first come vp, take: and when thou hast opened his mouth, thou shalt find a :: stater: take that, and giue it them for me and thee."

Rheims notes.

The note is, ":: This stater vvas a double didrachme, and therfore vvas payed for tvvo."

The annotation at the end of the chapter is, "A great mysterie in that he payed not only for him self, but for Peter bearing the Person of the Church, and in vvhom as the cheefe, the rest, vvere conteyned. Aug. q. ex no Test. q. 75 to 4."

At the end of the Acts of the Apostles is a table of the life of S. Peter, and another of S. Paul, with short notices of the other Apostles, ending with, "Before they departed one from an other al Twelue assembling together, and ſul of the Holy Ghost, eche laying downe his sentence, agreed vpon twelue principal Articles of the Christian ſaith, and appointed them for a rule to al beleeuers: VVhich is therfore called and is THE APOSTLES CREDE: *Not written in paper, as the Scripture, but from the Apostles deliuered by tradition.* VVhich, as of old, so at this day al solemnely professe in their Baptisme, either by them selves or by others: and al that be of age and capacitie, are bound to know and beleeue euerie article of the same. VVhich are these that followv:

Apostles' creed.

THE APOSTLES CREDE
or
Symbolvm Apostolorvm.

1. I beleeue in God the Father almightie, creator of heauen and earth
2. And in Iesvs Christ, his only Sonne, our Lord.
3. VVho was conceiued by the Holy Ghost, borne of the Virgin Marie.
4. Suffered vnder Pontius Pilate, was crucified, dead, and buried: Descended into hel.
5. The third day he rose againe from death.
6. Ascended into heauen: sitteth at the right hand of God the Father almightie.
7. From thence he shal come to iudge the quicke and the dead.
8. I beleeue in the Holy Ghost.
9. The holy Catholike Church: the communion of saincts.

10. Remission of sinnes.
11. Resurrection of the flesh.
12. Life euerlasting. Amen."

Then on page 377, "The Argvment of the Epistles in general," 2½ pages.

"The time vvhen the Epistle to the Romanes vvas vvritten, and the Argument therof;" in which it is said that the first Epistle written by S. Paul was to the Galatians. "So then, the Epistle to the Romanes was not the first that he wrote. But yet it is, and alwaies was set first, because of the primacie of that Church," &c.

Why the Epistle to the Romans placed first.

The translation of the Rheims Testament differs from all others on almost every page; for instance, in Hebrews xii. 18 Tyndale has, "For ye are not come vnto the mounte that can be touched, and vnto burnynge fyre, nor yet to myst and darknes, and tempest of wedder:" Coverdale, Matthew, Taverner, the Great, and the Bishops' Bible all read nearly the same; but this version has, "For you are not come to a palpable mount."

Difference in translations.

A very considerable number of the Rhemish renderings, which they introduced for the first time, were adopted by the revisers of King James's Bible of 1611, and still more by the revisers of the 1881 version.

The third edition of this version was issued in 12^{m} by James Seldenflach, Antwerp, 1621. The "Approbation" on reverse of title is dated "Antwerp, die 10 Aprilis, 1620," and is signed,

Third edition of the Rhemish New Testament.

"L. Beyerlink, Archipresbyter." After the title is a preface of 21 pages.

"The signification or meaning of the nvmbers and marke vsed in this Nevv Testament;" "The favltes in this text correct thvs," with a list of 21 printer's errors, 1 page.

The text is an accurate reprint of the previous quarto edition, without note or comment. The Apocalypse ends on page 285.

The annotations are placed at the end and occupy 349 pages.

The book concludes with, "A table for the controversies of these times;" "Places to proue that the Church hath alwayes visible pastors, &c.;" "The necessity of Baptisme."

On verso of last leaf is, "The favltes in the annotations correct thvs," and a list of 15 errors.

Fourth edition, quarto.

The fourth edition has two title-pages: the first an elaborate engraving of an entrance to a temple. The words in the centre are, "The New Testament of Jesus Christ." On one side is the figure of a man, and on the other of a woman. On the upper part is a crucifix. At the foot of the woman is the word "Ecclesia," and from her mouth proceed the words, "Absit mihi gloriari nisi in cruce." At the foot of the man, who is habited as a Jewish High Priest, is the word "Synagoga."

In an ornamental panel below are the words, "Printed By Iohn Cousturier, MDCXXXIII."

Title page of Cousturier's Testament.

The letterpress title is the same as the previous quarto, excepting that this is said to be, "The fourth Edition, enriched with Pictures."

Engravings.

My copy has seven full-page engravings :—

S. Matthew, with a winged man, and below,

"Divo Hominis facies Matthæo adstare videtur
Qui Christum verè natum hominum esse docet."

S. Mark, with a lion,

"Forma Leonis Marco : instar namq leonis,
Rugit et exclamat : sit via plana Dei."

S. Luke, with an ox,

"Effigies Vituli, Lvca, tibi conuenit : exstat
Zachariæ in scriptis mentio prima tuis."

S. John, with an eagle,

"Sanctus Ioannes, Aquilæ instar, celsa reuelat
Altinolans, Verbum prædicat esse Deum."

(All the four signed "Picquet, f.")

The day of Pentecost (no engraver's name),

"In nouissimis diebus Dominus, effundam de spū meo super oēm̄ carnem, et prophetabunt filii uestri, et filiæ uestræ."

S. Peter, with sword (Michel van Lochom, fecit),

"In medio Ecclesiæ aperuit os eius, et impeuit eum Dominus Spiritū : sapientiæ et intellectus."

S. John in Patmos (Michel van Lochom, f.),

"Ecce puer meus electus quem elegi posui super eum spiritum meum."

List of new words introduced.

At the end of the book is, "The explication of certaine words, &c." Many of these words have been incorporated into our language, and are now familiar to every one :

"Abstracted — *i.e.* drawen away.
Advent — the comming.
Adulterating — corrupting.
Allegorie — a mystical speech.
Amen.

Anathema.	
Assist.	
Assumption	Christ's departure out of this world.
Cathechize.	
Catechumens.	
Condigne.	
Co-operate	working with others.
Co-operation.	
Euangelize.	
Gratis	for nothing, freely.
Neophyte.	
Sacrament	mysterie.
Sancta Sanctorum	Holie of Holies.
Tetrarch	Gouernour of the fourth part of a countrie."

Mary, Queen of Scots, not allowed to take an oath on this Testament.

The hatred of this version of the New Testament by the dominant party of the day was so bitter that an oath sworn on it was not deemed valid. A touching incident in the life of the unfortunate Mary, Queen of Scots, about five years after the first edition was published, shows this. When Mary offered to pledge her word upon it that she had not conspired against the life of Queen Elizabeth, the Earl of Kent exclaimed, "The book is a popish Testament and of course an oath on it is of no value." "It is a Catholic Testament," rejoined the Queen, "and on that account I prize it the more, and therefore according to your own reasoning you ought to judge my oath the more satisfactory."

THE DOUAI OLD TESTAMENT.

THE title is, "The | Holie Bible | Faithfully trans lated into English | ovt of the avthentical Latin. | Diligently conferred with the Hebrew, Greeke, | and other Editions in diuers languages. With Argvments of the Bookes, and Chapters: | Annotations, Tables: and other helpes, | for better vnderstanding of the text: for discouerie of | corrvptions in some late translations: and | for clearing Controversies in Religion. | The Douai Bible, 1609-10, quarto.

By the English College of Doway.

Haurietis aquas gaudio de fontibus Saluatoris. Isaiæ 12.

You shal draw waters in ioy out of the Sauiours fountaines.

Printed at Doway by Lavrence Kellam, at the signe of the holi Lambe.

M.DC.IX."

On verso is "Approbatio;" dated "Duaci 8 Nouembris, 1609." Signed, "Gvilielmvs Estivs," "Bartholomævs Petrvs," "Georgivs Colvenerivs."

On sig. †2 is an address, "To the right vvelbeloved English reader, grace and glorie in Iesvs Christ everlasting."

First is an explanation of the cause of delay in setting forth this English Bible, viz.: "Our poore estate in banishment." "VVherfore we | Address to English readers.

nothing doubt, but you our dearest, for whom we haue dedicated our liues, wil both pardon the long delay, which we could not wel preuent, and accept now this fruict of our laboures, with like good affection, as we acknowledge them due, and offer the same vnto you."

"Now since Luther, and his folowers haue pretended, that the Catholique Romane faith and doctrine, should be contrarie to Gods written word, and that the Scriptures were not suffered in vulgar languages, lest the people should see the truth, and withal these new maisters corruptly turning the Scriptures into diuers tongues, as might best serue their owne opinions, against this false suggestion, and practise, Catholique Pastores haue, for one especial remedie, set forth true and sincere Translations in most languages of the Latin Church."

No early codex known at that time.

If it is asked, "VVhy we translate the Latin text, rather then the Hebrew, or Greke, which Protestantes preferre, as the fountaine tongues, wherin holie Scriptures were first written? To this we answer, that if in dede those first pure Editions were now extant, or if such as be extant were more pure then the Latin, we would also preferre such fountaines before the riuers, in whatsoeuer they should be found to disagree."

Care taken to correct errors.

They say the MSS. now existing are not as free from error as those used by S. Jerome were, and that while the Latin copies have remained more pure than any other, yet even they in long process of time have differed in words, and some also in sense, by the mistakes of their writers; therefore they have corrected the Latin Text, by restoring to the text words omitted by scribes, or placed in the margin; this they have done solely "for the more secure conseruation of the true text."

They then explain why some words are not translated into English.

Early English Bibles compared.

Next they compare the translation of English Bibles printed in 1552 and 1557 with the Bibles of 1579 and 1603, and show the earlier editions to be more correct than the latter.

In another place they point out the 1552 (N. Hylls quarto Great Bible) and the 1577 (Bishops' quarto) translate *Theraphim*, "images," which the 1603 (Genevan quarto) changes to "idols."

Dedication to the public.

They then dedicate this Bible to all English speaking people in these words, "VVith this then we wil conclude most deare (we speake to you al, that vnderstand our tongue, whether you be of contrarie opinions in faith, or of mundane feare participate with an other Congregation; or professe with vs the same Catholique Religion) to you al we present this worke: dayly beseaching God Almightie, the Diuine VVisedom, Eternal Goodnes, to create, illuminate, and replenish your spirites, with his Grace, that you may attaine eternal Glory, euery one in his measure, in those manie Mansions, prepared and promised by our Sauiour in his Father's house. Not only to those which first receiued, and folowed his Diuine doctrine, but to al that should afterwardes beleue in him, and kepe the same preceptes. For there is one God, one also Mediatour of God and men: Man Christ Iesus. VVho gaue himself a Redemption for al. VVherby appeareth his wil, that al should be saued."

"From the English College in Doway, the Octaues of al Sainctes, 1609."

This address fills 12 pages, "The Svmme and partition of the Holie Bible. With a brife note of the Canonical and Apochryphal Bookes."

The Bible contains all things necessary to be believed.

"By the vniform consent of al learned Diuines, the holi Bible, or written word of God, conteyneth expressed or implied, al thinges that man is to beleue, to obserue, and to auoide, for obtayning of eternal saluation. That is, al matters of faith and maners, by which we may know and serue God, and so be spiritually ioined with him in this life, and in eternitie."

The marginal notes are, "How the holie Scriptures conteine al knowlege necessarie to saluation. The Old and new Testament show the same God, Christ, Church, and other Mysteries of Religion."

"The old more obscurely, with lesse helpes, the new more expresly and yeldeth more grace."

Division of the Books.

"In both Testaments there are foure sortes of Bookes — Legal — Historical — Sapiential — Prophetical."

A list is then given of the Canonical Books.

Apocryphical Books are divided into two classes: First, Books not declared Canonical, such as the Prayer of Manasses, the Third Book of Esdras, and the Third Book of Maccabees; the second class are rejected as erroneous.

"The svmme of the old Testament, as it is distinguished from the new."

The marginal summary is, "The old Testament conteyneth figures of the new."

"A continual visible Church from the beginning of the world to Christ, the same Mystical bodie, but different in state." "Diuided into six ages,—

The first continued 1656 yeares.

The second 368 or 398.

The third about 430.

The fourth 480.

The fifth 430.

The sixth nere 640."

Six ages of the world.

"Of Moyses the Avthor of the fiue first bookes."

"The argvment of the Booke of Genesis" finishes the preliminary matter, 18 pages in all.

The text is in Roman type, not divided into verses, but numbered down the inner margins.

The first tome concludes with the Book of Job, sig. Ttttt 5, page 1114.

On the last leaf (1115) is the following address, "To the cvrteovs reader. We haue already found some faultes escaped in printing, but fearing there be more, and the whole

Address to the reader.

volume being ouerlong, to be examined agayne, we pray the curteous reader to pardon al, and amend them as they occure.

"Two tables, one of the times of the old Testament: an other of the principal matters in the Annotations therof, shal folow (God willing) with the other Tome: which we desire and hope to send you shortly. In the mean time the gentle reader may please to supplie the want therof, as he may by the Recapitulations of the Historie, and pointes of Religion, in the first fiue ages, already contayned in this Volume, in their proper places: in the pages 29, 47, 196, 701, and 934."

Second part of the Douai Bible, 1610, quarto.

The second volume of the Douai Bible has a title similar to the first, excepting that it begins, "The seconde tome of the Holie Bible," and in place of the quotation from Isaiah it has one from II. S. Peter i.,

"Spiritu Sancto inspirati, locuti sunt Sancti Dei homines.

"The holie men of God spake, inspired with the Holie Ghost."

The date is "M.DC.X."

Reverse, the same as first tome.

On sig. A 2, page 3, "Proemial Annotations vpon the Booke of Psalmes," which, after 11 pages of interesting matter, thus finishes:

"As for the name, S. Ierom, S. Augustin, and other Fathers teach, that wheras amongst innumerable musical instruments, six were more specially vsed in Dauids time, mentioned by him in the last Psalme, Trumpet, Psalter, Harpe, Timbrel, Organ, and Cimbal.

"This booke hath his name of the instrument called Psalter, which hath tenne strings, signifying the tenne commandements, and is made in forme (as S. Ierom, and S. Bede suppose) of the Greke letter Δ *delta*, because as that instrument rendreth sound from aboue, so we should attend to heauenlie vertues, which come from aboue: Likewise vsing the harpe, which signifyeth mortification of the flesh, & other ininstruments, which signifie and teach other vertues, we must finally referre al to Gods glorie, reioyce spiritually in hart, and render al praise to God."

The following is appended as an example of the Douai translation of the Psalms (the 23rd of all English versions except Coverdale's):

"Paslme (*sic*) xxij. xxij. Psalm.

A forme of thanksgeuing for al spiritual benefites (described vnder the metapher of temporal prosperitie) euen from a sinners conuersion, to final perseuerance, and eternal beatitude.

1. The Psalme of Dauid.

2. Ovr (*a*) Lord ruleth me, and nothing shal be wanting to me: in place (*b*) of pasture there he hath placed me.

(*a*) Christ the good pastor gouerneth, protecteth, (*b*) and feedeth his faithful flocke.

3. Vpon (*c*) the water of refection he hath brought me vp: he hath (*d*) conuerted my soule.

c Baptisme of regeneration *d* which is the first iustification.

He hath conducted me vpon (*e*) the pathes of justice (*f*) for his name.

(*e*) Gods precepts which the baptised must obserue. (*f*) Saluation is in the name and power of Christ, not in mans owne merites.

4. For, although I shal walke in the (*g*) middes of the shaddow of death, I wil (*h*) not feare euils: because thou art with me.

(*g*) In great danger of tentation to mortal sinne, (*h*) yet by Gods grace we may resist.

Thy (*i*) rod and thy (*k*) staffe, they haue comforted me.

(*i*) Gods direction and law is streight, (*k*) and strong.

5. Thou hast prepared in my sight (*l*) a table against them that truble me.

(*l*) Christ hath prepared for our spiritual foode the B Sacrament of the Eucharist.

Thou (*n*) hast fatted my head with oyle: and my (*o*) chalace inebriating how goodlie is it!

(*n*) Christian souls are also strengthened by the other Sacraments. (*o*) The B Sacrament and Sacrifice of Christs bodie and bloud.

6. And thy merce shal folow me (*p*) al the dayes of my life.

(*p*) Continual and final perseuerance is by Gods special grace

And that I may dwel in the house of our Lord, (*q*) in longitude of dayes.

(*q*) in eternal life."

Tables of the Douai Bible.

This Bible ends with IV. Esdras, chapter xvi., on page 1071, on verso of which is, "A table of the Epistles, taken forth of the old Testament, vpon certayne festiual dayes, &c.;" then follows a list of 22 festivals.

Next are 24 pages of "An historical table of the times, special persons, most notable thinges, and canonical bookes of the old Testament," divided into six ages; then 27 pages of "A particvlar table of the most principal thinges conteyned as wel in the holie text, as in the Annotations of both the Tomes of the old Testament."

On page 1124 is, "Censura trium Theologorum Anglorum, extra collegium commorantium." Signed, "Ioannes Wrightvs," "Matthævs Kellisonvs," "Gvilielmvs Harisonvs."

On recto of last leaf is, "You may please curteous reader) to amend the more especial errors happened in this Edition, by reading thus."

The second edition of the Douai version of the Old Testament was printed by John Cousturier in 1635, one hundred years after Coverdale's Bible appeared.

Second edition of the Douai Old Testament, 1635, quarto.

It may be described as an accurate reprint of the first edition. It has no colophon, but on the first title are the words, "Printed by Iohn Covstvrier Permissv Svperiorvm M.DC.XXXV."

Should the titles be missing, a copy of the second edition may be distinguished by having a double black line around each page, and the verse numbers being embodied in the text as they were in the quarto edition of the Bishops' Bible of 1569, the first edition having the numbers in the margin and not introduced into the text.

The reason the Douai version is sometimes called the "Rosin" Bible, is from the rendering of the last verse of the eighth chapter of "the prophecie of Ieremie:" "18. My sorow

"Rosin" Bible.

is aboue sorow, my hart mourning within me. 19. Behold the voice of the daughter of my people from a farre countrie: Is not our Lord in Sion, or is not her king in her? Why then haue they prouoked me to wrath in their sculptils, and in strange vanities? 20. The haruest is past, somner is ended: and we are not saued. 21. For the affliction of the daughter of my people I am afflicted, and made sorowful, astonishment hath taken me. 22. Is there noe rosin in Galaad? or is there no phisition there? Why then is not the wound of the daughter of my people closed?"

At the end of Cousterier's edition, after the errata, is: "Extraict dv privilege dv Roy. Par grace & priuilege du Roy, Il est permis à Iean le Covstvrier, Marchand Libraire & Imprimeur en ceste ville de Roüen, d'Imprimer, vendre & distribuer, pendant le temps & espace de dix ans, *la Bible en language Anglois*, de l'edition de Laurens Kellam Imprimeur de Douay, Et deffences sont faictes à tous Marchands Libraires & Imprimeurs de ce Royaume, d'en vendre, ny distribuer pendant le dit temps, d'autre Impression que de celle du dit Covstvrier, sur peine de 500 liures d'amende, & de confiscation des Exemplaires, ainsi que plus au long est contenu es-dites Lettres de Priuilege, Données à Paris le 3 iour d'Aoust, l'an de grace 1634. Et de nostre regne le 25. Signé, Par le Roy en son Conseil."

Translated from the Vulgate.

The Douai Bible is, as it professes to be, a literal translation of the Vulgate, and in some places more accurately hands down the very words of the inspired writers than any English translation then existing. This is owing to the Latin having been taken from earlier MSS. than were accessible to later translators.

The exact time the old Latin translation was made is not known, but in all probability it was used by the Church in North Africa in the second half of the second century.

Source of Authorised Version.

The text used by the revisers of our present version of the New Testament was Beza's fourth edition of the Greek Text, published in 1589, and the fourth edition of Stephens', published in 1557, or, as these editions were little more than reprints of preceding editions, they may be said to have used the third edition of Beza's Greek Testament of 1582, and Stephens' of 1550, and these followed the very imperfect and defective fourth edition of the Greek Testament of Erasmus, prepared by him in 1516, based on late and untrustworthy manuscripts, without regard to more ancient and accurate authorities that were even then within his reach. The text of Erasmus has been proved not accurately to represent the apostolic originals. Since the sixteenth century Greek MSS. have been discovered of far greater antiquity than those of Erasmus and Stephens, as well as others in Latin, Syriac, and Coptic, into which languages the Scriptures were translated before the fourth century; and long quotations occur in the works of the early fathers, from the original sacred text.

Discovery of Codex Sinaiticus.

which serve as a test of genuineness. The most ancient MS. was discovered by the late Professor Tischendorf in 1844, in the Monastery of St. Catherine, on Mount Sinai, and presented at his instance, in 1859, to the Emperor of Russia, Alexander II., by the monks of St. Catherine. It is known as the Codex Sinaiticus, and is in all probability one of the fifty copies of the Bible made in the year 331, under the care of Eusebius, by order of the Emperor Constantine. The readings in this MS., when tested by the quotations from the sacred writings in the works of SS. Ignatius, Irenæus, and Clement, agree in every particular. This MS. contains the Old Testament in the Septuagint version, and the whole of the New Testament; also the Epistle of Barnabas.

Agreement with quotations in writings of SS. Ignatius, Irenæus, and Clement.

It consists of 345 leaves, each page having four parallel columns. The Epistles of S. Paul are placed immediately after the Gospels, and before the Acts of the Apostles. As an example of the fidelity of the Rheims version, and its agreement with the ancient MSS., the following may be cited: In St. Luke ii. 14, in the A. V., "Glory to God in the highest, and on earth peace, good will towards men." S. Jerome gives it, "and on earth peace among men of good pleasure (or will)." The Alexandrian, the Vatican, and the Sinaitic Codices all agree with the Latin, which has handed down to us what is now generally acknowledged to be the true rendering of the very words of the song of the angels.

S. Jerome, by his great knowledge of languages, and his wonderful industry, did more than any other man that ever lived towards the interpretation of Holy Scripture. He was born in Stridon, in Dalmatia, about the year 329. In the deserts of Syria he perfected himself in the Hebrew language so as to be able to translate the Old Testament into Latin. He studied at Constantinople, under the great orator and theologian, S. Gregory of Nazianzum, and learned from his eloquent lips the great treasure to be found in the Scriptures. Afterwards, at Rome, he revised the Latin translations of the New Testament and the Psalter, which even at that early date, varied considerably from the original text. Considering it necessary for the preservation of religion that the ascetic and cloisteral life should be encouraged, he retired to a hermitage at Bethlehem, where he watched over the sacred deposit of the Scriptures, and devoted himself to its study and translation, until, at length, worn out by ceaseless toil and great age, he died in the year 420. S. Jerome.

S. Jerome's version was not universally accepted until the 8th century. In the beginning of the 9th century Alcuin revised the Vulgate, and by the aid of early MSS. restored it to its early purity.

Lanfranc, Archbishop of Canterbury, in the year 1089 orrected the text, and removed from it many clerical errors. Corrections of the text made by Lanfranc.

Early in the 16th century Cardinal Ximenes

made a considerable revision, and another was made by Pope Sixtus V. in 1590, but in passing through the press so many printer's errors were made that in 1592 Pope Clement VIII. issued a corrected edition.

Comparison of the 1610 and 1853 editions.

Greater changes have been made in the various editions of the Douai Bible than in any other English version. This will be at once seen by comparing any of the chapters. We append two in parallel columns as an example.

The version of 1610.

The Threnes
that is to say,
The lamentations of Ieremie the Prophet.

1 How doth the citie ful of people, sitte solitarie: how is the ladie of the Gentiles become as a widow: the princesse of prouinces is made tributarie?

2 Weeping she hath wept in the night, and her teares are on her cheekes: there is none to comfort her of al her deare ones: al her freindes haue despised her, and are become her enimies.

3 Iudas is gone into transmigration because of affliction, and the multitude of bondage; she hath dwelt among the Gentiles, neither hath she found rest: al her persecuters haue apprehended her within the straites.

The edition of 1853.

The lamentations of Jeremias.

1. How doth the city sit solitary, that was full of people! how is the mistress of the Gentiles become as a Widow, the princess of the provinces is made tributary!

2. Weeping she hath wept in the night and her tears are on her cheeks, there is none to comfort her, all her friends have despised her, and are become her enemies.

3. Juda hath removed her dwelling place because of her affliction, and the greatness of her bondage, she hath dwelt among the nations, and she hath found no rest, all her persecutors have taken her in the midst of straits.

4 The waies of Sion mourne, because there are none that come to the solemnitie: al her gates are destroyed: her priestes sighing: her virgins lothsome, and herself is oppressed with bitternes.

5 Her aduersaries are made in the head, her enemies are enriched: because our Lord hath spoken vpon her for the multitude of her iniquities: her little ones are led into captiuitie, before the face of the afflicter.

4. The ways of Zion mourn, because there are none that come to the solemn feast, all her gates are broken down, her priests sigh, her virgins are in affliction, and she is oppressed with bitterness.

5. Her adversaries are become her lords, her enemies are enriched, because the Lord hath spoken against her for the multitude of her iniquities, her children are led into captivity before the face of the oppressor.

King James's Version.

Hampton Court Conference.

AT the Hampton Court Conference between the Church party and the conforming Dissenters, held January 16th, 17th, and 18th, 1604, it was decided that a new translation of the Bible should be made.

This was at the suggestion of Dr. Reynolds, the leader of the Puritan party, who "moved his Majesty that there might be a new translation of the Bible, because those which were allowed in the reign of King Henry VIII. and Edward VI. were corrupt, and not answerable to the truth of the original."

King James's opinion of the early versions.

King James said he did not consider any translation into English, that had hitherto been made, to be satisfactory, but the worst of all versions was the Genevan; some of the notes of which were very partial, untrue, seditious, and savoured too much of dangerous and traitorous conceits.

Steps were immediately taken to carry the suggestions into effect. 54 translators were appointed, and divided into six companies.

They met at Oxford, Cambridge, and Westminster, and the following rules were framed for their guidance:—

"1. The ordinary Bible read in the Church, commonly called the Bishops' Bible, to be followed, and as little altered as the truth of the original will admit.

Rules to guide the revisers.

"2. The names of the prophets and the holy writers, with the other names of the text, to be retained as nigh as may be, accordingly as they were vulgarly used.

"3. The old ecclesiastical words to be kept, viz., the word *church* not to be translated *congregation*, &c.

"4. When a word hath divers significations, that to be kept which hath been most commonly used by the most of the ancient fathers, being agreeable to the propriety of the place and the analogy of the faith.

"5. The division of the chapters to be altered either not at all, or as little as may be, if necessity so require.

"6. No marginal notes at all to be affixed, but only for the explanation of the Hebrew or Greek words which cannot, without some circumlocution, so briefly and fitly be expressed in the text.

"7. Such quotations of places to be marginally set down as shall serve for the fit reference of one Scripture to another.

"8. Every particular man of each company to take the same chapter or chapters; and having translated or amended them severally by himself where he thinketh good, all to meet together, confer what they have done, and agree for their parts what shall stand.

"9. As any one company hath dispatched any one book in this manner, they shall send it to the rest to be considered of seriously and judiciously, for his Majesty is very careful in this point.

"10. If any company, upon the review of the book so sent, doubt or differ upon any place, to send them word thereof, note the place, and withal send the reasons; to which if they consent not, the difference to be compounded at the general meeting, which is to be of the chief persons of each company at the end of the work.

"11. When any place of special obscurity is doubted of, letters to be directed by authority to send to any learned man in the land for his judgment of such a place.

"12. Letters to be sent from every bishop to the rest of his clergy, admonishing them of this translation in hand, and to move and charge as many as being skilful in the tongues, and having taken pains in that kind, to send his particular observations to the company either at Westminster, Cambridge, or Oxford.

"13. The directors in each company to be the Deans of Westminster and Chester for that place, and the king's professors in the Hebrew or Greek in either university.

"14. These translations to be used when they agree better with the text than the Bishop's Bible: Tindale's, Matthew's, Coverdale's, Whitchurch's, Geneva.

"15. Besides the said directors before mentioned, three or four of the most ancient and grave divines in either of the universities, not employed in translating, to be assigned by the Vice-Chancellor upon conference with the rest of the Heads to be overseers of the translations, as well Hebrew as Greek, for the better observation of the fourth rule above specified."

The Bible was divided among the six companies as follows:–

1. Genesis to II. Kings.
2. I. Chronicles to Ecclesiastes.
3. Isaiah to Malachi.
4. The Apocrypha.
5. The Gospels, Acts, and Apocalypse.
6. The Epistles.

The Bible being the property of the Church, its translators were, very properly, remunerated for their work out of Church funds; Archbishop Bancroft and other Bishops presented the translators, or more correctly speaking the revisers, with Church preferment as vacancies arose.

This revision has long been commonly called "The Authorised Version," but it has been questioned whether it was ever formally authorised by Convocation, Council, or Parliament.

The version of 1611 never specially authorised.

Matthew's Bible of 1537 was licensed by the King, and the Great Bible was specially sanctioned by proclamation.

The Bishops' Bible was duly approved of by Convocation, and as the Bishops' Version was the legal successor of the Great Bible, it inherited royal authority.

So the Bible of 1611, being a revision of the 1602 edition of Parker's Bible, may justly be deemed to possess all the rights and privileges belonging to the version of which it was a revision; just as the Book of Common Prayer of 1604 was regarded as merely a revision of Elizabeth's book of 1559, and therefore to possess all the authority of its predecessor.

"Appointed to be read in Churches."

The words, "Appointed to be read in Churches," to be found on the title pages of all modern Bibles, are absent from many of the early issues, especially from the smaller editions not intended for use in Church, and they are absent from the New Testament title of the first folio edition of 1611. They are not to be seen on the title of the first 12mo Testament, the first octavo Bible, the second quarto, the folio of 1616 in Roman letter, the quarto of 1613-12, the octavos of 1615 and 1617, nor on the octavo of 1621 and others.

"Appointed" can hardly be regarded as synonymous with "Authorised." It only means that this version was to be read in the service of the Church for lessons, in place of the version which had then been in use for forty-three years.

Although the lessons were to be read from King James's Version, the Epistles and Gospels used at the Sacrament of the Altar were taken from the Great Bible until the year 1662.

First folio of King James's Bible.

The title of the first issue of King James's Bible is, "The Holy Bible, Conteyning the Old Testament, and the New: Newly Translated out of the Originall Tongues: and with the former Translations diligently compared and reuised by his Maiesties special Comandement. *Appointed to be read in Churches.* Imprinted at London by Robert Barker, Printer to the Kings most Excellent Maiestie. Anno Dom. 1611."

In some copies these words appear in a very handsome copper-plate engraving, representing Moses on one side and Aaron on the other, the four Evangelists at the corners, and the Sacred Name above. Title page not always the same.

The engraving is signed "Cornelius Boel fecit in Richmont."

In other copies the same words are printed within a woodcut (so frequently seen in the Genevan Bible) of the Twelve Apostles on the right hand, and the Twelve Tribes with their tents and armorial bearings on the left; at the corners are the Evangelists with their symbols, the same as were borne by the four divisions of the army of Israel; above is the Lamb triumphant, and, at the top of all, the Holy Name (Jehovah) in Hebrew characters.

This woodcut was used for the New Testament title in 1611; and for both titles in the large folios of 1613, 1617, 1634, and 1640.

The collation is as follows: verso of title blank; "The Epistle Dedicatorie," A 2, ending on A 3 recto; Verso, "The Translators to the Reader," extending to verso of B 4; "Kalender," 6 Leaves, C 1, A 2 (for C 2), &c.; "An Almanack for 39 years," on D 1; "Table to find Easter for ever," verso of D 1; "Table and Collation.

Kalender," D 2; Verso, "Proper Lessons;" "The names and order of all the Bookes," on verso of D 4, printed wholly in black. Then follow the "Genealogies" and map, 18 leaves, with distinct register. The text begins A 1. Gen. i. has the rose and thistle in the initial I. Apocrypha ends on C c c c 6 verso.

The New Testament has a separate register running from A to A a 6.

There are altogether 119 signatures and 714 leaves of text.

Title page of the New Testament.

The letterpress of the second title reads: "The Newe Testament of our Lord and Sauiour Iesvs Christ. ¶ Newly Translated out of the Originall Greeke: and with the former Translations diligently compared and reuised by his Maiesties speciall Commandment. Imprinted at London by *Robert Barker*, Printer to the Kings most Excellent Maiestie. Anno Dom. 1611."

The text is in black letter, the chapter headings and marginal references, as well as words supplied by the translators in the text, are in Roman type, and the alternative readings in Italic.

The issues of the folio of 1611.

There are three issues assigned to the year 1611, each of which bears that date on the New Testament title-page.

The first is the one already described. It is commonly known as the great "He" Bible, because it reads in Ruth iii. 15, "Also he said, Bring the vaile that thou hast vpon thee, and holde it. And when she helde it, he measured sixe measures of barley, and laide it on her: and he went into the citie."

This is the correct rendering of the Hebrew text; but the second issue and almost all subsequent editions read, "and she went into the citie."

There are several other passages which serve to differentiate the issues.

Every edition that has "she" has one series of errors, and all that read "he" have another series, no doubt owing to a "He" Bible being used as "copy" at one printing office, and a "She" Bible at another; for instance, the first quarto has "he"; the quarto of 1613-12 has "she"; the folio of 1613 has "she"; the quarto of 1613 has "he."

Some errata of first issue of 1611. — Errors of the "He" Bible.

Genesis x. 16, "Emorite" for "Amorite."

Exodus xiv. 10, Repetition of three lines.

Exodus xxxviii. 11, "hoopes" for "hooks."

Leviticus xiii. 56, "the plaine be" for "the plague be."

Leviticus xvii. 14, "ye shall not eat" for "ye shall eat."

Jeremiah xxii. 3, "deliver the spoiler" for "deliver the spoiled."

Ezra iii. 5, "offred, offered," repetition.

Micah iv., Heading "Ioel."

Ezek. vi. 8, "that he may have some" for "ye."

Ezek. xxiv. 7, "She poured it upon the ground" for "poured it not."

I. Esdras iv. "Anocrynha" for "Apocrypha."

S. Matthew xvi. 25, "his" repeated.

The "She" Bible, 1611.

The second and third folios bear a general resemblance to the first, but differ in the following particulars:—

The first page of the Dedication, "To the most high and mightie Prince," "OE" should be "OF," and in the eighth line, "Chkist" should be "Christ." On the page which faces the first chapter of Genesis, between "2 Kings" and "Ezrah" is placed "I. Corinthians," "II. Corinthians" for "Chronicles." Sig. D 2 of preliminary has a woodcut of Neptune and his sea-horses.

Exodus ix. 13 has, "let my people goe that they may serue thee" for "may serue me."

S. Matthew xxvi. 36, "Judas" for "Jesus."

In the upper part of the letter P beginning Psalm cxii. is Walsingham's crest.

None of the before-mentioned errata of the first issue are to be found in these Bibles, excepting the two in Ezekiel.

Third issue of King James's Bible of 1611.

From the third issue the first title is so often absent that it is difficult to say positively what date it ought to bear, but most likely it should be 1613. In the British Museum is a copy, once the property of Lea Wilson, with the date 1611; but it looks like an insertion. At Oriel College, Oxford, is a copy of this issue, with a title dated 1613, and a similar one at All Souls' College, Oxford, is also dated 1613, and several others in private hands bear the same date.

These 1613–11 Bibles differ in every sheet from the first issue, sometimes in minute points, but always sufficiently to indicate a separate setting up.

The two "She" issues are in most of their sheets identical, but some of them have been reprinted.

Different copies are most curiously and capriciously mixed up in respect of these varying sheets, it being almost impossible to find two copies made up exactly alike; for instance, two British Museum copies contain between them almost all the "reprints," but very seldom is the same reprinted sheet found in both.

Reprinted sheets in third issue of 1611.

The following are the sheets which have been found to be "reprints:" E 3, 4; P 2, 3, 4, 5; X 2, 5; Aa 2, 3, 4, 5; the whole of the sheets Bb to Ee; Ff 1, 3, 4, 6; Gg 3, 4; Hh; Ii; Kk 2, 3, 4, 5; from Ll to Ss and Vv to Zz; Aaa 1, 3, 4, 6; Bbb 1, 2, 5, 6; from Ccc to Hhh; Iii 1, 3, 4, 6; Kkk; Lll 2, 3, 4, 5; Mmm; Nnn; Ooo 1, 6; Ppp; Qqq 1, 2, 5, 6; Rrr 1, 2, 5, 6; the whole of Ttt to Yyy; Zzz 1, 2, 5, 6; Iiii 1, 6; Ssss 4; Xxxx 2, 5.

The following table gives tests for distinguishing between the three large folio Bibles, with the date 1611 on the New Testament title page.

It has been drawn up by a comparison between four Bibles in the collection of the Rev. W. E. Smith, M.A., Vicar of Corton. One of these is a Bible of the first issue ("He"). Two are almost exactly like each other, and represent the standard second issue ("She"). The fourth contains most of the "reprint" sheets which are so curiously divided between the two British Museum copies.

		First Issue, 1611.	Second Issue, without Reprints.	Second Issue, with Reprints.
E 3	Genesis			
	46. 32. mrg.	† Hebr. they	† Heb. they	† Heb they
	47. 27.	possessions	possession	possessions
P 2	Numbers			
	21. 4. mrg.	shortened	shortned	shortned
	21. 18.	*direction*	*directions*	*direction*
E e 6	2 Samuel			
	6. 8. marg.	Uzzah	Uzzah	Vzzah
	6. 9.	Arke of the Lord	Arke of God	Arke of the Lord
	6. 16.	citie of Dauid	house of Dauid	citie of Dauid
I i 2	1 Kings			
	9. 22.	no bondmen	no bondman	no bondmen
	9. 25. mrg.	† Hebr. vp-	† Heb. vp.	† Heb. vp-
L l 3	2 Kings			
	5. 12.	he turned,	hee returned,	hee turned,
N n 1	2 Kings			
	19. 15.	before	vnto	before
	19. 18.	work	worke	worke
O o 1	1 Chron.			
	4. 14. marg. and text.	craftesmen	craftsmen	craftsmen
	4. 30.	and at Hormah,	and Hormah,	and at Hormah,
N n n 2	Isaiah			
	18. 3.	see yee,	see ye,	see yee,
	19. 5.	riuer	riuers	riuer
Q q q 1	Isaiah			
	59. 14.	a farre off	farre off	a farre off
T t t 2	Jeremiah			
	29. 1.	the words	the words	ye words
	29. 11. mrg.	† Hebr. ende	† Hebr. end	† Hebr. end
X x x 1	Jeremiah			
	48. 34.	Nimrim shall be	Nimrim shall be	Nimrim shalbe
Y y y 3	Ezekiel			
	5. 3. marg.	† Hebr. wings.	† Hebr. wings.	† Heb. wings.
	5. 5.	This *is*	Thus *is*	This *is*

The three issues distinguished above, as well as the folio editions of 1617, 1634, and 1640, all bear a strong resemblance to each other. The type is so set up that each leaf ends with the same word: hence the sheets can be mixed together at pleasure, and much trouble is thereby caused to the collator.

First quarto edition of King James's Bible, 1612.

The first quarto edition of the Bible of 1611 was printed in Roman letter in 1612.

The title page is a reduced copy, on copper, of the first issue; it has the Agnus Dei on the upper part, and the pelican feeding her young from her own blood at the lower. It is signed, "Jasper Isac, fecit." It is on very smooth paper, without water mark or wire lines, quite different to the paper on which the rest of the book is printed.

The New Testament title is within a heart-shaped woodcut border, with the crowned letters "I. R." at the bottom. It was taken from the "He" Bible.

At the end is the Metrical Psalms, "with apt notes to sing them with all," printed the same year (1612) "for the Companie of Stationers."

Two editions of this book were issued. In one the head line of sig. H 5 verso is, "The Galatians reproued. To the Galaitans. The Law a Scholemaster to Christ." In the other, "The Galatians reproooued. To the Galatians. The Law a Schoolemaster to Christ."

The orthography of the two editions is totally different, and the initial letters are not from the same fount.

First octavo of 1612.

The first octavo was also printed in 1612.

The same woodcut used for the numerous editions of Tomson's New Testament, produced by R. Barker, was utilised for this Bible.

It was again issued the same year with slight variations.

First quarto New Testament, 1612.

The first quarto New Testament came out this year (1612).

It is a handsome book, printed in rather heavy black letter type on good paper.

It has a man, a lion, an ox, and an eagle, at the corners of the title page, without pictures of the Evangelists, and "Fides" and "Hvmilitas" represented by full length female figures at the sides. "The names and order of all the Bookes of the New Testament, with the number of their Chapters" is on verso. There is no preliminary matter.

One would suppose that the Testament of 1631 was a re-issue of this book, but close investigation shows that although both read together, and appear to be printed from the same type, there are minute differences in the setting up; for instance, the fourth line of S. Matt. i. 2 reads in the 1612, "Abraham begat Isaac, and"; but the 1631 has, "Abraham begat Isaac, and I-."

Folio of 1613, No. 10 (Rev. W. J. Loftie's).

The folio of 1613 was printed with smaller type, and has 72 instead of 59 lines to a full column. The Psalms begin on Kk, Job ending on the twenty-first line of the previous page. The Prophets end on Ggg2 verso.

The Apocrypha ends on T t t 5 recto, verso being blank. The New Testament begins on V v v 1, the title being T t t 6, and ends on N n n n 4. There is no colophon.

It is full of mistakes, as the following list, which might easily be made longer, will show:

Errata in Folio of 1613.

Genesis xxvii. 44, "passe" for "turn."
Leviticus vii. 25, "fast" for "fat."
I. Samuel x. 10, "water" for "matter."
I. Kings iii. 15, four words omitted.
II. Kings xxii. 3, "were" for "year."
II. Chronicles vi. 10, "throne" for "roome."
Nehemiah x. 31, "not leave" for "leave."
Job xxix. 3, "shined" for "walked."
Psalm xi. 1, "flie" for "flee."
Ezekiel xxiii. 7, "delighted" for "defiled."
Habakkuk ii. 5, six words omitted.
Ecclus. xvi. 13, 14, both verses omitted.
S. Matthew xiii. 8, three words omitted.
S. Matthew xvi. 11, seven words omitted.
S. Matthew xxvi. 68, two words omitted.
S. John xx. 25, ten words omitted.
Acts xiii. 51, four words omitted.
I. Corinthians xi. 17, "I praise you" for "I praise you not."
I. Corinthians xvi. 14, "doings" for "things."
II. Corinthians ii. 8, "continue" for "confirm."
II. Timothy iv. 16, the word "not" omitted.
I. S. Peter i. 22, "selves" for "souls."

First quarto of 1613, No. 11.

The first quarto Bible of King James's revision printed in black letter is dated 1613. It was taken from the "He" Bible, and has the usual errors of that edition.

Black letter quarto of 1613-14. No. 14 (Mr. Loftie's).

The black letter quarto of 1613-14 reads in Isaiah xxviii. 9. "Milke and drawen from the beasts" instead of "drawn from the breasts."

It is singular that in this edition the date on the New Testament title is a year later than that on the first title.

Roman letter quarto, 1614-15, No. 18.

Like the last edition noticed, the colophon of this book is dated the succeeding year to that in which the Old Testament was printed, viz., 1614. The first title has "The Bible" only, like the earliest versions. All the rest of R. Barker's editions have the words "Holy Bible" on the title page.

First folio in Roman letter, 1616, No. 24.

The first Bible of King James's revision in small folio size was issued by Robert Barker in 1616. My copy begins with the Genealogies by J[ohn] S[peed], 34 pages; after which comes the double-page map of Canaan so frequently missing. The title page has the old woodcuts so often used by Christopher Barker, with the initials "C.B." still at the bottom, in spite of the book having been printed by Robert Barker. The lion and unicorn on each side the words, "Cum Privilegio Regiæ Majestatis," cannot be mistaken.

There are 16 pages of preliminary. On verso of "The names and order" is the full-page engraving of the Tree of Knowledge found in some editions of the Bishops' Bible.

The New Testament title is exactly like the first title, excepting the letterpress.

It is a beautifully printed book with wide margins, and has very tasteful headpieces found in no other Bible. This edition is the first in which any serious attempt was made to revise the text.

The large folio of 1617 closely resembles the rest of this series. The title has the Twelve Tribes on the left hand and the Twelve Apostles on the right, with large pictures of SS. Matthew, Mark, Luke, and John, all engaged in writing. The Agnus Dei is below the Sacred Name, and the Dove below it. Large black letter folio of 1617, No. 27.

It has 68 pages of preliminary, the Prayer Book, &c., coming after the Dedication and Preface. The New Testament title is like the first, but in my copy is a much finer impression. Jeremiah xviii. 3, has "Whelles" for "Wheels."

The first duodecimo Bible of this version was printed by R. Barker in 1617. First 12mo., 1617. No. 29.

There is an architectural border to title page.

It is without the words, "Appointed to be read in Churches," and has no chapter headings. Dedication on sig. A. On verso is "Names and order of Bookes." Genesis begins on Sig. A 2. Sig. B 3 is by mistake printed A 3. New Testament ends on verso of Xxij. It has no colophon.

Bonham Norton and John Bill succeeded Robert Barker as Bible printers late in the year 1618. Norton and Bill's first quarto, 1619, No. 32.

The first time the names of Norton and Bill are seen on a colophon, is in the Bishops' New Testament of 1618; but the first complete Bible they printed was the quarto of 1619. It has the Book of Common Prayer at the beginning, in the Litany of which King James, Prince Charles, Frederick the Prince Elector Palatine, and the Lady Elizabeth, his wife, are prayed for. Both titles are alike. The Metrical Psalter at the end, dated 1619, was printed by the Company of Stationers.

Black letter quarto, 1619-20, No. 36.

The Old Testament title of "Holy Bible, London, 1619-20," has on it, "Norton and Bill, 1619." The New Testament title has the names of "Robert Barker and John Bill, 1620." The colophon is without either Norton's or Bill's name; it has Robert Barker only.

Black letter quarto, 1619 20-24, No. 37.

A Bible composed of portions of several editions was next issued. It is a black letter quarto. It has on the first title, "Norton and Bill, 1619." The second title has the names of "Barker and Bill, 1620." The colophon has, "Norton and Bill, 1624."

In one place "Corinthians" reads "Coainthans."

This mistake occurs also in the black letter quarto of 1620-1.

12mo. and 18mo. New Testaments.

A number of small black letter New Testaments came out about this time, all printed by Norton and Bill; a 12mo. in 1621, and similar ones the two following years.

In 1625 another 12mo. came out, and in 1626 an 18mo. After this rather larger sizes began to be printed, and octavos were produced in 1627 and 1628.

After this date we find the names of other Bible printers appear. A small octavo Testament was issued at Edinburgh, by the Heirs of Hart, in 1628 (the Andro Hart whose "Breeches" Bibles were so highly esteemed).

This is the first Testament printed in Scotland of King James's Version.

Although the Universities always claimed the right to print the Bible, Cambridge had not exercised that right since the year 1589; but in 1628 a duodecimo Testament was published at Cambridge, by the printers to the University, and the following year Thomas and John Buck issued the first Cambridge Bible.

First Cambridge N. T. of the 1611 version, 12mo., 1628.

First Cambridge Bible, 1629.

It is small folio size, Roman letter, the copper-plate title page is a very fine work of art. There is a globe at the top, and an angel at each side holding a scroll with the words, "And God saw everything that he had made, and behold it was very good." Below is a representation of the institution of the Holy Eucharist.

The engraving is smaller than usually seen in folios, and was afterwards used for quarto issues. The New Testament title is a very plain one; it has the Cambridge arms in an oval, with "Alma mater Cantabrigia," and "Hinc lvcem et pocvla sacra."

This is the first Bible containing the misprint in I. S. Timothy iv. 16, "Take heed unto thyself and unto *thy* doctrine," instead of "the doctrine," which was copied into such a vast number of succeeding editions.

This edition was carefully revised, and many blemishes of the first edition were removed, but the inordinate use of Italics was introduced;

and since then insignificant words have been Italicised with minute accuracy more pedantic than scholarly.

The climax of absurdity in this respect is reached by the Cambridge Paragraph Bible, as will be seen by the following table, giving the number of Italicised words and phrases in S. Matthew's Gospel:—

Table of the number of words in Italics.

Place of Issue.	Year.	No. of Italic Words.
London	1611	43
Cambridge	1629	165
"	1638	224
"	1762	352
Oxford	1739	375
Cambridge	1870	583

About the year 1630 several small Bibles were printed by "Robert Barker and assigns of John Bill," notably the octavo of 1631, commonly called the "Wicked" Bible, from the word "not" having been omitted from the seventh commandment.

"Wicked" Bible, octavo, 1631, No. 84.

We often find the statement that there are only two copies, or only four copies, in existence; but this is a "Queen Anne's farthing" story, for I know of several: one is in the possession of H. J. Akinson, Esq., M.P., of Gunnersbury House, Acton, W.

This error must have been discovered before the printing of the edition was finished, for I have several copies in which the seventh commandment is correctly printed; no doubt the correction was made during the passage of the sheets through the press.

The quarto black letter Testament, in long lines, printed by Robert Barker and assignes of John Bill, 1631, reads with the first quarto; from which it can only be distinguished (if the title and imprint are missing) by the spelling of certain words, the division of a few words at the end of some lines, and from the type used for the running titles and numbering the pages being rather larger in the 1631 than in the 1612. Black letter New Testament, in long lines, quarto, 1631, No. 88.

The first complete Bible printed in Scotland of King James's revision, was the Roman letter octavo, "printed by the printers to the King's most excellent Majestie: cum privilegio," in 1633. First Bible printed in Scotland, 1633, No. 1[illegible].

It had in it a number of woodcuts, not printed with the book, but inserted in some copies during the process of binding. They are Dutch work, and were originally intended for a history of the Bible.

The Puritans were enraged at these pictures being bound up with the Bible, although they thought it no harm to insert in the Bible the productions of Luther and Calvin.

At the trial of Archbishop Laud, these pictures were brought as a serious charge against him, and formed one excuse for his martyrdom.

Most likely they were only bound up with a portion of the edition, for I have two copies in original binding into which no pictures were ever inserted.

The title page is engraved. It has a "Jesse tree," and in the corners of the plate are four ovals, with the usual representation of the Evangelists. The Sacred Trine is above, with the Holy Name. The Dedication is on Sig. A 2, with, on verso, "The Order of the Books." Text begins on A 3 and ends on recto of M m m 4.

The New Testament title has, on verso, the arms of Scotland, quartering France with England in the second place, and Ireland in the third, within the garter.

As there are three editions of the same date and very much alike, it may be well to notice that Archbishop Laud's Bible has the first five psalms on a page.

Buck and Daniel.

In the year 1635, Thomas Buck and Roger Daniel, of Cambridge, printed two quarto Bibles, one in black letter and the other in Roman; and Robert Young, of Edinburgh, printed a 12mo. black letter New Testament.

Foreign printed Bibles.

Many editions of the Bible circulated about this time were printed at Amsterdam, some arrangement having been made with the holders of the Bible patent to allow the words, "Barker and assignes of Bill, London," to be placed on the title page and imprint.

The compositors' work must have gone uncorrected to the press, for errors appear on almost every page.

The 12mo. of 1638 has the following in addition to other misprints:—

Errata in the 12mo. of 1638.

Genesis i. 26, "Let us make men" for "man."

Genesis xxxvii. 2, "sons of Belial" for "Bilhah."

Numbers xxv. 18, "vex you with their wives" for "wiles."

Numbers xxvi. 10, "two thousand" for "hundred."

II Samuel xxiii. 20, "slew two lions like men" for "lion-like men."

II Chronicles xxxiv. 2, "that which was evill" for "that which was right."

II. Chronicles xxxvi. 14, "had polluted" for "hallowed."

Nehemiah iv. 9, "read our prayer" for "made our prayer."

Isaiah i. 6, "purifying sores" for "putrifying."

Isaiah xxix. 13, "taught by the people" for "taught by the precepts."

Isaiah xlix. 22, "their sons" for "thy sons."

Ezekiel v. 11, "any piety" for "any pity."

S. Luke vii. 47, "her sins which are many are forgotten" for "forgiven."

S. Luke xix. 29, "ten of his disciples" for "two."

S. John xviii. 29, "Pilate then went not" for "went out."

I. Corinthians vii. 34, "praise her husband" for "please."

I. S. Timothy ii. 9, "shamefulness" for "shamefastnesse."

The folio published in 1638, by Thomas Buck and Roger Daniel, the University printers, is in clear but rather small Roman type. Most of the copies are hand ruled with red lines. Cambridge Bible of 1638, No. 145.

The text was carefully revised by Dr. Goad, Dr. Ward, Mr. Boyse, and Mr. Mead.

Mr. Kilburne (1659) calls it, "the authentic corrected Cambridge Bible, revised *Mandato Regio.*"

The mistakes in the issue of 1611 are for the most part corrected, and but few new ones introduced; it, however, continues the serious mistranslation of the first Cambridge Bible in Acts vi. 3, "Look ye out among you seven men of honest report, full of the Holy Ghost and wisdome, whom ye may appoint over this businesse," instead of "whom we (the Apostles) may appoint."

It is probably the best edition of King James's Version ever published.

Barker's last black letter folio, 1640.

The last of Barker's grand series of black letter folios was brought out in 1640. Its appearance is improved by the alternative readings in the margin being in Roman letter (a peculiarity of this edition).

A comparison of this book with those that preceded it, shows the change that was gradually taking place in the mode of spelling; for instance, in the earlier black letter Bibles "u" is used in the middle of a word, and "v" as an initial letter; but in the 1640 edition, as in modern black letter, "u" is used for the vowel and "v" as the consonant, without regard to their position in the word; *e.g.*, in the 1611 we find "vnto, haue," but in this book, "unto, have" is used.

A copy of this edition may be recognised by

the words, "To the Most High," in the first line of the Dedication, being in capital letters.

As before stated, many Bibles bearing English imprints were imported from Holland, and the first Bible said to be printed in America, has the imprint of "Mark Baskett, London."

Amsterdam Bibles, with Geneva notes.

In the year 1642, a folio edition of King James's Version was printed at Amsterdam by "Joost Broersz, dwelling in the Pijlsteegh, in the Druckerije." The title is a full-page engraving of the nave and chancel of a church; on the altar are two lights, but where the cross or crucifix should be is an enormous alms-dish. Below is a representation of the institution of the Holy Eucharist, with the Apostles reclining around a square table. At the top of the page is a picture of the Ascension.

After the Dedication, "To the most high and mighty Prince," and the Translators' Preface, comes, "A briefe table of the interpretation of the proper names, &c.," and a second table of principal things, concluding with the verses,

"Here is the spring where waters flow,
To quench our heat of sin," &c.,

and the usual prayer. On verso is, "The names and order of all the books," followed by another large engraving of the Garden of Eden. The notes of King James's Bible are omitted, and the arguments and annotations of the "Breeches" Bible are inserted in their place.

The New Testament has "Brief summaries and expositions of Theod. Beza upon the hard places. Together with the annotations of Fr. Junius upon the Revelation of S. John. The which notes have never been till now set forth with this new translation. Placed in order by I. C." (John Canne).

Many Bibles and Testaments were afterwards introduced from Amsterdam to England (mostly in small sizes), known as Canne's Bibles, from their having a prologue, or address, written by John Canne, a prominent leader among the Brownists.

Canne's Bibles.

There seems to be no alteration made in the text, but the margins are loaded with references to parallel passages, Canne holding that "Scripture is the best interpreter of Scripture."

Commonwealth Bibles.

During the Commonwealth many editions of the Bible were published, nearly all very badly printed, and full of errors, containing such statements as, "The unrighteous shall inherit the kingdom of God."

Many of these corruptions were exposed by William Kilburn, Finsbury, in a tract printed in the year 1659.

The first Bible printed at Oxford.

The University of Oxford did not begin to print Bibles until the year 1675, when the first was issued in quarto size; the spelling was revised by Dr. John Fell, Dean of Oxford.

It has two titles, both to the Old and the New Testament. The first is an engraving representing the Transfiguration of our Blessed Lord. The words, "The Holy Bible," are in a label across the centre.

In the foreground are two seated female figures, the one veiled representing "The Law," the other, with a nimbus, "The Gospell."

On the base of a broken column are the words, "At the Theater in Oxon." The second title is an ordinary letterpress one, with the date 1675.

New Testament title of the first Oxford Bible.

The first New Testament title is a rather good engraving of an obelisk, on which an angel is writing with an arrow, "The Law of Loue from the Hill of Sion." A label, supported by angels, has the inscription, "The New Testament." On a step below are the words, "At the Theater in Oxford, A° 1675."

This title is followed by a printed one.

The colophon of my copy is, "At the Theater in Oxford, MDCLXXIII."; but in other copies the colophon is dated 1675.

The Apocrypha is printed in smaller type than the rest of the Bible.

Two editions of the "Vinegar" Bible.

In the year 1717, J. Baskett printed a large folio Bible, in two volumes, known as the "Vinegar" Bible, from the head line of S. Luke, chapter xx., having the word "Vinegar" in mistake for "Vineyard"—"The parable of the Vinegar."

Several copies were printed on vellum. It is a beautifully printed book, and contains many copperplate illustrations of considerable merit.

Baskett issued two Bibles nearly the same size, and both contain the same mistake. They may be distinguished by noticing that the first has the date 1717 on the first title and 1716 on the New Testament title, while the other has 1717 on both title pages.

The illustrations in the second are not as numerous nor as well executed as in the first issue.

In 1762 was published a Bible in folio and quarto, 2 vols., printed by Joseph Bentham, printer to the University of Cambridge. It was edited by Dr. Paris, and is of great importance, as being in the main the foundation of our modern Bible. The use of Italics was considerably extended, the language was modernised, many marginal references were added. Much care was expended over it, but it may well be doubted whether it was an improvement upon the Cambridge edition of 1638.

It is reported that all the folio copies except six were destroyed by fire. There is one copy in the British Museum, another in the Library of Corpus Christi College, Cambridge, and a third in the Ewing collection at Glasgow. Probably a little research would reveal the existence of many more than the traditional six copies. The quarto edition is not uncommon.

A fine copy of the 1762 folio is in my collection.

In 1768 a Bible was published at Oxford, also in folio and quarto, edited by Dr. Blayney, following very much the same lines as that of

Dr. Paris, but carrying the alterations a little further.

These Bibles were issued with no small pretensions to excellence ("many errors that were found in former editions have been corrected, and the text reformed to such a standard of purity, as, it is presumed, is not to be met with in any other edition hitherto extant"). They are larger and handsomer books than the Cambridge Bible of 1762, and they are commonly regarded as the standard from which modern Bibles are printed.

This, however, is happily not the case in one conspicuous respect. Dr. Blayney writes: "Considerable alterations have been made in the Heads or Contents prefixed to the Chapters, as will appear on inspection; and though the editor is unwilling to enlarge on the labour bestowed by himself in this particular, he cannot avoid taking notice of the peculiar obligations, which both himself and the public lie under, to the Principal of Hertford College, Mr. Griffith, of Pembroke College, Mr. Wheeler, Poetry Professor, and the late Warden of New College, so long as he lived to bear a part in it; who with a prodigious expense of time, and inexpressible fatigue to themselves, judiciously corrected and improved the rude and imperfect Draughts of the Editor." It is a pity the learned men did not spare themselves this "inexpressible fatigue;" for their endeavours to reduce the chapter headings to the standard of 18th century taste cannot be pronounced altogether a success, as will appear from a comparison of Dr. Blayney's headings to the first four chapters of the Epistle to the Romans with those of 1611.

1611.	1769.
CHAP. I.	CHAP. I.
1 Paul commendeth his calling to the Romanes, 9 and his desire to come to them. 16 What his Gospel is, and the righteousnesse which it sheweth. 18 God is angry with all maner of sin. 21 What were the sinnes of the Gentiles.	Paul, commending to the Romans his calling, greeteth them, 8 and professeth his concern for, and desire of coming to see, them. 16 He sheweth that the gospel is for the justification of all mankind through faith; 18 and having premised that sinners in general are obnoxious to God's wrath, he describeth at large the corruption of the Gentile world.
CHAP. II.	CHAP. II.
1 They that sinne, though they condemne it in others, cannot excuse themselues, 6 and much lesse escape the iudgement of God, 9 whether they be Iewes or Gentiles. 14 The Gentiles cannot escape, 17 nor yet the Iewes, 25 whom their Circumcision shall not profit, if they keepe not the Law.	1 They that condemn sin in others, and are guilty of the like themselves, cannot escape God's judgement; 6 which will be according to every man's deserts, without distinction of Jew or Gentile. 14 The Gentiles are not left without a rule of conduct. 17 The Jew, who boasteth of greater light, is doubly criminal in sinning against it; nor will circumcision profit him except he keep the law.

CHAP. III.

1 The Iewes prerogatiue: 3 which they haue not lost: 9 Howbeit the Law conuinceth them also of sinne: 20 Therefore no flesh is iustified by the Law, 28 but all, without difference, by faith onely: 31 And yet the Law is not abolished.

CHAP. III.

1 The Jew's prerogative: 3 which is not vacated by the unbelief of some; 5 nor is God's justice impeached in punishing their sinfulness. 9 The law itself convinceth the Jews also universally of sin; 20 so that no flesh is justified by the deeds of the law; 21 but all indiscriminately by God's grace through faith in Christ: 31 yet without annulling the obligations of the law.

CHAP. IIII.

1 Abrahams faith was imputed to him for righteousnesse, 10 before he was circumcised. 13 By faith only hee and his seed receiued the promise. 16 Abraham is the father of all that beleeue. 24 Our faith also shall be imputed to vs for righteousnes.

CHAP. IV.

1 Abraham himself was justified by faith: 9 which was imputed to him for righteousness before circumcision, that he might be the common father of believers, whether circumcised or not. 13 The promise was not given him through the law, else had it been void from the very nature of the law; but being of faith by grace is sure to all the destined seed, and not to those of the law only. 18 The acceptableness of Abraham's faith; 23 which stands recorded not for his sake only, but for the sake of all who shall profess a like faith in God through Christ.

Probably the printers of later editions considered it an "inexpressible fatigue" to print such wordy "copy," so they soon reverted to the 1611 headings, which are to be found in all modern Bibles.

The running headings at the top of each page are necessarily modified to suit the paging of each edition. This is doubtless the reason why we have entirely lost those of 1611. These are so terse and vigorous that they might well be restored as far as circumstances admit.

The very rare black letter New Testament issued in the year 1679, without place or printer's name, affords an instance of the different classification of the size of a book adopted by competent authorities.

My copy measures $6\frac{1}{4}$ by 4 inches. The Rev. W. J. Loftie, in his "Century of Bibles," page 161, calls this book a 16mo.

In Lea Wilson's list it is described as a 12mo, and in the list of the Canterbury Cathedral Library it is called an octavo.

By Mr. Francis Fry's rule this book would be classed as a small quarto, because the wire lines go across the leaf.

The signature is in twelves; seven numbered, and five blank.

The headings and the initial letter of each chapter are in Roman letter.

In 1833 was published at Oxford, "The Holy Bible, an exact reprint page for page of the Authorized Version published in the year MDCXI." This is a very useful, because extremely exact, reprint of the first issue of 1611.

It is a large quarto, and, so far as it goes, represents the edition of 1611 so completely that it may be consulted with as much confidence as an original. The spelling, punctuation, italics, capitals, and distribution into lines and pages are all followed with the most scrupulous care. It is, however, printed in Roman instead of black letter type, the ornamental initials at the beginning of the chapters are mere fancy work, which does not attempt to imitate the original, and (gravest defect of all) the register of the original is not given, but in its place is substituted the quarto register of the reprint.

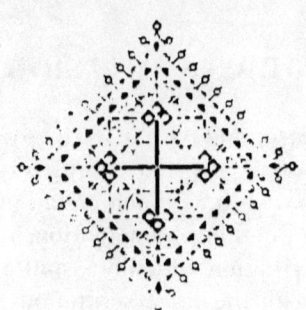

Appendix No. 1.

Preface to King James's Bible of 1611.

THE TRANSLATORS TO THE READER.

The best things have been calumniated.

ZEAL to promote the common good, whether it be by devising any thing our selves, or revising that which hath been laboured by others, deserveth certainly much respect and esteem, but yet findeth but cold entertainment in the world. It is welcomed with suspicion in stead of love, and with emulation in stead of thanks: and if there be any hole left for cavil to enter, (and cavil, if it do not finde a hole, will make one) it is sure to be misconstrued, and in danger to be condemned. This will easily be granted by as many as know story, or have any experience. For, was there ever any thing projected, that savoured any way of newness or renewing, but the same endured many a storm of gainsaying, or opposition? A man would think that Civility, wholesome laws, learning and eloquence, Synods, and Church maintenance, (that we speak of no more things of this kind) should be as safe as a Sanctuary, and out of the danger of the dart, as they say, that no man would lift up the heel, no, nor dog moove his tongue against the motioners of them. For by the first, we are distinguished from brute beasts led with sensuality: By the second, we are bridled and restrained from outragious behaviour, and from doing of injuries, whether by fraud or by violence: by the third, we are enabled to inform and reform others, by the light and feeling that we have attained unto our selves: Briefly, by the fourth being brought together to a parle face to face, we sooner compose our differences then by writings, which are endlesse: And lastly, that the Church be sufficiently provided for, is so agreeable to good reason and conscience, that those mothers are holden to be lesse cruell, that kill their children assoon as they are born, then those nourcing fathers and mothers (wheresoever they be) that withdraw from them who hang upon their brests (and upon whose breasts again themselves do hang to receive the Spirituall and sincere milk of the word) livelihood and support fit for their estates. Thus it is apparent, that these things which we speak of, are of most necessarie use, and therefore, that none, either without absurdity can speak against them, or without note of wickednesse, can spurn against them.

Yet for all that, the learned know that certain worthy men have been brought to untimely death for none other fault, but for seeking to reduce their country-men to good order and discipline: and that in some Common-weals it was made a capitall crime, once to motion the making of a new Law for the abrogating of an old, though the same were most pernicious: And that certain, which would be counted pillars of the State, and paterns of Vertue and Prudence, could not be brought for a long time to give way to good Letters and refined speech, but bare themselves as averse from them, as from rocks, or boxes of poison: And fourthly, that he was no babe, but a great cleark, that gave forth (and in writing to remain to posteritie) in passion peradventure, but yet he gave forth, that he had not seen any profit to come by any Synode, or meeting of the Clergie, but rather the contrary: And lastly, against Church-maintenance and allowance, in such sort, as the Embassadours and messengers of the great King of kings should be furnished, it is not unknown what a fiction or fable (so it is esteemed, and for no better by the reporter himself, though superstitious) was devised: Namely, that at such time as the professours and teachers of Christianitie in the Church of Rome, then a true Church, were liberally endowed, a voyce forsooth was heard from heaven, saying; Now is poyson poured down into the Church, &c. Thus not onely as oft as we speak, as one saith, but also as oft as we do any thing of note or consequence, we subject our selves to every ones censure, and happy is he that is least tossed upon tongues: for utterly to escape the snatch of them it is impossible. If any man conceit, that this is the lot and portion of the meaner sort onely, and that Princes are priviledged by their high estate, he is deceived. As *the sword* determined either on the one or the other, as it is in *Samuel*, nay as the great Commander charged his souldiers in a certaine battell, to strike at no part of the enemie, but at the face; And as the King of *Syria* commanded his chief captaines *to fight neither with small nor great, save onely against the King of Israel:* so it is too true, that Envie striketh most spitefully at the fairest, and at the chiefest. *David* was a worthy Prince, and no man to be compared to him for his first deeds, and yet for as worthy an act as ever he did, (even for bringing back the Ark of God in solemnitie) he was scorned and scoffed at by his own wife. *Solomon* was greater then *David*, though not in vertue, yet in power: and by his power and wisdome he built a Temple to the LORD, such a one as was the glory of the land of Israel, and the wonder of the whole world. But was that his magnificence liked of by all? We doubt of it. Otherwise, why do they lay it in his sonnes dish, and call unto him for easing of the burden, *Make*, say they, *the grievous servitude of thy father, and his sore yoke, lighter.* Belike he had charged them with some levies, and troubled them with some cariages; Hereupon they raise up a Tragedie, and wish in their heart the Temple had never been built. So hard a thing it is to please all, even when we please God best, and do seek to approove our selves to every ones conscience.

If we will descend to latter times, we shall finde many the like examples of such kind, or rather unkind acceptance. The first Roman Emperour did never do a more pleasing deed to the learned, nor more profitable to posteritie, for conserving the record of times in true supputation, then when he corrected the Calender, and ordered the yeer according to the course of the Sunne; and yet this was imputed to him for noveltie, and arrogancie, and procured to him great obloquie. So the first Christned Emperour (at the leastwise that openly professed the faith himself, and allowed others to do the like) for strengthning the Empire at his great charges, and providing for the Church, as he did, got for his labour the name *Pupillus*, as who would say, a wastefull Prince, that had need of a Guardian, or overseer. So the best Christened Emperour, for the love that he bare unto peace, thereby to enrich both himself and his subjects, and because he did not seek war but find it, was judged to be no man at arms (though in deed he excelled in feats of chivalry, and shewed so much when he was provoked) and condemned for giving himself to his ease, and to his pleasure. To be short, the most learned Emperour of former times, (at the least, the greatest politician) what thanks had he for cutting off the superfluities of the laws, and digesting them into some order

The best things have been calumniated

and method? This, that he hath been blotted by some to be an Epitomist, that is, one that extinguished worthy whole volumes, to bring his abridgements into request. This is the measure that hath been rendred to excellent Princes in former times, even *Cum benefacerent, male audire.* For their good deeds to be evill spoken of. Neither is there any likelihood, that envie and malignity died, and were buried with the ancient. No, no, the reproof of *Moses* taketh hold of most ages; *You are risen up in your fathers stead, an increase of sinfull men. What is that that hath been done? that which shall be done: and there is no new thing under the Sunne*, saith the wise man: and S. *Steven, As your fathers did, so do you.* This, and more to this purpose, His Majestie that now reigneth (and long, and long may he reign, and his off-spring for ever, *Himself, and children, and childrens children alwayes)* knew full well, according to the singular wisdome given unto him by God, and the rare learning and experience that he hath attained unto; namely, that whosoever attempteth any thing for the publike (specially if it pertain to Religion, and to the opening and clearing of the word of God) the same setteth himself upon a stage to be glouted upon by every evill eye, yea, he casteth himself headlong upon pikes, to be gored by every sharp tongue. For he that medleth with mens Religion in any part, medleth with their custome, nay, with their freehold; and though they finde no content in that which they have, yet they cannot abide to hear of altering. Notwithstanding his Royall heart was not daunted or discouraged for this or that colour, but stood resolute, *as a statue immoveable, and an anvile not easie to be beaten into plates*, as one saith; he knew who had chosen him to be a Souldier, or rather a Captain, and being assured that the course which he intended, made much for the glory of God, and the building up of his Church, he would not suffer it to be broken off for whatsoever speeches or practises. It doth certainly belong unto Kings, yea, it doth specially belong unto them, to have care of Religion, yea, to know it aright, yea, to professe it zealously, yea, to promote it to the uttermost of their power. This is their glory before all nations which mean well, and this will bring unto them a farre most excellent weight of glory in the day of the Lord Jesus. For the Scripture saith not in vain, *Them that honour me, I will honour*, neither was it a vain word that *Eusebius* delivered long ago, that piety towards God was the weapon, and the onely weapon that both preserved *Constantines* person, and avenged him of his enemies.

His Majesties constancie notwithstanding calumniation, for the survey of the English translations.

The praise of the holy Scriptures.

But now what piety without trueth? what trueth (what saving trueth) without the word of God? what word of God (whereof we may be sure) without the Scripture? The Scriptures we are commanded to search, Joh. 5. 39. Esa. 8. 20. They are commended that searched and studied them, Act. 17. 11. and 8. 28, 29. They are reproved that were unskilfull in them, or slow to beleeve them, Mat. 22. 29., Luk. 24. 25. They can make vs wise unto salvation, 2 Tim. 3. 15. If we be ignorant, they will instruct vs; if out of the way, they will bring us home; if out of order, they will reform us; if in heavinesse, comfort us; if dull, quicken us; if cold, inflame us. *Tolle, lege; Tolle, lege*, Take up and read, take up and read the Scriptures, (for unto them was the direction) it was sayd unto S. *Augustine* by a supernaturall voyce. *Whatsoever is in the Scriptures, beleeve me*, saith the same S. *Augustine*, *is high and divine; there is verily truth, and a doctrine most fit for the refreshing and renewing of mens mindes, and truely so tempered, that every one may draw from thence that which is sufficient for him, if he come to draw with a devout and pious minde, as true Religion requireth.* Thus S. *Augustine*. And S. *Hierome*, *Ama Scripturas, & amabit te sapientia*, &c. Love the Scriptures, and wisdome will love thee. And S. *Cyril* against *Julian*; *Even boyes that are bred up in the Scriptures, become most religious*, &c. But what mention we three or foure uses of the Scripture, whereas whatsoever is to be beleeved or practised, or hoped for, is conteined in them? or three or foure sentences of the Fathers, since whosoever is worthy the name of a Father, from Christs time downeward, hath likewise written not onely of the riches, but also of the perfection of the Scripture? *I adore the fulnesse of the Scripture*, saith *Tertullian* against *Hermogenes*. And againe, to *Apelles* an Heretike of the like stampe, he sayth, *I doe not admit that which thou bringest in* (or concludest) *of thine owne* (head or store, *de tuo*) without Scripture. So Saint *Justin Martyr* before him; *We must know by all means*, (saith he) *that it is not lawfull* (or possible) *to learne* (any thing) *of God or of right pietie, save onely out of the Prophets, who teach us by divine inspiration.* So Saint *Basill* after *Tertullian*, *It is a manifest falling away from the Faith, and a fault of presumption, either to reject any of those things that are written, or to bring in* (upon the head of them, ἐπεισάγειν) *any of those things* that are not written. We omit to cite to the same effect, S. *Cyril* B. of *Hierusalem* in his 4. *Cataches.*, S. *Hierome* against *Helvidius*, Saint *Augustine*, in his third book against the letters of *Petilian*, and in very many other places of his works. Also we forbeare to descend to latter Fathers, because we will not weary the reader. The Scriptures then being acknowledged to be so full and so perfect, how can we excuse our selves of negligence, if we do not studie them, of curiosity, if we be not content with them? Men talk much of εἰρεσιώνη, how many sweet and goodly things it had hanging on it: of the Philosophers stone, that it turneth copper into gold: of *Cornucopia*, that it had all things necessary for food in it, of *Panaces* the herb, that it was good for all diseases: of *Catholicon* the drugge, that it is in stead of all purges: of *Vulcans* armour, that it was an armour of proof against all thrusts, and all blows, &c. Well, that which they falsely or vainly attributed to these things for bodily good, we may justly and with full measure ascribe unto the Scripture, for spirituall. It is not onely an armour, but also a whole armory of weapons, both offensive, and defensive; whereby we may save our selves, and put the enemy to flight. It is not an herb, but a tree, or rather a whole paradise of trees of life, which bring forth fruit every moneth, and the fruit thereof is for meat, and the leaves for medicine. It is not a pot of *Manna*, or a cruse of oyl, which were for memory onely, or for a meals meat or two, but as it were a showre of heavenly bread, sufficient for a whole host, be it never so great; and as it were a whole cellar full of oyl vessels, whereby all our necessities may be provided for, and our debts discharged. In a word, it is a Panary of wholesome food against fenowed traditions; a Physitions shop (Saint *Basil* calleth it) of preservatives against poysoned heresies; a Pandect of profitable Laws against rebellious spirits; a treasury of most costly jewels, against beggerly rudiments; Finally, a fountain of most pure water springing up unto everlasting life. And what marvell? The originall thereof being from heaven, not from earth; the author being God, not man; the enditer, the holy spirit, not the wit of the Apostles or Prophets; the Pen-men such as were sanctified from the womb, and endued with a principall portion of Gods spirit; the matter, verity, piety, purity, uprightnesse; the form, Gods word, Gods testimony, Gods oracles, the word of trueth, the word of salvation, &c. the effects, light of underderstanding, stablenesse of perswasion, repentance from dead works, newnesse of life, holinesse, peace, joy in the holy Ghost; lastly, the end and reward of the studie thereof, fellowship with the Saints, participation of the heavenly nature, fruition of an inheritance immortall, undefiled, and that never shall fade away: Happy is the man that delighteth in the Scripture, and thrice happy that meditateth in it day and night.

Translation necessary.

But how shall men meditate in that, which they cannot understand? How shall they understand that, which is kept shall men pray in an unknowen tongue? as it is written, *Except I know the power of the voyce, I shall be to him that speaketh, a Barbarian, and he that speaketh, shall be a Barbarian to me.* The Apostle excepteth no tongue: not Hebrew the ancientest, not Greek the most copious, not Latine the finest. Nature taught a naturall man to confesse, that all of us in those tongues which we do not understand, are plainly deaf; we may turn the deaf ear unto them. The *Scythian* counted the *Athenian*, whom he did not understand, barbarous: so the *Roman* did the *Syrian*, and the *Jew*, (even Saint *Hierome* himself calleth the Hebrew tongue barbarous, belike because it was strange to so many) so the Emperour of *Constantinople* calleth the *Latin* tongue, barbarous, though Pope *Nicolas* do storm at it: so the *Jews* long before *Christ*, called all other nations, *Lognazim*, which is little better then barbarous. Therefore as one complaineth, that alwayes in the Senate of *Rome*, there was one or other that called for an interpreter: so lest the Church be driven to the like exigent, it is necessary to have translations in a readinesse. Translation it is that openeth the window, to let in the light; that breaketh the shell, that we may eat the kernell; that putteth aside the curtain, that we may look into the most holy place; that removeth the cover of the well, that we may come by the water, even as *Jacob* rolled away the stone from the mouth of the well, by which means the flocks of *Laban* were watered. Indeed without translation into the vulgar tongue, the unlearned are but like children at *Jacobs* well (which was deep) without a bucket, or something to draw with: or as that person mentioned by *Esay*, to whom when a sealed book was delivered, with this motion, *Read this, I pray thee*, he was fain to make this answer, *I cannot, for it is sealed.*

While God would be known onely in *Jacob*, and have his Name great in *Israel*, and in none other place, while the dew lay on *Gideons* fleece onely, and all the earth besides was dry; then for one and the same people, which spake all of them the language of *Canaan*, that is, *Hebrew*, one and the same originall in *Hebrew* was sufficient. But when the fulnesse of time drew neer that the Sunne of righteousnesse, the Sonne of God should come into the world, whom God ordained to be a reconciliation through faith in his blood, not of the *Jew* onely, but also of the *Greek*, yea, of all them that were scattered abroad; then lo, it pleased the Lord to stirre up the spirit of a *Greek* Prince, (*Greek* for descent and Language) even of *Ptolome Philadelph* King of *Egypt*, to procure the translating of the Book of God out of *Hebrew* into *Greek*. This is the translation of the *Seventy* Inter- The translation of the Old Testament out of the Hebrew into Greek.

preters, commonly so called, which prepared the way for our Saviour among the Gentiles by written preaching, as Saint *John* Baptist did among the *Jews* by vocall. For the *Grecians* being desirous of learning, were not wont to suffer books of worth to lye moulding in Kings Libraries, but had many of their servants, ready scribes, to copie them out, and so they were dispersed and made common. Again, the *Greek* tongue was well known, and made familiar to most inhabitants in *Asia*, by reason of the conquests that there the *Grecians* had made, as also by the Colonies, which thither they had sent. For the same causes also it was well understood in many places of *Europe*, yea, and of *Afrike* too. Therefore the word of God being set forth in *Greek*, becometh hereby like a candle set upon a candlestick, which giveth light to all that are in the house, or like a proclamation sounded forth in the market place, which most men presently take knowledge of; and therefore that language was fittest to contain the Scriptures, both for the first Preachers of the Gospel to appeal unto for witnesse, and for the learners also of those times to make search and triall by. It is certain, that that Translation was not so sound and so perfect, but that it needed in many places correction; and who had been so sufficient for this work as the Apostles or Apostolike men? Yet it seemed good to the holy Ghost and to them, to take that which they found, (the same being for the greatest part true and sufficient) rather then by making a new, in that new world and green age of the Church, to expose themselves to many exceptions and cavillations, as though they made a Translation to serve their own turn, and therefore bearing witnesse to themselves, their witnesse not to be regarded. This may be supposed to be some cause, why the Translation of the *Seventy* was allowed to passe for currant. Notwithstanding, though it was commended generally, yet it did not fully content the learned, no not of the *Jews*. For not long after *Christ*, *Aquila* fell in hand with a new Translation, and after him *Theodotion*, and after him *Symmachus*: yea, there was a fift and a sixt edition, the Authours whereof were not known. These with the *Seventie* made up the *Hexapla*, and were worthily and to great purpose compiled together by *Origen*. Howbeit the Edition of the *Seventy* went away with the credit, and therefore not onely was placed in the midst by *Origen* (for the worth and excellency thereof above the rest, as *Epiphanius* gathereth) but also was used by the *Greek* Fathers for the ground and foundation of their Commentaries. Yea, *Epiphanius* above named doeth attribute so much unto it, that he holdeth the Authours thereof not onely for Interpreters, but also for Prophets in some respect:

and *Justinian* the Emperour enjoyning the *Jews* his subjects to use specially the Translation of the *Seventie*, rendreth this reason thereof, because they were as it were enlightened with propheticall grace. Yet for all that, as the *Egyptians* are said of the Prophet to be men and not God, and their horses flesh and not spirit; so it is evident (and Saint *Hierome* affirmeth as much) that the *Seventy* were interpreters, they were not Prophets; they did many things well, as learned men, but yet as men they stumbled and fell, one while through oversight, another while through ignorance, yea, sometimes they may be noted to adde to the Originall, and sometimes to take from it; which made the Apostles to leave them many times, when they left the *Hebrew*, and to deliver the sence thereof according to the trueth of the word, as the Spirit gave them utterance. This may suffice touching the *Greek* Translations of the old Testament.

There were also within a few hundred yeers after CHRIST, translations many into the Latine tongue: for this tongue also was very fit to convey the Law and the Gospel by, because in those times very many countreys of the West, yea, of the South, East, and North, spake or understood Latine, being made Provinces to the *Romanes*. But now the Latine Translations were too many to be all good, for they were infinite (*Latini Interpretes nullo modo numerari possunt*, saith Saint *Augustine*.) Again, they were not out of the *Hebrew* fountain (we speak of the *Latine* Translations of the Old Testament) but out of the *Greek* stream, therefore the *Greek* being not altogether clear, the *Latine* derived from it, must needs be muddie. This moved S. *Hierome* a most learned father, and the best Linguist, without controversie, of his age, or of any that went before him, to undertake the translating of the Old Testament, out of the very fountains themselves, which he performed with that evidence of great learning, judgement, industry and faithfulnesse, that he hath for ever bound the Church unto him, in a debt of speciall remembrance and thankfulnesse.

The translating of the Scripture into the vulgar tongue.

Now though the Church were thus furnished with *Greek* and *Latine* Translations, even before the faith of CHRIST was generally embraced in the Empire; (for the learned know that even in S. *Hieromes* time, the Consull of *Rome* and his wife were both Ethnicks, and about the same time the greatest part of the Senate also) yet for all that the godly-learned were not content to have the Scriptures in the Language which themselves understood, *Greek* and *Latine*, (as the good Lepers were not content to fare well themselves, but acquainted their neighbours with the store that God had sent, that they also might provide for themselves) but also for

Translation out of Hebrew and Greek into Latine.

the behoof and edifying of the unlearned, which hungred and thirsted after Righteousnesse, and had soules to be saved aswell as they, they provided Translations into the vulgar for their Countrymen, insomuch that most nations under heaven did shortly after their conversion, hear CHRIST speaking unto them in their mother tongue, not by the voice of their Minister onely, but also by the written word translated. If any doubt hereof, he may be satisfied by examples enough, if enough will serve the turn. First Saint *Hierome* saith, *Multarum gentium linguis Scriptura ante translata, docet falsa esse quæ addita sunt, &c.* i. *The Scripture being translated before in the languages of many Nations, doeth shew that those things that were added* (by *Lucian* or *Hesychius*) *are false.* So S. *Hierome* in that place. The same S. *Hierome* elswhere affirmeth, that he, the time was, had set forth the translation of the *Seventy*, *suæ linguæ hominibus* i. for his countreymen of *Dalmatia.* Which words not onely *Erasmus* doeth understand to purport, that Saint *Hierome* translated the Scripture into the *Dalmatian* Tongue, but also *Sixtus Senensis*, and *Alphonsus a Castro* (that we speak of no more) men not to be excepted against by them of *Rome*, do ingenuously confesse as much. So S. *Chrysostome* that lived in S. *Hieromes* time giveth evidence with him: *The doctrine of S. John* (saith he) *did not in such sort* (as the Philosophers did) *vanish away: but the Syrians, Egyptians, Indians, Persians, Ethiopians, and infinite other nations being barbarous people, translated it into their (mother) tongue, and have learned to be (true) Philosophers*, he meaneth Christians. To this may be added *Theodoret*, as next unto him, both for antiquity, and for learning. His words be these, *Every country that is under the Sunne, is full of these words*, (of the Apostles and Prophets) *and the Hebrew tongue* (he meaneth the Scriptures in the *Hebrew* tongue) *is turned not only into the Language of the Grecians, but also of the Romans, and Egyptians, and Persians, and Indians, and Armenians, and Scythians, and Sauromatians, and briefly into all the Languages that any Nation useth.* So he in like manner, *Vlpilas* is reported by *Paulus Diaconus* and *Isidor* (and before them by *Sozomen*) to have translated the Scriptures into the *Gothicke* tongue: *John* Bishop of *Sivil* by *Vasseus*, to have turned them into *Arabick*, about the yeer of our Lord 717: *Beda* by *Cistertiensis*, to haue turned a great part of them into *Saxon: Ethnard* by *Trithemius*, to have abridged the French Psalter, as *Beda* had done the *Hebrew*, about the yeer 800: King *Alured* by the same *Cistertiensis*, to have turned the Psalter into *Saxon: Methodius* by *Aventinus* (printed at *Ingolstad*) to have turned the Scriptures into *Sclavonian*: *Valdo*, Bishop of *Frising*, by *Beatus Rhenanus*, to have caused about that time, the Gospels to be translated into *Dutch*-rithme, yet extant in the library of *Corbinian*: *Valdus*, by divers to have turned them himself, or to have gotten them turned into *French*, about the yeere 1160: *Charles* the fift of that name, surnamed *The wise*, to have caused them to be turned into *French*, about 200 yeers after *Valdus* his time, of which translation there be many copies yet extant, as witnesseth *Beroaldus*. Much about that time, even in our King *Richard* the seconds dayes, *John Trevisa* translated them into *English*, and many *English* Bibles in written hand are yet to be seen with divers, translated, as it is very probable, in that age. So the *Syrian* translation of the New Testament is in most learned mens Libraries, of *Widminstadius* his setting forth; and the Psalter in *Arabick* is with many, of *Augustinus Nebiensis* setting forth. So *Postel* affirmeth, that in his travail he saw the Gospels in the *Ethiopian* tongue. And *Ambrose Thesius* alledgeth the Psalter of the *Indians*, which he testifieth to have been set forth by *Potken* in *Syrian* Characters. So that, to have the Scriptures in the mother tongue, is not a quaint conceit lately taken up, either by the Lord *Cromwell* in *England*, or by the Lord *Radevile* in *Polonia*, or by the Lord *Ungnadius* in the Emperours dominion, but hath been thought upon, and put in practice of old, even from the first times of the conversion of any Nation; no doubt, because it was esteemed most profitable to cause faith to grow in mens hearts the sooner, and to make them to be able to say with the words of the Psalm, *As we have heard, so we have seen*.

Now the Church of Rome would seem at the length to bear a motherly affection towards her children, and to allow them the Scriptures in their mother tongue: but indeed it is a gift, not deserving to be called a gift, an unprofitable gift: they must first get a Licence in writing before they may use them, and to get that, they must approve themselves to their Confessor, that is, to be such as are, if not frozen in the dregs, yet soured with the leaven of their superstition. Howbeit, it seemed too much to *Clement* the 8. that there should be any Licence granted to have them in the vulgar tongue, and therefore he overruleth and frustrateth the grant of *Pius* the fourth. So much are they afraid of the light of the Scripture, (*Lucifugae Scripturarum*, as *Tertullian* speaketh) that they will not trust the people with it, no not as it is set forth by their own sworn men, no not with the Licence of their own Bishops and Inquisitors. Yea, so unwilling they

The unwillingness of our chief adversaries, that the Scripture should be divulged in the mother tongue, &c.

are to communicate the Scriptures to the peoples understanding in any sort, that they are not ashamed to confesse, that wee forced them to translate it into English against their wills. This seemeth to argue a bad cause, or a bad conscience, or both. Sure we are, that it is not he that hath good gold, that is afraid to bring it to the touch-stone, but hee that hath the counterfeit; neither is it the true man that shunneth the light, but the malefactour, lest his deeds should be reproved: neither is it the plain-dealing Merchant that is unwilling to have the weights, or the meteyard brought in place, but he that vseth deceit. But we will let them alone for this fault, and return to translation.

The speeches and reasons, both of our brethren, and of our Adversaries against this worke.

Many mens mouthes haue been open a good while, (and yet are not stopped) with speeches about the Translation so long in hand, or rather perusals of Translations made before: and ask what may be the reason, what the necessitie of the employment: Hath the Church been deceived, say they, all this while? Hath her sweet bread been mingled with leaven, her silver with drosse, her wine with water, her milk with lime? *(Lacte gypsum malè miscetur*, saith S. *Ireney.)* We hoped that we had been in the right way, that we had had the Oracles of God delivered unto us, and that though all the world had cause to be offended and to complain, yet that we had none. Hath the nurse holden out the breast, and nothing but winde in it? Hath the bread been delivered by the Fathers of the Church, and the same proved to be *lapidosus*, as *Seneca* speaketh? What is it to handle the word of God deceitfully, if this be not? Thus certain brethren. Also the adversaries of *Judah* and *Hierusalem*, like *Sanballat* in *Nehemiah*, mock, as we hear, both at the work and workmen, saying; *What do these weak Jews, &c. will they make the stones whole again out of the heaps of dust which are burnt? although they build, yet if a fox go up, he shall even break down their stony wall.* Was their Translation good before? Why do they now mend it? Was it not good? Why then was it obtruded to the people? Yea, why did the Catholicks (meaning Popish *Romanists,)* alwayes go in ieopardie, for refusing to go to heare it? Nay, if it must be translated into English, Catholickes are fittest to do it. They have learning, and they know when a thing is well, they can *manum de tabula.* We will answere them both briefly: and the former, being brethren, thus, with S. *Hierome*, *Damnamus veteres? minimè, sed post priorum studia in domo Domini, quod possumus laboramus.* That is, *Do we condemn the ancient? In no case: but after the endevours of them that were before vs, we take the best paines we can in the house of God.* As if he said, Being provoked by the example of the learned that lived before my time, I have thought it my duetie, to assay whether my talent in the knowledge of the tongues, may be profitable in any measure to Gods Church, lest I should seeme to have laboured in them in vain, and lest I should be thought to glory in men, (although ancient,) above that which was in them. Thus S. *Hierome* may be thought to speak.

A satisfaction to our brethren.

And to the same effect say we, that we are so farre off from condemning any of their labours that traveiled before us in this kinde, either in this land or beyond sea, either in King *Henries* time, or King *Edwards* (if there were any translation, or correction of a translation in his time) or Queene *Elizabeths* of ever-renouned memorie, that we acknowledge them to have been raised up of God, for the building and furnishing of his Church, and that they deserve to be had of us and of posteritie in everlasting remembrance. The judgement of *Aristotle* is worthy and well knowen: *If Timotheus had not bene, we had not had much sweet musicke; but if Phrynis (Timotheus* his master) *had not been, we had not had Timotheus.* Therefore blessed be they, and most honoured be their name, that breake the yce, and give the onset upon that which helpeth forward to the saving of soules. Now what can be more availeable thereto, then to deliver Gods booke unto Gods people in a tongue which they understand? Since of an hidden treasure, and of a fountaine that is sealed, there is no profit, as *Ptolemee Philadelph* wrote to the Rabbines or masters of the Jews, as witnesseth *Epiphanius*: and as S. *Augustine* saith; *A man had rather be with his dog then with a stranger* (whose tongue is strange unto him.) Yet for all that, as nothing is begun and perfited at the same time, and the later thoughts are thought to be the wiser: so if we building upon their foundation that went before us, and being holpen by their labours, do endeavour to make that better which they left so good, no man, we are sure, hath cause to mislike us; they, we perswade our selves, if they were alive, would thanke us. The vintage of *Abiezer*, that strake the stroake: yet the gleaning of grapes of *Ephraim* was not to be despised. See *Jud.* 8. verse 2. *Joash* the king of *Israel* did not satisfie himself, till he had smitten the ground three times; and yet he offended the Prophet, for giving over then. *Aquila*, of whom we spake before, translated the Bible as carefully, and as skilfully as hee could; and yet he thought good to go over it again, and then it got the credit with the Jews, to be called κατ' ἀκρίβειαν, that is, acurately done, as Saint *Hierome* witnesseth. How many bookes of profane learning have been gone over again and again, by the same translators, by others? Of one and the same book of *Aristotles* Ethikes, there are exstant not so few as sixe or seven severall translations. Now if this cost may be bestowed upon the gourd, which affordeth us a little shade, and which to day flourisheth, but to morrow is cut downe; what may we bestow, nay, what ought we not to bestow vpon the Vine, the fruit whereof maketh glad the conscience of man, and the stemme whereof abideth for ever? And this is the word of God, which we translate. *What is the chaffe to the wheat, saith the Lord? Tanti vitreum, quanti verum Margaritum?* (saith *Tertullian)* if a toy of glasse be of that reckoning with us, how ought we to value the true pearl? Therefore let no mans eye be evill, because his Majesties is good; neither let any be grieved, that we have a Prince that seeketh the increase of the spirituall wealth of Israel (let *Sanballats* and *Tobiahs* do so, which therefore do bear their just reproof) but let us rather blesse God from the ground of our heart, for working this religious care in him, to have the translations of the Bible maturely considered of and examined. For by this means it cometh to passe, that whatsoever is sound already (and all is sound for substance, in one or other of our editions, and the worst of ours far better then their authentike vulgar) the same will shine as gold more brightly, being rubbed and polished; also, if any thing bee halting, or superfluous, or not so agreeable to the originall, the same may be corrected, and the trueth set in place. And what can the King commaund to be done, that will bring him more true honour then this? and wherein could they that have been set a worke, approve their duetie to the King, yea their obedience to God, and love to his Saints more, then by yeelding their service, and all that is within them, for the furnishing of the work? But besides all this, they were the principall motives of it, and therefore ought least to quarrell it: for the very Historicall trueth is, that upon the importunate petitions of the Puritans, at his Majesties comming to this Crown, the Conference at Hampton Court having been appointed for hearing their complaints: when by force of reason they were put from all other grounds, they had recourse at the last, to this shift, that they could not with good conscience subscribe to the Communion book, since it maintained the Bible as it was there translated, which was, as they sayd, a most corrupted translation. And although this was judged to be but a very poor and emptie shift; yet even hereupon did his Majestie begin to bethink himself of the good that might ensue by a new translation, and presently after gave order for this Translation which is now presented unto thee. Thus much to satisfie our scrupulous Brethren.

Now to the later we answer; that we do not denie, nay we affirme and avow, that the very meanest translation of the Bible in English, set forth by men of our profession (for we have seen none of theirs of the whole Bible as yet) containeth the word of God, nay, is the word of God. As the Kings Speech which he uttered in Parliament, being translated into French, Dutch, Italian and Latin, is still the Kings Speech, though it be not interpreted by every Translator with the like grace, nor peradventure so fitly for phrase, nor so expresly for sense, every where. For it is confessed, that things are to take their denomination of the greater part; and a naturall man could say, *Verum ubi multa nitent in carmine, non ego paucis offendor maculis*, &c. A man may be counted a vertuous man, though he have made many slips in his life, (els, there were none vertuous, for *in many things we offend all*) also a comely man and lovely, though he have some warts upon his hand, yea, not only freakles upon his face, but also skarres. No cause therefore why the word translated should be denied to be the word, or forbidden to be currant, notwithstanding that some imperfections and blemishes may be noted in the setting forth of it. For what ever was perfect under the Sunne, where Apostles or Apostolike men, that is, men indued with an extraordinarie measure of Gods spirit, and privileged with the priviledge of infallibilitie, had not their hand? The Romanists therefore in refusing to heare, and daring to burne the Word translated, did no lesse then despite the spirit of grace, from whom originally it proceeded, and whose sense and meaning, as well as mans weaknesse would enable, it did expresse. Judge by an example or two. *Plutarch* writeth, that after that *Rome* had been burnt by the *Galles*, they fell soon to build it againe: but doing it in haste, they did not cast the streets, nor proportion the houses in such comely fashion, as had been most sightly and convenient; was *Catiline* therefore an honest man, or a good Patriot, that sought to bring it to a combustion? or *Nero* a good Prince, that did indeed set it on fire? So, by the story of *Ezra*, and the prophesie of *Haggai* it may be gathered, that the Temple built by *Zerubbabel* after the returne from *Babylon*, was by no means to be compared to the former built by *Solomon* (for they that remembred the former, wept when they considered the later) notwithstanding, might this later either have been abhorred and forsaken by the *Jews*, or prophaned by the *Greeks*? The like we are to think of Translations. The translation of the *Seventy* dissenteth from the Originall in many places, neither doth it come neer it, for perspicuitie, gravitie, majestie; yet which of the Apostles did condemn it?

An answer to the imputations of our Adversaries.

Condemn it? Nay, they used it, (as it is apparant, and as Saint *Hierome* and most learned men do confesse) which they would not have done, nor by their example of using it, so grace and commend it to the Church, if it had been unworthy the appellation and name of the word of God. And whereas they urge for their second defence of their vilifying and abusing of the *English* Bibles, or some pieces thereof, which they meet with, for that heretikes (forsooth) were the authors of the translations, (heretikes they call us by the same right that they call themselves Catholikes, both being wrong) we marveile what divinitie taught them so. We are sure *Tertullian* was of another minde: *Ex personis probamus fidem, an ex fide personas?* Do we trie mens faith by their persons? we should trie their persons by their faith. Also S. *Augustine* was of an other minde: for he lighting upon certain rules made by *Tychonius* a *Donatist*, for the better understanding of the word, was not ashamed to make use of them, yea, to insert them into his own book, with giving commendation to them so farre forth as they were worthy to be commended, as is to be seen in Saint *Augustines* third book *de doctrina Christiana*. To be short, *Origen*, and the whole Church of God for certain hundred yeers, were of an other minde: for they were so farre from treading under foot, (much more from burning) the Translation of *Aquila* a Proselyte, that is, one that had turned *Jew*; of *Symmachus*, and *Theodotion*, both *Ebionites*, that is, most vile heretikes, that they joyned them together with the *Hebrew* Originall, and the Translation of the *Seventy*, (as hath been before signified out of *Epiphanius*) and set them forth openly to be considered of and perused by all. But we weary the unlearned, who need not know so much, and trouble the learned, who know it already.

Yet before we end we must answere a third cavill and objection of theirs against us, for altering and amending our Translation so oft; wherein truely they deal hardly, and strangely with us. For to whom ever was it imputed for a fault (by such as were wise) to go over that which he had done, and to amend it where he saw cause? Saint *Augustine* was not afraid to exhort Saint *Hierome* to a *Palinodia* or recantation; the same S. *Augustine* was not ashamed to retractate, we might say, revoke, many things that had passed him, and doeth even glory that he seeth his infirmities. If we will be sonnes of the Trueth, we must consider what it speaketh, and trample upon our own credit, yea, and upon other mens too, if either be any way an hinderance to it. This to the cause: then to the persons we say, that of all men they ought to be most silent in this case. For what varieties have they, and what alterations have they made, not onely of their Service books, Portesses and Breviaries, but also of their Latine Translation? The Service Book supposed to be made by Saint *Ambrose (Officium Ambrosianum)* was a great while in speciall use and request: but Pope *Hadrian* calling a Council with the ayd of *Charles* the Emperour, abolished it, yea, burnt it, and commanded the Service Book of Saint *Gregorie* universally to be used. Well, *Officium Gregorianum* gets by this means to be in credit, but doeth it continue without change or altering? No, the very *Romane* Service was of two fashions, the New fashion, and the Old, (the one used in one Church, the other in another) as is to be seen in *Pamelius* a Romanist, his Preface, before *Micrologus*. The same *Pamelius* reporteth out of *Radulphus de Rivo*, that about the yeer of our Lord, 1277, Pope *Nicolas* the third removed out of the Churches of *Rome*, the more ancient books (of Service) and brought into use the Missals of the Friars Minorites, and commaunded them to be observed there; insomuch that about an hundred yeers after, when the above-named *Radulphus* happened to be at *Rome*, he found all the books to be new, (of the new stamp.) Neither was there this chopping and changing in the more ancient times onely, but also of late: *Pius Quintus* himself confesseth, that every Bishoprick almost had a peculiar kinde of service, most unlike to that which others had: which moved him to abolish all other Breviaries, though never so ancient, and priviledged, and published by Bishops in their Dioceses, and to establish and ratifie that onely which was of his own setting forth, in the yeer 1568. Now, when the father of their Church, who gladly would heal the sore of the daughter of his people softly and sleightly, and make the best of it, findeth so great fault with them for their oddes and jarring; we hope the children have no great cause to vaunt of their uniformity. But the difference that appeareth between our Translations, and our often correcting of them, is the thing we are specially charged with; let us see therefore whether they themselves be without fault this way, (if it be to be counted a fault, to correct) and whether they be fit men to throw stones at us: *O tandem maior parcas insane minori*: they that are less sound themselves, ought not to object infirmities to others. If we should tell them that *Valla*, *Stapulensis*, *Erasmus*, and *Vives* found fault with their vulgar Translation, and consequently wished the same to be mended, or a new one to be made, they would answer peradventure, that we produced their enemies for witnesses against them; albeit, they were in no other sort enemies, then as Saint *Paul* was to the *Galatians*, for telling them the truth : and it were to be wished, that they had dared to tell it them plainlier and oftner. But what will they say to this, that Pope *Leo* the tenth allowed *Erasmus* Translation of the New Testament, so much different from the vulgar, by his Apostolike Letter and Bull ; That the same *Leo* exhorted *Pagnin* to translate the whole Bible, and bare whatsoeuer charges was necessary for the work? Surely, as the Apostle reasoneth to the *Hebrews*, that *if the former Law and Testament had been sufficient, there had been no need of the latter :* so we may say, that if the old vulgar had been at all points allowable, to small purpose had labour and charges been undergone, about framing of a new. If they say, it was one Popes private opinion, and that he consulted onely himself ; then we are able to go further with them, and to averre, that more of their chief men of all sorts, even their own *Trent*-champions *Paiva* and *Vega*, and their own Inquisitor *Hieronymus ab Oleastro*, and their own Bishop *Isidorus Clarius*, and their own Cardinall *Thomas a Vio Caietan*, do either make new Translations themselves, or follow new ones of other mens making, or note the vulgar Interpreter for halting ; none of them fear to dissent from him, nor yet to except against him. And call they this an uniform tenour of text and judgement about the text, so many of their Worthies disclaiming the now received conceit? Nay, we will yet come neerer the quick : doth not their *Paris* edition differ from the *Lovaine*, and *Hentenius* his from them both, and yet all of them allowed by authority? Nay, doth not *Sixtus Quintus* confesse, that certain Catholikes (he meaneth certain of his own side) were in such an humour of translating the Scriptures into *Latine*, that Satan taking occasion by them, though they thought of no such matter, did strive what he could, out of so uncertain and manifold a varietie of Translations, so to mingle all things, that nothing might seem to be left certain and firm in them, &c? Nay further, did not the same *Sixtus* ordain by an inviolable decree, and that with the counsell and consent of his Cardinals, that the *Latine* edition of the Old and New Testament, which the Councill of *Trent* would have to be authentike, is the same without controversie which he then set foorth, being diligently corrected and printed in the Printing house of *Vatican?* Thus *Sixtus* in his Preface before his Bible. And yet *Clement* the eight his immediate successour, to accompt of, publisheth another edition of the Bible, containing in it infinite differences from that of *Sixtus*, (and many of them weighty and materiall) and yet this must be authentike by all means. What is to have the faith of our glorious Lord JESUS CHRIST with Yea and Nay, if this be not? Again, what is sweet harmony and consent, if this be? Therefore as *Demaratus* of *Corinth* advised a great King, before he talked of the dissensions among the *Grecians*, to compose his domestick broils: (for at that time his Queen and his son and heir were at deadly feud with him) so all the while that our adversaries do make so many and so various editions themselves, and do jarre so much about the worth and authority of them, they can with no shew of equity challenge us for changing and correcting.

But it is high time to leave them, and to shew in brief what we proposed to our selves, and what course we held in this our perusall and survey of the Bible. Truely (good Christian Reader) we never thought from the beginning, that we should need to make a new Translation, nor yet to make of a bad one a good one, (for then the imputation of *Sixtus* had been true in some sort, that our people had been fed with gall of Dragons in stead of wine, with whey in stead of milk,) but to make a good one better, or out of many good ones, one principall good one, not justly to be excepted against; that hath been our indeavour, that our mark. To that purpose there were many chosen, that were greater in other mens eyes then in their own, and that sought the trueth rather then their own pryse. Again, they came or were thought to come to the work, not *exercendi causa* (as one saith) but *exercitati*, that is, learned, not to learn: For the chief overseer and ἐργοδιώκτης under his Majestie, to whom not only we, but also our whole Church was much bound, knew by his own wisdome, which thing also *Nazianzen* taught so long ago, that it is a preposterous order to teach first and to learn after, yea that τὸ ἐν πίθῳ κεραμίαν μανθάνειν, to learn and practise together, is neither commendable for the workman nor safe for the work. Therefore such were thought upon, as could say modestly with Saint *Hierome*, *Et Hebraeum Sermonem ex parte didicimus, & in Latino pene ab ipsis incunabulis &c. detriti sumus*. *Both we have learned the Hebrew tongue in part, and in the Latine we have been exercised almost from our verie cradle.* Saint *Hierome* maketh no mention of the *Greek* tongue, wherein yet he did excell, because he translated not the old Testament out of *Greek*, but out of *Hebrew*. And in what sort did these assemble? In the trust of their own knowledge, or of their sharpness of wit, or deepness of judgement, as it were in an arm of flesh? At no hand. They trusted in him that hath the key of *David*, opening and no man shutting; they prayed to the Lord the Father of our Lord, to the effect that Saint *Augustine* did; *O let thy Scriptures be my pure delight, let me not be deceived in them, neither let me deceive by*

The purpose of the Translators, with their number, furniture, care, &c.

them. In this confidence, and with this devotion did they assemble together; not too many, lest one should trouble another; and yet many, lest many things haply might escape them. . If you ask what they had before them, truly it was the *Hebrew* text of the Old Testament, the *Greek* of the New. These are the two golden pipes, or rather conduits, wherethrough the olive branches emptie themselves into the gold. Saint *Augustine* calleth them precedent, or originall Tongues; Saint *Hierome*, fountains. The same S. *Hierome* affirmeth, and *Gratian* hath not spared to put it into his Decree, That *as the credite of the old Books* (he meaneth of the Old Testament) *is to be tried by the Hebrew Volumes, so of the New by the Greek tongue*, he meaneth by the originall *Greek*. If trueth be to be tried by these tongues, then whence should a translation be made, but out of them? These tongues therefore, the Scriptures we say in those tongues, we set before us to translate, being the tongues wherein God was pleased to speak to his Church by his Prophets and Apostles. Neither did we run over the work with that posting haste that the *Septuagint* did, if that be true which is reported of them, that they finished it in seventy two dayes; neither were we barred or hindred from going over it again, having once done it, like Saint *Hierome*, if that be true which himself reporteth, that he could no sooner write any thing, but presently it was caught from him, and published, and he could not have leave to mend it: neither, to be short, were we the first that fell in hand with translating the Scripture into English, and consequently destitute of former helps, as it is written of *Origen*, that he was the first in a manner, that put his hand to write Commentaries upon the Scriptures, and therefore no marveil, if he over-shot himself many times. None of these things: the work hath not been hudled up in seventy two dayes, but hath cost the workmen, as light as it seemeth, the pains of twise seven times seventie two dayes and more: matters of such weight and consequence are to be speeded with maturitie: for in a businesse of moment a man feareth not the blame of convenient slacknesse. Neither did we think much to consult the Translators or Commentators, *Chaldee, Hebrew, Syrian, Greek* or *Latine*, no nor the *Spanish, French, Italian*, or *Dutch;* neither did we disdain to revise that which we had done, and to bring back to the anvill that which we had hammered: but having and using as great helps as were needfull, and fearing no reproach for slownesse, nor coveting praise for expedition, we have at the length, through the good hand of the Lord upon us, brought the work to that passe that you see.

Some peradventure would have no varietie of sences to be set in the margine, lest the authoritie of the Scriptures for deciding of controversies by that shew of uncertaintie, should somewhat be shaken. But we hold their judgement not to be so sound in this point. For though, *whatsoever things are necessary, are manifest*, as S. *Chrysostome* saith, and as S. *Augustine*, *In those things that are plainely set downe in the Scriptures, all such matters are found that concerne Faith, Hope, and Charitie.* Yet for all that it cannot be dissembled, that partly to exercise and whet our wits, partly to weane the curious from loathing of them for their every-where-plainenesse, partly also to stirre up our devotion to crave the assistance of Gods Spirit by prayer, and lastly, that we might be forward to seek ayd of our brethren by conference, and never scorne those that be not in all respects so compleate as they should be, being to seek in many things our selves, it hath pleased God in his divine providence, here and there to scatter words and sentences of that difficultie and doubtfulnesse, not in doctrinall points that concern salvation (for in such it hath been vouched that the Scriptures are plain) but in matters of lesse moment, that fearfulnesse would better beseeme us then confidence, and if we will resolve, to resolve upon modestie with Saint *Augustine*, (though not in this same case altogether, yet upon the same ground) *Melius est dubitare de occultis, quam litigare de incertis*, it is better to make doubt of those things which are secret, then to strive about those things that are uncertain. There be many words in the Scriptures, which be never found there but once, (having neither brother nor neighbour, as the *Hebrewes* speak) so that we cannot be holpen by conference of places. Again, there be many rare names of certain birds, beasts and precious stones, &c. concerning which the *Hebrewes* themselves are so divided among themselves for judgement, that they may seem to have defined this or that, rather because they would say something, then because they were sure of that which they said, as Saint *Hierome* somewhere saith of the *Septuagint*. Now in such a case, doth not a margine do well to admonish the Reader to seek further, and not to conclude or dogmatize upon this or that peremptorily? For as it is a fault of incredulitie, to doubt of those things that are evident: so to determine of such things as the Spirit of God hath left (even in the judgement of the judicious) questionable, can be no lesse then presumption. Therefore as Saint *Augustine* saith, that varietie of Translations is profitable for the finding out of the sense of the Scriptures: so diversitie of signification and sence in the margine, where the text is not so clear, must needs do good, yea, is necessary as we are

Reason moving us to set diversity of senses in the margin, where there is great probability for each.

perswaded. We know that *Sixtus Quintus* expresly forbiddeth, that any varietie of readings of their vulgar edition, should be put in the margine (which though it be not altogether the same thing to that we have in hand, yet it looketh that way) but we think he hath not all of his own side his favourers, for this conceit. They that are wise, had rather have their judgements at libertie in differences of readings, then to be captivated to one, when it may be the other. If they were sure that their hie Priest had all laws shut up in his breast, as *Paul* the second bragged, and that he were as free from errour by speciall priviledge, as the Dictators of *Rome* were made by law inviolable, it were another matter: then his word were an Oracle, his opinion a decision. But the eyes of the world are now open, God be thanked, and have been a great while, they finde that he is subject to the same affections and infirmities that others be, that his body is subject to wounds, and therefore so much as he prooveth, not as much as he claimeth, they grant and imbrace.

Reasons inducing us not to stand curiously upon an identity of phrasing.

Another thing we think good to admonish thee of (gentle Reader) that we have not tyed our selves to an uniformitie of phrasing, or to an identitie of words, as some peradventure would wish that we had done, because they observe, that some learned men somewhere, have been as exact as they could that way. Truly, that we might not varie from the sense of that which we had translated before, if the word signified the same thing in both places (for, there be some words that be not of the same sense everywhere) we were especially carefull, and made a conscience, according to our dutie. But, that we should expresse the same notion in the same particular word; as for example, if we translate the *Hebrew* or *Greek* word once by *Purpose*, never to call it *Intent*; if one where *Journeying*, never *Travelling*; if one where *Think*, never *Suppose*; if one where *Pain*, never *Ache*; if one where *Joy*, never *Gladnesse*, &c. Thus to mince the matter, we thought to favour more of curiosity then wisedome, and that rather it would breed scorn in the Atheist, then bring profit to the godly Reader. For is the kingdome of God become words or syllables? why should we be in bondage to them if we may be free, use one precisely when we may use another no lesse fit, as commodiously? A godly Father in the Primitive time shewed himself greatly moved, that one of newfanglenes called κράββατον σκίμπους, though the difference be little or none; and another reporteth, that he was much abused for turning *Cucurbita* (to which reading the people had beene used) into *Hedera*. Now if this happen in better times, and upon so small occasions, we might justly feare hard censure, if generally we should make verball and unnecessary changings. We might also be charged (by scoffers) with some unequall dealing toward a great number of good English words. For as it is written of a certaine great Philosopher, that he should say, that those logs were happie that were made images to be worshipped; for their fellowes, as good as they, lay for blocks behinde the fire: so if we should say, as it were, unto certaine words, Stand up higher, have a place in the Bible alwayes, and, to others of like qualitie, Get ye hence, be banished for ever, we might be taxed peradventure with *S. James* his words, namely, *To be partiall in our selves, and Judges of evill thoughts*. Adde hereunto, that nicenesse in words was alwayes counted the next step to trifling, and so was to be curious about names too; also that we cannot follow a better patterne for elocution then God himselfe; therefore he using divers words, in his holy writ, and indifferently for one thing in nature: we, if we will not be superstitious, may use the same libertie in our English versions out of *Hebrew* and *Greek*, for that copie or store that he hath given us. Lastly, we have on the one side avoided the scrupulositie of the Puritanes, who leave the old Ecclesiasticall words, and betake them to other, as when they put *washing* for *Baptisme*, and *Congregation* in stead of *Church*: as also on the other side, we have shunned the obscuritie of the Papists, in their *Azimes*, *Tunike*, *Rational*, *Holocausts*, *Præpuce*, *Pasche*, and a number of such like, whereof their late Translation is full, and that of purpose to darken the sence, that since they must needs translate the Bible, yet by the language thereof, it may be kept from being understood. But we desire that the Scripture may speake like it selfe, as in the language of *Canaan*, that it may be understood even of the very vulgar.

Many other things we might give thee warning of (gentle Reader) if we had not exceeded the measure of a Preface alreadie. It remaineth, that we commend thee to God, and to the Spirit of his grace, which is able to build further then we can aske or thinke. He removeth the scales from our eyes, the vaile from our hearts, opening our wits, that we may understand his word, enlarging our hearts, yea correcting our affections, that we may love it above gold and silver, yea that we may love it to the end. Ye are brought unto fountaines of living water which ye digged not; doe not cast earth into them with the Philistines, neither preferre broken pits before them with the wicked Jews. Others have laboured, and you may enter into their labours; O receive not so great things in vaine! O despise not so great salvation! Be not like swine to tread under foote so precious things, neither yet like dogs to teare and abuse holy things. Say not to our

Saviour with the *Gergesites*, Depart out of our coasts, neither yet with *Esau*, Sell your birthright for a measse of pottage. If light be come into the world, love not darknesse more then light: if food, if clothing be offered, go not naked, starve not yourselves. Remember the advice of *Nazianzene*, *It is a grievous thing* (or dangerous) *to neglect a great faire, and to seeke to make markets afterwards:* also the encouragement of S. *Chrysostome*, *It is altogether impossible, that he that is sober (and watchfull) should at any time be neglected:* Lastly, the admonition and menacing of S. *Augustine*, *They that despise Gods will inviting them, shall feel Gods will taking vengeance of them.* It is a fearfull thing to fall into the hands of the living God: but a blessed thing it is, and will bring us to everlasting blessednesse in the end, when God speaketh unto us, to hearken; when he setteth his word before us, to read it; when he stretcheth out his hand and calleth, to answere, Here am I; here we are to do thy will, O God. The Lord worke a care and conscience in us to know him and serve him, that we may be acknowledged of him at the appearing of our Lord JESVS CHRIST, to whom with the holy Ghost, be all praise and thanksgiving. Amen.

Appendix No. 2.

Notes on Welsh Bibles.

THIS year 1888 being the tercentenary of the first version of the Bible in the Welsh language, a few notes may be interesting anent the editions that have appeared. These are not numerous. During the sixteenth century only one translation of the New Testament by itself, and one of the whole Bible, were issued; the first in quarto, and the second in small folio. For nearly one hundred years after the Reformation, no Welsh Bible of a convenient size was in existence; and during the whole of the seventeenth century, and a good way into the eighteenth, there were but two folios and four octavo editions printed. None of these editions consisted of a considerable number of copies. It is estimated that the whole of the impressions did not amount to more than 30,000; a very small number for the use of 370,000 persons.

Only one manuscript translation of any part of the Bible into Welsh has been known, and that was a Welsh version of the Pentateuch.

In the year 1551 some detached portions of the Bible were translated from the Vulgate into the Welsh language. They are entitled: *Certain portions of Scripture appointed to be read in Churches in the time of Communion and Public Worship.* In the year 1563 it was enacted by Parliament (5 Eliz., c. 28), "That the Bible, containing the New Testament and the Old, together with the Book of Common Prayer and the administration of the Sacraments, should be translated into the British or Welsh tongue . . . . should be viewed, perused, and allowed by the Bishops of S. Asaph, Bangor, S. David, Landaff and Hereford . . . should be printed and used in the churches by the 1st of March, in the year 1566, under a penalty, in case of failure, of forty pounds, to be levied on each of the above Bishops. That one printed copy at least of this translation should be had for and in every cathedral, collegiate, and parish church and chapel of ease throughout Wales, to be read by the Clergy in time of Divine service, and at other times for the benefit and perusal of any who had a mind to go to church for that purpose, as the inhabitants of Wales, being no small part of the realm, are utterly destituted (*sic*) of God's Holy Word, and do remain in the like, or rather more, darkness and ignorance than they were in the time of Papistry." "That till this version of the Bible and Book of Common Prayer should be completed and published, the Clergy of that country should read in time of worship, the Epistles and Gospels, the Lord's Prayer, the Articles of the Christian Faith, the Litany, and such other parts of the Common Prayer Book, in the Welsh tongue, as should be directed and appointed by the above-mentioned Bishops."

"And not only during this interval but ever after, English Bibles and Common Prayers should be had and remain in every church and chapel throughout that country, with the Welsh translation, so that such as do not understand the English language may, by conferring both tongues together, the sooner attain to the knowledge of the English tongue, anything in this Act to the contrary notwithstanding."

One year after the expiration of the time appointed by the above Act of Parliament, namely, in the year 1567, the first New Testament in Welsh was issued. It was printed by Henry Denham, at the cost and charges of Humphrey Toy, in a handsome quarto volume of 399 leaves, similar to the Blank Stone Mole, and Engraver's-mark editions of Tyndale; black-letter type, not divided into verses, but with arguments and contents to each chapter and book. In the margins are alternative renderings of certain words, but no references to parallel passages. In the preliminary matter is a "calendar" and a dedication in English to "the most vertuous and noble Prince (*sic*) Elizabeth," and a long Epistle in Welsh, by the Bishop of S. David's to his countrymen. This version is said to have been made from the original Greek, and the Vulgate. This *Editio princeps* being now excessively rare, it may be worth while to append its dedication:—

"To the most vertuous and noble Prince Elizabeth, by the grace of God of England, France, and Ireland, Queene, defender of the Faith, etc.

"When I call to remembrance, as well the face of the corrupted religion in England, at what tyme Paules Churcheyarde in the citie was occupied by makers of alabaster images to be set up in churches; and they of Pater noster rowe earned their lyving by makyng of Pater noster bedes only; they of Aue lane by selling Aue bedes; of Crede lane by makyng Crede bedes: As also the vaine rites crepte into our countrey of Wales, when, instede of the lyving God, men worshipped dead images of wood and stones, belles and bones, with other such uncertain reliques I wot not what; and withal consider our late general revolt from Goddes most holy worde once receaued, and dayly heare of the lyke enforced uppon our brethern in forain countryes, having most piteously susteined great calamities, bitter afflictions and merciles persecutions: under which verye many doe yet styll remain; I cannot, most Christian Prince, and gracious Soueraine, but even as dyd the poore blynde Bartimeus or Samaritane lepre to our Sauiour, so I com before your Majesties feete, and there lying prostrate, not onely for my selfe, but also for the deliuery of many thousandes of my countrey folkes, from the spiritual blyndnes of ignoraunce and fowl infection of the old idolatrie and false superstition, most humbly and dutifully to acknowlege your incomparable benefite bestowed upon vs in graunting the sacred Scriptures the verye remedie and salve of our ghostly blyndness and leprosie to be had in our best knowen tongue; which as far as euer I can gather (thoughe Christ's trewe religion sometyme floorished emong our auncesters the old Britons) yet were neuer so entierlye and uniuersallye had, as we now God be thanked have them.

"Our countreymen in tymes passed were indede most loth (and that not wythout good cause) to receaue the Romish religion, and yet haue they nowe synce (such is the domage of euyll custome) bene loth to forsake the same, and to receaue the gospell of Christ. But after that thys nation, as it is thought, for their apostasie had ben sore-plagued wyth long warres, and finally vanquished, and by rigorous lawes kept under, yet at the last it pleased God of his accustomed clemencie to looke down agayne upon them, sending a most godly and noble David and a wyse Solomon, I meane Henry the Seventh and his sonne Henry the Eighth (both kynges of most famous memorie, and your Grace's father and grandfather), who graciously released their paynes and mitigated their intolerable burthens, the one with charters of liberties, and the other with Acts of Parlyament, by abandoning from them al bondage and thraldom, and incorporating them wyth his other louing subjects of England.

"Thys, no doubt, was no small benefit touchyng bodyly welth; but thys benefit of your Maiesties prouidence and goodnesse excedeth that other so far as the soule doeth the bodye. Certaine noble women (whereof some were chiefe rulers of thys nowe your isle of Britain), are by antiquitie vnto us for their singuler learning and heroical vertues highely commended, as Cambra the Fayre, Martia the Good, Bunducia the Wariar, Claudia Rufina mentioned in S. Paules epistle, and Helena, mother of the great and first Christian emperor Constantinus Magnus, and S. Ursula of Cornwals, with such others who are also at thys day styl renowned; but of your Maiestie, I may as I thynk, right well use the wordes of that king who surnamed himself Lemuel. Many doughters have don vertuously; but thou surmountest them all. Fauour is deceiptfull, and beautie is vanitie: but a woman that feareth the Lord, she shall be praysed. For if M. Magdalen for the bestowing of a boxe of material oyntment, to annoynt Christes carnal body, be so famous throwe out all the world where the gospell is preached, howe muche more shall your munificence by conferring the unction of the holy ghost to annoynct his spiritual body the churche, be ever had in memorie?

"But to conclude and to drawe neare to offer up my vowe: where as I, by our most vigilant pastours the Bishopes of Wales, am called and substituted, though unworthy, somewhat to deale in the perusing and setting fourth of thys so worthy a matter, I thynk it my most bounden duetie here in their name, to present to your Maiestie (as the chiefest fyrst fruicte) a booke of the New Testament of our Lorde Jesus Christ, translated into the British language, which is our vulgare tongue, wyshing and most humbly praying, it it shall so seme good to your wysedome, that it myght remayne in your M. Librarie, for a perpetual monument of your graciouse bountie shewed herein to our countrey, and the churche of Christ there. And would to God that your Graces subiectes of Wales might also have the whole booke of God's woord brought to like passe: then might their felow subiectes of England reioycingly pronounce of them in these wordes, The people that sate in darknes, have seen a great lyght; they that dwelled in the land of the shadowe of death upon them hath the lyght shyned. Blessed are the people that be so, yea blessed are the people whose God is the Lord. Yea than wold they both together thus brotherly say, Come, and let us go up to the mountaine of the Lord, and he wyll teache us hys wayes, and we wyll walke in his pathes, &c.

"And thus to ende, I beseeche Almyghtye God, that as your Grace's circumspect providence doth perfectlye accomplish and discharge your princely vocation and gouvernaunce towardes all your humble subiects, that we also on our part may towards God and your highness demeane our selves in such wyse, that His iustice abrydge not these halcyons and quiet days which hetherto since the begynning of your happie reigne have most calmely and peaceably continued: but that we may long enioy your gracious presence and most prosperous reigne over us: which we beseche God, for our Saviour Jesus Christes sake moste mercifullye to graunt us. Amen.

Your Maiestie's
Most humble and
Faithfull subiect
WILLIAM SALESBURY."

The translators of this Testament were:

W. S.—William Salesbury;

T. H. C. M.—Thomas Huet, Chantor Menevensis;

D. R. D. M.—Dr. Richard Davis, Menevensis.

The Bishop of S. David's took the second Epistle to S. Timothy, the Hebrews, S. James, and the first and second Epistle of S. Peter; Thomas Huet, Precentor of S. David's, translated the Apocalypse; and William Salesbury the rest of the book. All three were men of eminent learning, and their work has ever been regarded as accurate but inelegant. Dr. Davis was a native of Denbigh, and was educated at Oxford. He left England at the death of Edward VI. On his return early in the reign of Elizabeth, he was consecrated Bishop of St. Asaph (January 21st, 1560), and translated to the See of S. David May 21st, 1561. He was one of the Bishops selected by Archbishop Parker to revise the Bible of 1568, commonly called the Bishops' Version. His share was the Books of Joshua, Judges, and Ruth. He died November 7th, 1581, aged eighty years.

The first complete Bible in Welsh is known as "Morgan's" Bible. It is small folio size, and is dated 1588. It contains the Old Testament, Apocrypha, and New Testament. The chapters are divided into verses. It has a table of contents prefixed to each chapter, and marginal references. A long dedication in Latin, to Queen Elizabeth, signed GVLIELMVS MORGANVS, also a calendar and other tables. Like the Welsh New Testament of 1567, it is numbered, not by pages, but by leaves, of which there are 555. It was printed at London by Christopher Barker. The title is, *Y Beibl Cyssegr-Lan, Sef yr hen Destament a'r Newydd.*

It has always been uncertain by whom Myles Coverdale was employed to translate the first English Bible, and it is equally doubtful by whom Morgan was induced to undertake the task of translating the Bible into Welsh. He mentions in his preface the support and encouragement he received from Whitgift, Archbishop of Canterbury. He would have sunk, he says, under his difficulties and relinquished the work, or would only have published the five books of Moses, had it not been for the Archbishop's help. Little is known of Coverdale's assistants in the work of translating, although it is almost impossible he could have accomplished it single-handed, and Morgan's assistants are equally unknown. Morgan speaks of, as his patrons, the Archbishop of Canterbury, the Bishops of St. Asaph and Bangor; Dean Goodman, of Westminster; Dr. David Powel; Archdeacon Edmund Prys, of Merioneth, author of the Welsh Psalms in metre; and the Rev. Richard Vaughan, Rector of Lutterworth, afterwards Bishop of Bangor, Chester, and of London. During the time the book was going through the press, Morgan resided with the Dean of Westminster. The exact number of copies of which the edition consisted is not known; there is reason to believe they did not exceed one thousand.

The statute of 1562 evidently does not contemplate a household Bible but one for church use.

A quarto edition of the Prayer Book and Psalter, beautifully printed in black letter, was printed the same year 1588. It is now a very rare book, much more difficult to procure than Salesbury's Testament, or Morgan's Bible.

At the commencement of the seventeenth century, a revision of Morgan's Bible was undertaken by his successor in the See of S. Asaph, Dr. Richard Parry. This new version was printed in London in 1620, by Bonham Norton and John Bill, who had purchased the patent right of Robert Barker to print the Bible. It is a grand folio volume, printed in clear black letter type, on good paper. The marginal references are taken from King James's Bible of 1611. The signatures of the Old Testament and the Apocrypha run to Eeee 3, and the New Testament from A to Y 2. Bishop Parry dedicated his Bible in Latin, to the Most Holy and Undivided Trinity, and to King James I. In it he says, that the copies of Morgan's Bible being exhausted, and many or most of the Welsh Churches being without Bibles, or having only worn or imperfect copies, he set about revising the Welsh Bible, as the English Bible had recently been revised, for the sake of providing for his countrymen a better and more correct version than they had ever possessed. Dr. John Davis, the learned Chaplain of the Bishop of S. Asaph, had a considerable share in the work of revision. He was admirably suited for the purpose, being well versed in Hebrew and Greek, and complete master of the Welsh language. This is important, as from one rendering in the Apocalypse it has been supposed it was translated solely from the English version into Welsh, without the original languages being consulted. The verse referred to is the eighth of the fifth chapter of the Revelation of S. John the Divine, which, in Morgan's Bible of 1588, reads: "The four-and-twenty elders fell down before the Lamb, having every one of them harps and golden fiddles full of odours," etc. "Crythau," which signifies fiddles or violins, being used instead of "phialau," the Welsh word for vials. The translator, it has been imagined, having only the English Bible before him, mistook "vials" for "viols." This may have been a printer's error, like one recently made in a rubric of a French Canon of Mass, which orders that "*Ici le prêtre ôte sa culotte*," instead of "*Ici le prêtre ôte sa calotte.*"

The first octavo Bible in the Welsh language is said on the title page to be, "Printiedig yn Llvndain. Robert Barker, Printiwr i Ardderchoccaf fawrhydi y Brenin: a chan Assignes Iohn Bill, A.D. 1630." It has four pages of Bishop Parry's Latin dedication; this is followed by four pages in smaller type of Morgan's address to "Illustrissimæ, Potentissimæ, serenissimæque Principi Elizabethæ D. G. Angliæ, Galliæ et Hiberniæ Reginæ, fidei veræ, et Apostolicæ Propugnat," etc.; then an address in Welsh of two pages, and on recto of last leaf of preliminary, "Nomina eorum qui præ cæteris hoc opus promouere conati sunt;" and on verso, "Henwav a threfn Llyfrav 'r hen Destament a'r Newydd, a rhifedi pennodau pob Llyfr." The text is printed in Roman type. The only woodcut is the "Temptation in the Garden of Eden." The book is without pagination, and is printed in double columns, having seventy-three lines to a full column. It was undertaken, like other Welsh Bibles, not by any public authority, but by private individuals, on their own responsibility and risk. Sir Thomas Middleton, and Mr. Rowland Heylyn, both Aldermen of London, and natives of Wales, co-operating with two other gentlemen, undertook to supply the great want that had been so long felt of a Bible of a size suitable for family and private reading.

The reason the Bible in Welsh was so sparingly supplied, was to induce the Welsh people to study the English language for the sake of obtaining a knowledge of the Scriptures, and thus gradually to banish the ancient British language from the principality, and to substitute for it the English tongue.

The third folio edition of the Holy Scriptures in Welsh is commonly known as "Lloyd's" Bible. It was printed at the Theatre, Oxford, 1690, in Roman letter. It has two title pages to the Old Testament: one, the usual plate engraving usual in Oxford Bibles of this date; the other, a letter press title. There are also two titles to the New Testament. It is well printed, on good paper, but not nearly so handsome a book as Parry's Bible of 1620.

Why Bishop Lloyd should have the credit of this edition it is difficult to say. It was brought out under the superintendence of Mr. Pierce Lewis, an Anglesea man, who discharged his trust accurately and well. It does not pretend to be a new translation, but merely a faithful reprint of the Bible of 1620.

The octavo edition of the Welsh Bible, issued in 1654, consisted of 6,000 copies. This is the first record we have of the exact number of copies of which any edition was made up. Numerous as it was, it soon became exhausted, and in 1677 another octavo edition was produced of 8,000 copies. One thousand were distributed gratuitously among the poor, and the remainder were offered for sale at four shillings each. An edition of the Book of Common Prayer in Welsh was published in 1664, in black letter. Many errors having been made in reprinting one edition after another, Mr. Stephen Hughes, of Swansea, undertook to act as editor of the 1677 octavo, and a better man for the purpose could not have been selected, as he had long been engaged in publishing Welsh literature, amongst other books the popular Welsh poetry of the Rev. Rhys Richard, of Llandovery. A great many copies of this edition were put into circulation by Mr. Thomas Gouge, a benevolent man, who always gave away two thirds of his income, and managed to live on the remainder, which amounted to rather less than a pound a week. When over sixty years of age he used to travel about Wales, and personally distribute his bounty among the poor and needy. His funeral sermon was preached by Archbishop Tillotson, and afterwards published. In this sermon Tillotson states that, aided by the contributions of others, Mr. Gouge established a great number of schools in the principality, and liberally supplied them with Welsh books, particularly with the Prayer Book, the New Testament, and the octavo Welsh Bible. Mr. Gouge died in 1681, and his colleague, Mr. Hughes, in the year 1687.

Sir Thomas Middleton and Mr. Rowland Heylyn were not the only Aldermen of London who exerted themselves to supply the inhabitants of Wales in their mother tongue, for in a copy of this Bible in Earl Spencer's library there is the following note:—"Presented by the Publisher to Sir Richard Clayton, of the City of London, Knt., Alderman and Mayor thereof, anno 1679, in thankfull acknowledgement of his former bounty to Wales, in contributing towards the printing of this Bible, and teaching many hundreds of poor children to read, and some to write."

The next edition of the Welsh Bible came out in quarto, in the year 1689, and was the last issued in the seventeenth century. It was printed by Bill and Newcombe, London, on rather poor paper, and from small and badly cast type. Its editor was Mr. David Jones. A considerable portion of the expense was defrayed by the Earl of Warton, once a member of Queen Anne's Cabinet. Ten thousand copies of this edition were speedily distributed.

The first edition issued in the eighteenth century was an octavo one, dated 1718. It has two engraved maps, signed, "Llundain. Ioan Basged." It was edited by the Rev. Moses Williams, Vicar of Dyfynog, Brecon, an excellent scholar, who assisted Dr. Wotton in publishing the *Leges Wallicæ*. He added to this Bible a table of interpretation of Hebrew and Greek names into Welsh. To the Society for Promoting Christian Knowledge is due the honour of publishing this and the two following editions. The second edition is dated 1727. This is small octavo size, without contents of chapters or marginal references, and was for this reason very little valued by Welsh people. The next was printed by J. Bentham, Caer Grawnt, 1746, in octavo. In addition to the Apocrypha, the Old and New Testament, it has the Prayer-Book, and a Metrical Psalter, by Archdeacon

Prys. This Prayer-Book contains the Acts of Uniformity of Elizabeth and Charles II. The table dates from 1746 to 1785. Great prominence is given to the ornaments rubric. It is printed in larger type than any other part of the book, and occupies an entire page. The Epistles and Gospels are all given in full. The authorisation of the State services is signed, "Townshend, 1728;" then follows the Ordinal and Canons of 1603. The last page has a table of affinity and consanguinity that "let" marriage. At the end of the New Testament are twenty-three pages of chronological and five of other tables. The Psalter has a fresh signature, and after it are sundry prayers.

In 1752, under the care of Mr. Morris, Baskett produced an octavo edition, which could not be spoken of as some of Baskett's Bibles have been, as Basketfuls of errors, for it is considered the most correct Welsh Bible ever printed.

In 1770 a quarto was printed at Carmarthen with a Welsh concordance, some notes in which were supposed to favour Sabellianism.

The last Welsh Bibles to be mentioned are the octavos of 1770 and 1799. The latter consisted of 10,000 copies, and, like the 1746 issue, contained the Book of Common Prayer and the Psalms in metre. The Psalms in metre were published separately several times. Thomas Salesbury's version in 1603, and Archdeacon Pryse's in 1648. The New Testament was also issued by itself in 1647 in 12mo.; in 1654 in 4to.; in 1672, and again by the Society for Promoting Christian Knowledge, in 1752 and 1769.

Appendix No. 3.

THE following is an early English version of the Epistle to the Laodiceans, which was ordered by S. Paul to be also read to the church at Colosse. It is now considered Apocryphal :—

"Paul apostil not of men, ne bi man, but bi Iesu Crist, to the Britherin that bin at Laodice; grace to yhou, and pees of God the Fadir, and the Lord Iesu Crist. I do thankyngis to my God, bi al myn orisoun that ye bin dwellynge and lastynge in hym, abidinge the biheeste in the dai of doom. For neithir the vein spekynge of somme unwise men, hath lettyed yhou the whiche wolden turne yhou fro the treuthe of the Ghospel that is preched of me, and now bin of me to the profight of the truthe of the Ghospel. God schal make deseroynge and doynge benygnyte of workis of heelthe of everlastynge lyf. And now mi boondis bin open which I suffre in Crist Iesu: in whiche I glade and joye, and that is to me everlastynge heelthe, that this same thinge bin doon by yhoure preiers and mynystringe of the Holy Goost eithir bi lyf, eithir bi deeth. Forsothe to me is lyf to lyve in Crist, and to die joye withouten ende. And his merci schal do in yhou that same thing, that ye mun have the same lovynge, and that yhe be of o will.

"Therfore yhe weel beloved britheren, hold yhe, and do yhe in the drede of God, as yhe han herde in the presence of me, and lyf schal bin to yhou withouten ende.

"Sotheli it is God that worcketh in yhou. And my weel beloved britheren do yhe withouten ony withdrawynge what evere thinge is that yhe doon. Ioye yhe in Crist and eschewe yhe man defouled with lucre, eithir foul wynnynge.

"Be alle yhour thingis open anentis God, and be yhe stidefast in the witt of Crist, and do yhe thos thingis that bin hool, and trewe, and just, and lovable. And kepe yhe in herte thos thingis yhe have herd, and pees shal be to yhou. All holi men greeten yhou. The grace of our Lord Iesu Crist be with yhoure spirit. Do yhe that pistil of colosensis bin red to yhou. Amen."

Appendix No. 4.

LIST OF ENGLISH BIBLES AND TESTAMENTS IN THE AUTHOR'S COLLECTION.

TYNDALE'S VERSION.

Title.	Size.	Date.	Printer.	Remarks.
N. T.	Quarto	1536	Printer unknown	Blank stone.
,,	,,	1538-7	Powell	2 copies.
,,	Octavo	1550	Gaultier	I. C.
,,	Quarto	1552	Jugge.	
,,	,,	1553	,,	
,,	,,	-	Watkins.	

COVERDALE'S VERSION.

Title.	Size.	Date.	Printer.	Remarks.
Bible	Folio	1535	Meterin	A fragment.
N. T.	12mo	1538	Crom	Imperfect.
,,	Quarto	1538	Nicolson.	
Bible	,,	1550	Hester	Large paper.

MATTHEW'S VERSION.

Title.	Size.	Date.	Printer.	Remarks.
Bible	Folio	1537.		
,,	,,	1549	Raynalde & Hyll.	
,,	,,	1549	Daye and Seres	2 copies.

TAVERNER'S VERSION.

Title.	Size.	Date.	Printer.	Remarks.
Bible	Folio	1551	Daye	2 copies.

GREAT BIBLE.

Title.	Size.	Date.	Printer.	Remarks.
Bible	Folio	1539	Grafton & Whitchurch.	
,,	,,	1540	,, ,,	April.
,,	,,	1541	,, ,,	May.
,,	,,	1541	,, ,,	December.

GREAT BIBLE—*continued.*

Title.	Size.	Date.	Printer.	Remarks.
Bible -	Folio -	1540 -	Whitchurch.	
,, -	,, -	1553 -	,,	
,, -	Quarto -	1553 -	Grafton.	
,, -	,, -	1561 -	Cawoode.	
,, -	,, -	1562 -	Harrison.	
,, -	Folio -	1566 -	Hamilton, Carmarden.	

GENEVAN VERSION.

Title.	Size.	Date.	Printer.	Remarks.
N. T. -	12mo -	1557 -	Badius.	
Bible -	Quarto -	1560 -	Hall - -	2 copies.
,, -	Folio -	1562 ?		
,, -	Quarto -	1568 -	Crespin.	
N. T. -	Octavo -	1575 -	Vautroulier.	
Bible -	Folio -	1576 -	Barker.	
N. T. -	Octavo -	1576 -	,, - -	Tomson.
,, -	,, -	1577 -	,, - -	,,
Bible -	Folio -	1578 -	,,	
,, -	Quarto -	1579 -	,,	
N. T. -	Octavo -	1580 -	,,	,,
,, -	,, -	1582 -	,,	,,
Bible -	Quarto -	1582 -	,,	
N. T. -	,, -	1583 -	,, -	
Bible -	,, -	1585 -	,,	
,, -	,, -	1587 -	,,	
,, -	,, -	1589 -	,,	
N. T. -	12mo -	1589 -	,, - -	,,
Bible -	Octavo -	1592 -	,, - -	Unique.
N. T. -	Quarto -	1593 -	,, - -	Tomson.
Bible -	,, -	1594 -	,, - -	1495.
N. T. -	,, -	1595 -	,, - -	Tomson.
Bible -	Octavo -	1596 -	,,	
,, -	Quarto -	1599 -	,, - -	5 editions.
,, -	Octavo -	1601 -	,,	
,, -	Quarto -	1602 -	,,	
,, -	Octavo -	1606 -	,,	
,, -	Folio -	1610 -	,,	
,, -	,, -	1611 -	,,	
N. T. -	Octavo -	1613 -	,,	
Bible -	Quarto -	1614 -	,,	
,, -	,, -	1615 -	,,	
,, -	Folio -	1616 -	,,	
N. T. -	Octavo -	1616 -	,,	
Bible -	Folio -	1641 -	Stafford.	
,, -	,, -	1644 -	,,	

BISHOPS' VERSION.

Title.	Size.	Date.	Printer.	Remarks.
Bible	Folio	1568	Jugge	Imperfect.
,,	Quarto	1569	,,	
,,	Folio	1572	,,	
,,	Quarto	1573	,,	
,,	Folio	1574	,,	With map.
,,	Sm. folio	1575	,,	
,,	Quarto	1576	,,	
,,	,,	1577	,,	Wants 1st title.
,,	Octavo	1577	,,	
,,	Folio	1578	Barker.	
N. T.	12mo	1581	,,	
Bible	Folio	1584	,,	
,,	Quarto	1584	,,	
,,	Folio	1595	,,	
,,	,,	1602	,,	
N. T.	12mo	1614	,,	Tyndale's notes.
,,	,,	1617	,,	,,
,,	,,	1619	Norton & Bill	,,

RHEIMS AND DOUAI VERSIONS.

N. T.	Quarto	1582	Fogny.	
,,	,,	1600	Veruliet.	
O. T.	,,	1609-10	Kellam	2 vols.
N. T.	12mo	1621	Seldenslach.	
,,	Quarto	1633	Cousturier.	
O. T.	,,	1635	,,	2 vols.

KING JAMES'S VERSION.

Bible	Folio	1611	Barker	3 issues.
,,	Quarto	1612	,,	Roman letter.
,,	Octavo	1612	,,	,,
N. T.	Quarto	1612	,,	Black letter.
Bible	Folio	1613	,,	
,,	Quarto	1613	,,	Black letter.
,,	Octavo	1613	,,	
,,	Folio	1616	,,	Roman letter.
,,	,,	1617	,,	
,,	Quarto	1619	Norton & Bill.	
,,	Folio	1629	Buck.	

KING JAMES'S VERSION—*continued.*

Title.	Size.	Date.	Printer.	Remarks.
N. T.	Quarto	1631	Barker & Bill.	
Bible	Octavo	1633	K.g.'s Prntr., Edinburgh.	
..	Folio	1634	Barker & Bill.	
..	..	1638	Buck & Daniel.	
..	..	1641	Barker & Bill.	
..	..	1642	[illegible]	Genevan notes.
N. T.	Octavo	1647	[illegible]	
Bible	12mo	1653	Field.	
..	Quarto	[illegible]	..	
..	..	1675	Theatre, Oxford.	
N. T.	Octavo	[illegible]		Black letter.
Bible	Quarto	1683	Theatre, Oxford.	
..	Folio	1717	Baskett	2 issues, "Vinegar."
..		1762	Bentham	2 vols.

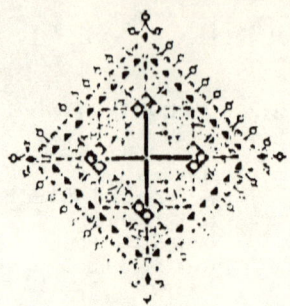

Printed by Eyre & Spottiswoode, *Queen's Printers*, Downs Park Road, Hackney.

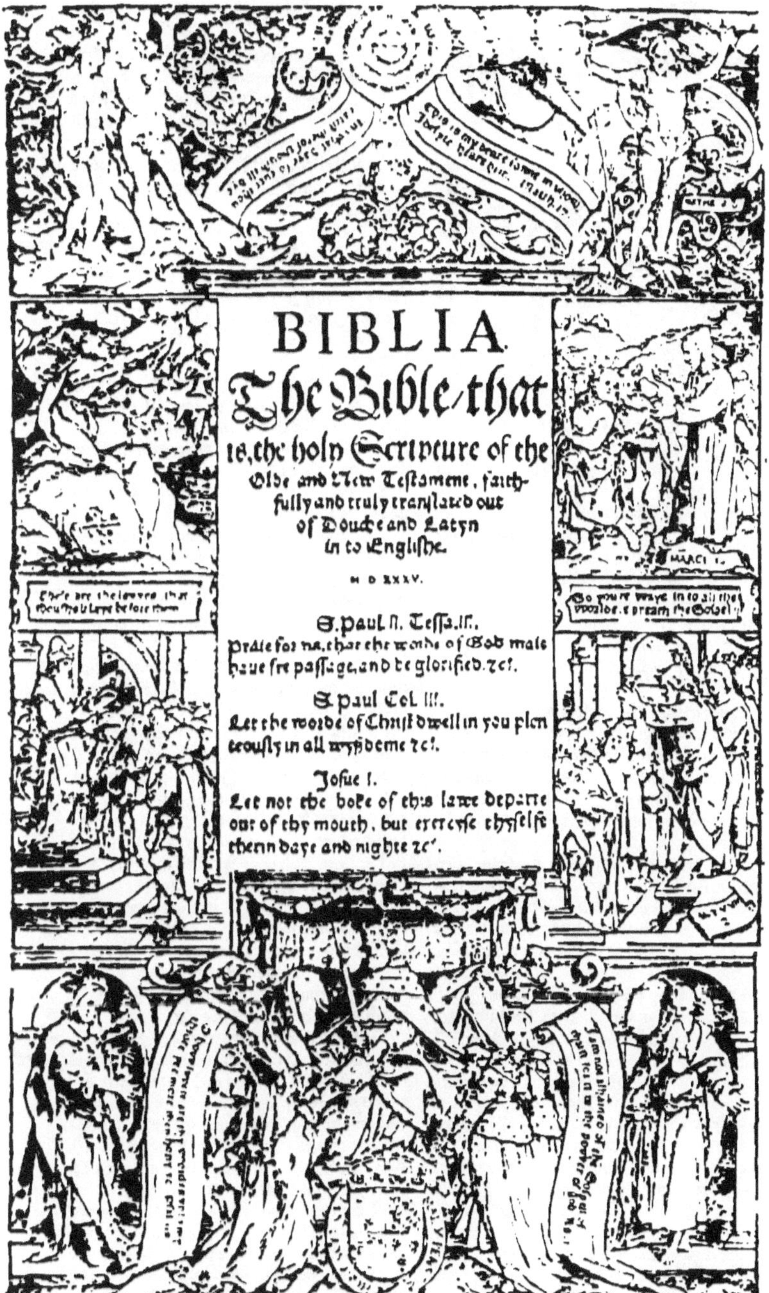

TITLE TO COVERDALE'S BIBLE, 1535.

Size of Original, 12¼ × 8 in. See page [illegible].)

The gospell of S. Marke.

The first Chapter.

A This is the begynnyn
ge of the gospell of
Iesus Christ the son
ne of God, as it is
Mal.3.a wrytte in the prophe
Mat.11.b tes. Beholde, I sen
Luc.7.c de my messaunger be
fore thy face, which
Esa.40.a shal prepare thy waye before the. The voy
Mat.3.a ce of a cryer is in the wyldernes: Prepare
Luc.3.a the waye of the LORDE, make his pathes
Iohã.1.b straight.
Ihon was in the wyldernes, and bapty-
Iohã 3.d sed, and preached the baptyme of amend-
ment, for the remyssion of synnes. And the-
re wente out vnto him the whole londe of
Iewry, and they of Ierusalem, and were
all baptysed of him in Iordan, and knowle-
ged thar synnes.
Ihon was clothed with Camels heer,
Mat.3.a and with a lethren gerdell aboute his loy-
nes, and ate locustes and wylde hony, and
preached, and sayde: There commeth one
Mat.3.b after me, which is stronger then I: before
Luc.3.c whom I am not worthy to stoupe downe,
Iohã.1.c and to lowse vp ẏ lachet of his shue. I bap
tyse you with water, but he shal baptyse
you with the holygoost.
Mat.3.b And it happened at the same tyme, that
Luc.3.c Iesus came out of Galile from Nazareth,
Iohã.1.d and was baptysed of Ihon in Iordan. And
as soone as he was come out of the water,
he sawe that the heauens opened, and the
Some goost as a doue comynge downe vpon him.
reade: And there came a voyce from heauē: Thou
*In whō art my deare sonne, *in whom I delyte.
I am pacified.
B And immediatly the sprete droue him in
Mat.4.a to the wyldernes: and he was in the wylder
Luc.4.a nes fourtye dayes, and was tempted of Sa
than, and was with the wylde beestes. And
the angels mynistred vnto him.
But after that Ihon was taken, Iesus Mat.4.b
came in to Galile, and preached the gospell Luc.4.b
of the kyngdome of God, and sayde: the ty
me is fulfylled, and the kyngdome of God is
at hande: Amende youre selues, and beleue
the gospell.
So as he walked by the see of Galile, he Mat.4.c
sawe Symon and Andrew his brother, cas Luc.5.a
tinge their nettes in the see, for they were
fysshers. And Iesus sayde vnto thē: Folowe
me, and I wil make you fysshers of mē. And Iere.16.c
immediatly they left thar nettes, and fo- Eze.47.b
lowed him.
And when he was gone a lytle further
from thence, he sawe Iames the sonne of
Zebede, and Ihon his brother, as they were
in the shyppe mendynge their nettes. And
anone he called them. And they left their fa
ther Zebede in the shyppe with the hyred ser
uauntes, and folowed him.
And they wente in to Capernaum, and Luc.4.d
immediatly vpon the Sabbathes, he entred Iohã.2.b
in to the synagoge, and taught. And they Mat.7.c
were astonnyed at his doctryne: for he
taught them as one hauynge power, and
not as the Scrybes.
And in their synagoge there was a man C
possessed with a foule sprete, which cried and Luc.4.d
sayde: Oh what haue we to do with the,
thou Iesu of Nazareth. Art thou come to
destroye vs? I knowe that thou art euen ẏ
holy one of God. And Iesus reproued him,
and sayde: holde thy tonge, and departe
out of him. And the foule sprete tare him,
and cried with a loude voyce, and departed
out of him. And they were all astonnyed, in
so moch that they axed one another amonge thē selues, & sayde: What is this? What
new lernynge is this? For he cōmaundeth
the foule spretes with power, and they are
obedient vnto him. And immediatly the fa
me of him was noysed rounde aboute in the
coastes and borders of Galile.
And forth with they wente out of the sy- Mat.8.b
nagoge, and came in to the house of Symō Luc.4.d
and Andrew, wt Iames and Ihon. And Sy
mons mother in lawe laye, & had the feuers,
and anone they tolde him of her. And he ca
me to her, and set her vp, and toke her by ẏ
hande, and the feuer left her immediatly.
And she mynistred vnto them.
At euen whan the Sonne was gone Mat.8.b
downe, they brought vnto him all that we- Luc.4.e
re sick and possessed, and the whole cite
was gathered together at the dore, and

PAGE OF COVERDALE'S BIBLE, 1535.

(*Size of Original*, 12½ × 8 *in.* *See page* 91.)

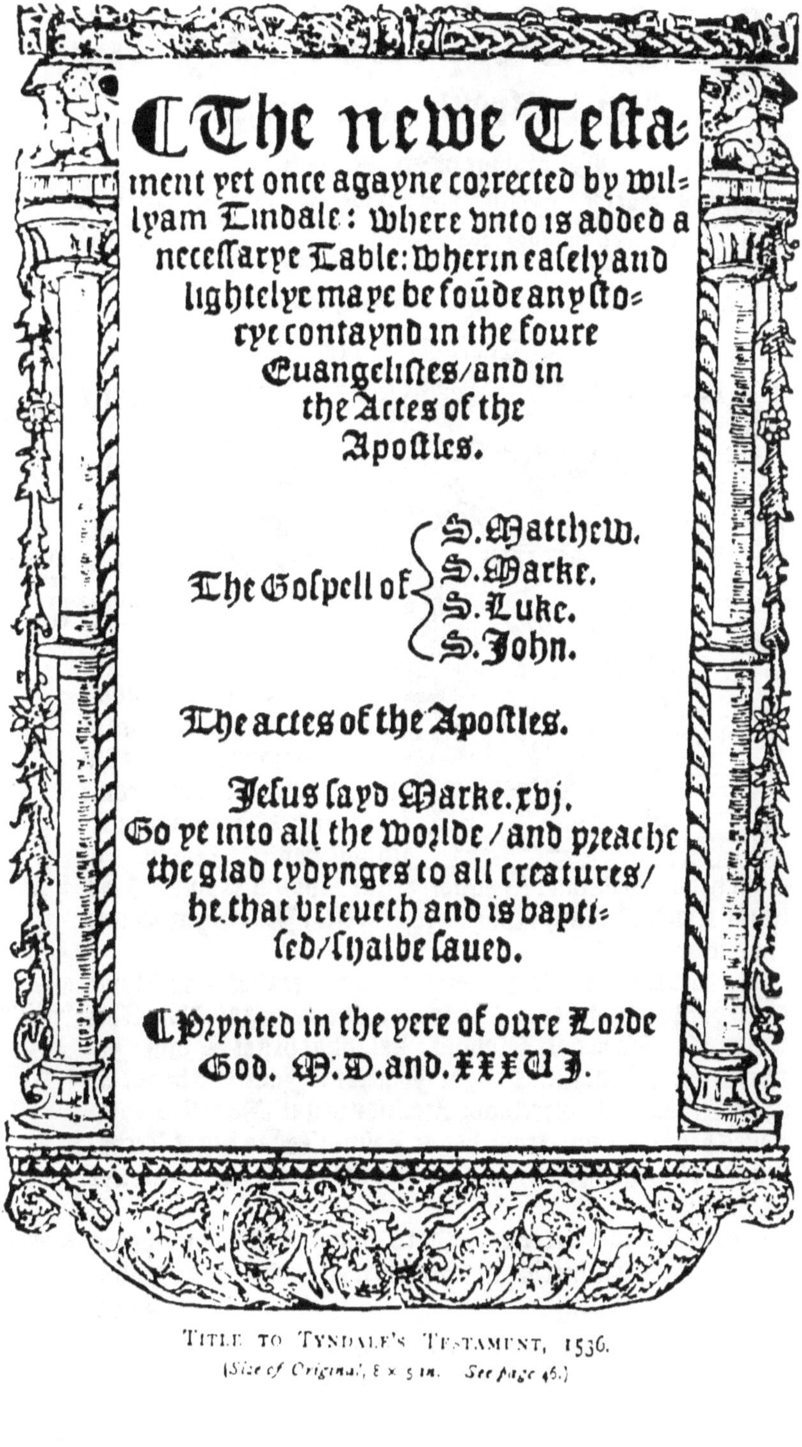

¶ The newe Testament yet once agayne corrected by willyam Tindale: where vnto is added a necessarye Table: wherin easely and lightelye maye be foūde any storye contaynd in the foure Euangelistes/and in the Actes of the Apostles.

The Gospell of { S. Matthew. S. Marke. S. Luke. S. John.

The actes of the Apostles.

Jesus sayd Marke.xvj.
Go ye into all the worlde/and preache the glad tydynges to all creatures/ he that beleueth and is baptised/shalbe saued.

¶ Prynted in the yere of oure Lorde God. M.D.and.XXXVJ.

TITLE TO TYNDALE'S TESTAMENT, 1536.

(Size of Original, 8 × 5 in. *See page 46.)*

¶ The Gospell of S. Mathew the Apostle and Euangelist.

¶ A prologe of S. Mathew.

As touchynge the Euangelistes: ye se in the new Testament clearly what they were. Fyrst Matthew (as ye reade Matthew. ix. Mar. ii. Luke. v.) was one of Christes Apostles/ and was with Christ all the tyme of his preachynge/ and sawe and heard his awne selfe all/ most all that he wrote.

¶ The generacion of Jesu Christ. The byrth of Christ.

¶ The fyrst Chapter.

A This is the boke of the generació of Jesus Christe the sonne of Dauid/ ye Luc.iii.c Ge.xxi.a
sone also of Abraham. Abraham begat Isaac: Isaac begat Jacob: Jacob begat Judas and his brethré: Judas begat Phares and zaram of Thamar: Phares begat Hesrom: Hesrom begat Aram: Aram begat Aminadab: Aminadab begat Naassó: Naasson begat Salmon: Salmon begat Boos of Rahab: Boos begat Obed of Ruth: Obed begat Jesse: Jesse begat Dauid the kynge. Genesis xxxviii. i.par.ii.a Ruth. iiii.d.
B Dauid the kynge begat Salomon/ of her that was ye wyfe ii.re.xii.c i.par.iii b
of Ury: Solomon begat Roboam: Roboam begat Abia: Abia begat Asa: Asa begat Josaphat: Josaphat begat Joram: Joram begat Osias: Osias begat Joatham: Joatham begat Achas: Achas begat Ezechias: Ezechias begat Manasses: Manasses begat Amon: Amon begat Josias: Josias begat Jechonias and his brethren aboute ye tyme they were caryed awaye to Babylon.
a And after they were brought to Babyló/ Jechonias begat ii. parali: pe.xxxvi. i.par.iii.c
Salathiel: Salathiel begat zorobabel: zorobabel begat Abiud:

a Abiud

PAGE OF TYNDALE'S TESTAMENT, 1536.

(Size of Original, 7½ × 5 in. See page 45.)

: The newe Testament in Englyshe & in Latin

NOVVM TESTAMENTVM ANGLICE ET LATINE.

Anno Dñi. 1538.

TITLE TO TYNDALE'S TESTAMENT, 1538.

(*Size of Original, 7 × 4½ in. See page 4[illegible].*)

The newe tes-
tament both in Latine and
Englyshe eche correspondent e to
the other after the vulgare texte, com-
munely called S. Jeromes. Fayth-
fullye translated by Johan
Hollybushe.

Anno.M.CCCCC.XXXVIII.

Jeremie. xxxi.
Is not my worde lyke a fyre sayeth the
Lorde, and lyke an hammer that
breaketh the harde stone.

Prynted in Southwarke
by James Nicolson.

Set forth wyth the Kyn-
ges moost gracious lycence.

TITLE TO HOLLYBUSHE'S TESTAMENT, 1538.

(*Size of Original, 7 × 4¾ in.* *See page 101.*)

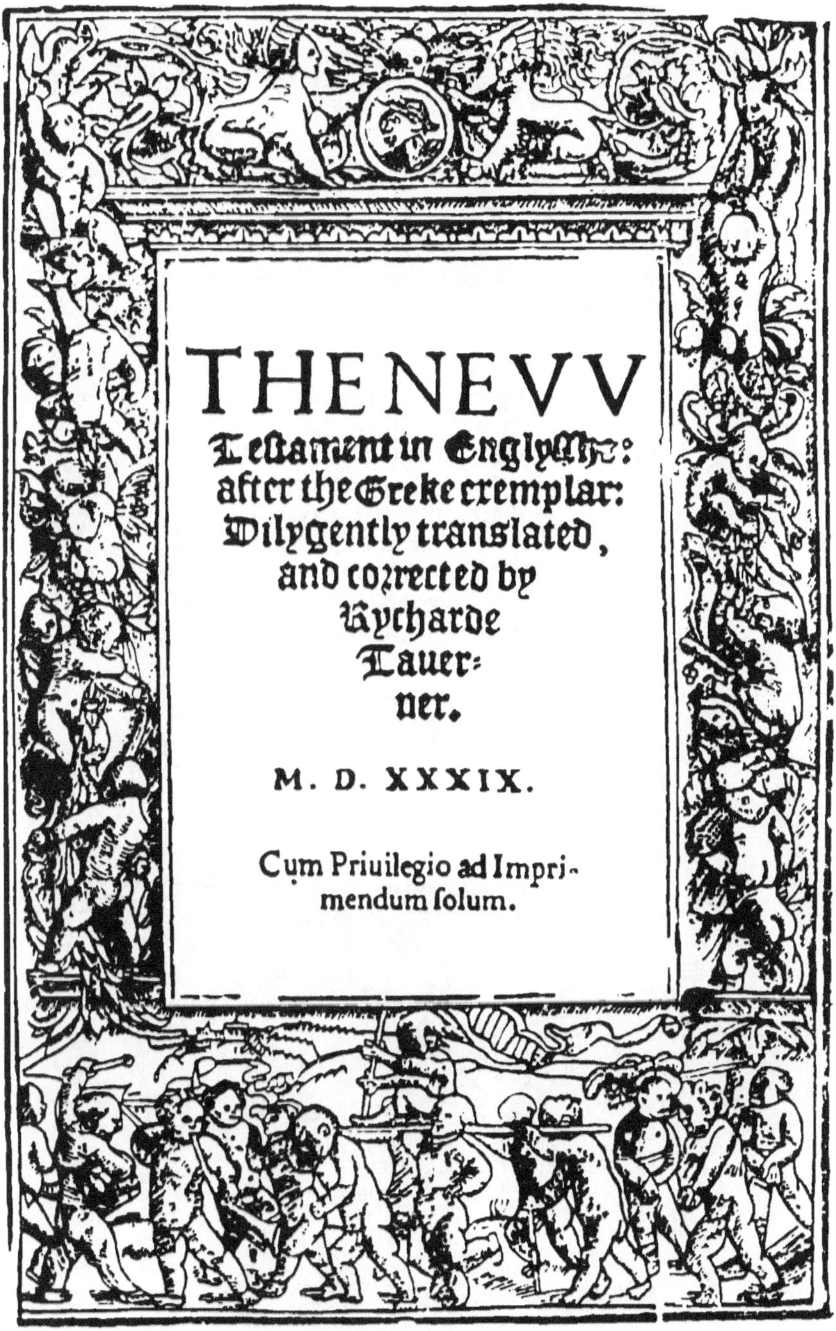

THE NEVV
Testament in Englyshe:
after the Greke exemplar:
Dilygently translated,
and corrected by
Rycharde
Tauer-
ner.

M. D. XXXIX.

Cum Priuilegio ad Impri-
mendum solum.

Title to Taverner's Testament, 1539.
(Size of Original, 7 × 4¾ in. *See page 142.)*

TITLE TO GREAT BIBLE, 1540.

(*Size of Original*, 10½ × 6⅞ *in.* *See page* 171.)

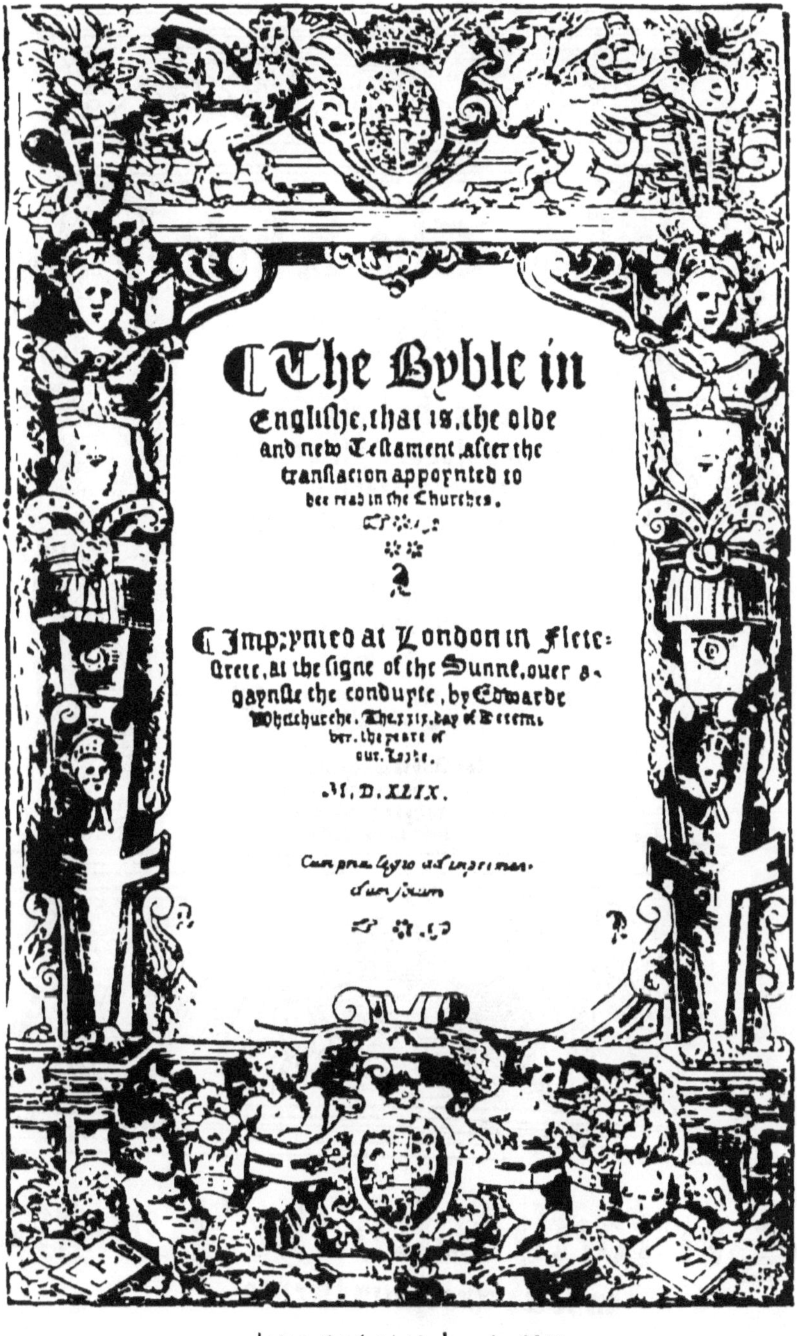
¶The Byble in Englishe, that is, the olde and new Testament, after the translacion appoynted to bee read in the Churches.

¶Imprynted at London in Fletestrete, at the signe of the Sunne, over agaynste the conduyte, by Edwarde Whitchurche. The xxix. day of Decemb. the yeare of our Lorde.

M.D.XLIX.

Cum privilegio ad imprimendum solum

TITLE TO GREAT BIBLE, 1540.
([illegible])

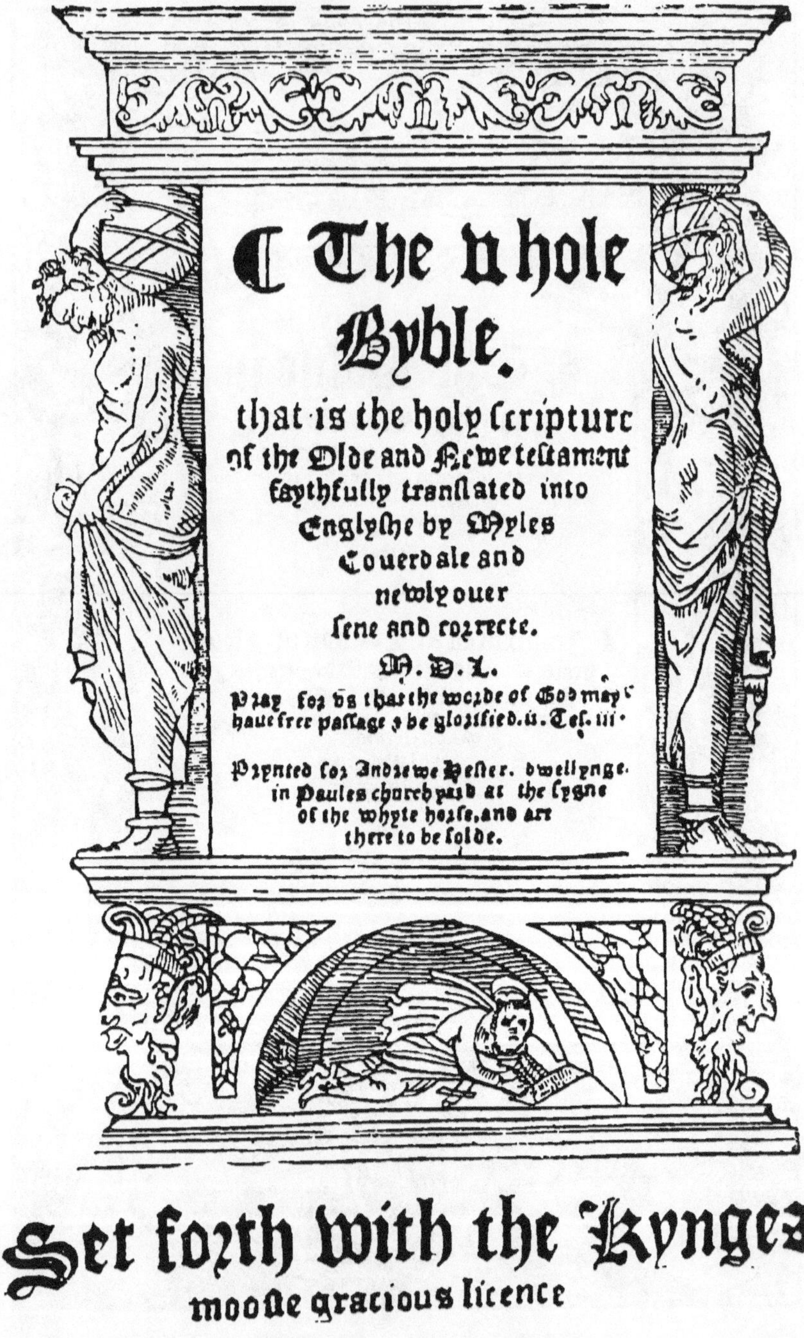
¶ The whole Byble.

that is the holy scripture of the Olde and Newe testament faythfully translated into Englyshe by Myles Couerdale and newly ouer sene and correcte.

M. D. L.

Pray for vs that the worde of God may haue free passage & be glorified. ii. Tes. iii.

Prynted for Andrewe Hester. dwellynge in Paules churchyard at the sygne of the whyte horse, and are there to be solde.

Set forth with the Kynges moste gracious licence

TITLE TO HESTER'S (COVERDALE'S) BIBLE, 1550.

(*Size of Original, 9½ × 7½ in.* *See page* 104.)

¶ The byble in Englishe, that is to say, the contente of all the holy scripture, bothe of the olde and newe Testament, accordyng to the translacion that is appointed to be read in Churches.

¶ Imprinted at London by Edwarde Whytchurche.

¶ Cum privilegio ad imprimendum solum.

Title to Cranmer's Great Bible, 1553

Size of Original, [illegible] in. See page [illegible]

THE

NEVVE TESTA-
MENT OF OVR LORD IE-
sus Christ.

Conferred diligently with the Greke, and best approued translations.

VVith the arguments aswel before the chapters, as for euery Boke & Epistle, also diuersities of readings and moste profitable annotations of all harde places, wherunto is added a copious Table.

GOD BY TYME RESTORETH TRUTH

AND MAKETH HER VICTORIOUS.

AT GENEVA
Printed By Conrad Badius.
M. D. LVII.

TITLE TO WHITTINGHAM'S NEW TESTAMENT, 1557.
(*Same size as Original.* *See page 189.*)

TO THE MOSTE VERTVOVS AND NOBLE QVENE ELISABET,

Quene of England, France, and Ireland, &c. Your humble subiects of the English Churche at Geneua, wish grace and peace from God the Father through Christ Iesus our Lord.

HOW hard a thing it is, and what great impedimentes let, to enterprise any worthie act, not only dailie experience sufficiently sheweth (moste noble and vertuous Quene) but also that notable prouerbe doeth confirme the same, which admonisheth vs, that all thīgs are hard which are faire and excellēt. And what enterprise can there be of greater importance, and more acceptable vnto God, or more worthie of singuler commendation, then the building of the Lords ‖ Temple, the ‖ house of God, the ‖ Church of Christ, whereof the ‖ Sonne of God is the head and perfection?

When Zerubbabel went about to builde the material Temple, according to the commandement of the Lord, what difficulties and stayes ‖ daily arose to hinder his worthy indeuours, ẏ bookes of Ezra & Esdras playnely witnesse: how that not only he and the people of God were sore molested with ẏ foreyn aduersaries, (whereof some maliciously ‖ warred against them, and corrupted the Kings officers: and others craftely practised vnder ‖ pretence of religion) but also at home with domestical enemies, as ‖ false Prophetes, ‖ craftie worldlings, faint hearted soldiers, and ‖ oppressors of their brethren, who aswel by false doctrine and lyes, as by subtil counsel, cowardies, and extortion, discouraged the heartes almoste of all: so that the Lords worke was not only interrupted and left of for ‖ a long tyme, but scarcely at the length with great labour and danger after a ‖ sort broght to passe.

Which thing when we weigh aright, and consider earnestly how muche greater charge God hath laid vpon you in making you a builder of his spiritual Temple, we can not but partely feare, ‖ knowing the crafte and force of Satan our spiritual enemie, and the weakenes and vnabilitie of this our nature: and partely be feruent in our prayers toward God that he wolde bring to perfection this noble worke which he hath begon by you: and therefore we indeuour our selues by all meanes to ayde, & to bestowe our whole force vnder your graces stādard, whome God hath made as our Zerubbabel for the erecting of this most excellent Temple, and to plant and maynteyn his holy worde to the aduancement of his glorie, for your owne honour and saluatiō of your soule, and for the singuler comfort of that great flocke which Christ Iesus the ‖ great Shepherd hath boght with his ‖ precious blood, and committed vnto your charge to be fed both in body and soule.

Considering therefore how many enemies there are, which by one meanes or other, as the ‖ aduersaries of Iudah and Beniamin went about to stay the building of that Temple, so labour to hinder the course of this building (whereof some are Papistes, who vnder pretence of fauoring Gods worde, traiterously seke to erect idolatrie and to destroy your maiestie: some are worldlings, who as ‖ Demas haue forsakē Christ for the loue of this worlde: others are ambitious prelates, who as ‖ Amasiah & ‖ Diotrephes can abide none but them selues: and as ‖ Demetrius many practise sedition to maynteyne their errors) we persuaded our selues that there was no way so expedient and necessarie for the [illegible] of the one and [illegible] of

(margin: The enemies labour to stay religion.)

PART OF THE LETTER IN GENEVAN BIBLE, 15[illegible]

[illegible]

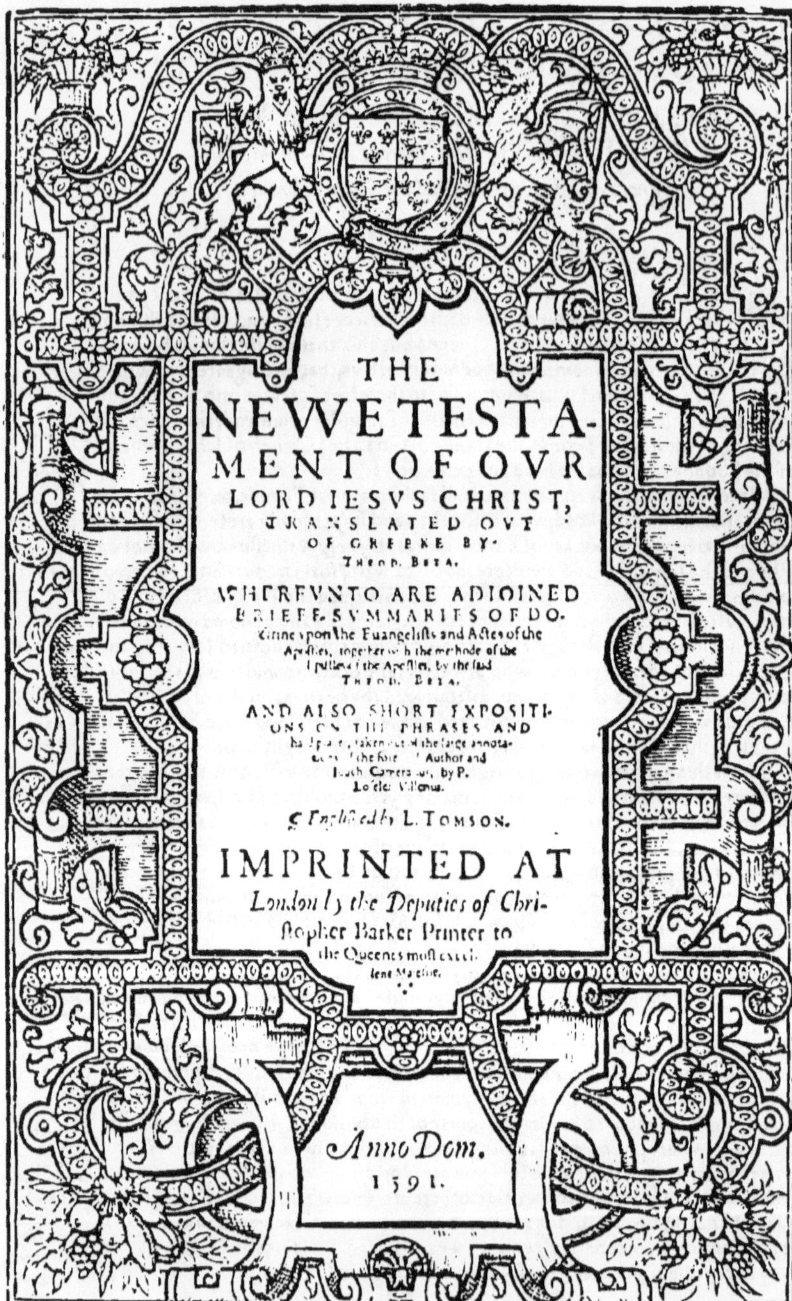

THE
NEWE TESTA-
MENT OF OVR
LORD IESVS CHRIST,
TRANSLATED OVT
OF GREEKE BY
THEOD. BEZA.

WHEREVNTO ARE ADIOINED
BRIEFE SVMMARIES OF DO-
ctrine vpon the Euangelists and Actes of the
Apostles, together with the methode of the
Epistles of the Apostles, by the said
THEOD. BEZA.

AND ALSO SHORT EXPOSITI-
ONS ON THE PHRASES AND
hard places, taken out of the large annota-
tions of the foresaid Author and
Ioach. Camerarius, by P.
Loseler Villerius.

Englished by L. TOMSON.

IMPRINTED AT
*London by the Deputies of Chri-
stopher Barker Printer to*
the Queenes most excel-
lent Maiestie.

Anno Dom.
1591.

TITLE TO TOMSON'S TESTAMENT, 1591.
(*Size of Original*, 9¾ × 6 *in.* *See page* 227.)

ROYAL ARMS IN FOLIO BIBLE, 1611.

(Size of Original, [illegible] × 7 in. See page 3[illegible])

THE

NEW TESTA-
MENT OF OVR

Lord Iesus Cl.rist, Translated

out of Greeke by *Theod Beza.*

WHEREVNTO ARE ADIOYNED
briefe Summaries of doctrine vpon the Euangelists
and Acts of the Apostles, together with the Methode of the
Epistles of the Apostles, by the sayd
THEOD. BEZA.

And also short expositions on the phrases and hard places,
taken out of the large Annotations of the foresaid Author
and Ioach. Camerarius, by P. Lo. Villerius.

Englished by L. Tomson.

¶ *Together with the Annotations of* FR IVNIVS *vpon the*
Reuelation of S. IOHN.

IMPRINTED AT LON-
DON BY ROBERT BARKER,
Printer to the Kings most excellent
Maiestie. 1616.

¶ *Cum priuilegio.*

TITLE OF TOMSON'S TESTAMENT, 1616.
(*Size of Original*, $10\frac{3}{8} \times 5\frac{1}{2}$ *in.* *See page* 230.)

www.ingramcontent.com/pod-product-compliance
Lightning Source LLC
Chambersburg PA
CBHW051737300426
44115CB00007B/596